Sociocultural and Power-Relational Dimensions of Multilingual Writing

NEW PERSPECTIVES ON LANGUAGE AND EDUCATION
Founding Editor: Viv Edwards, *University of Reading, UK*
Series Editors: Phan Le Ha, *University of Hawaii at Manoa, USA* and
Joel Windle, *Monash University, Australia.*

Two decades of research and development in language and literacy
education have yielded a broad, multidisciplinary focus. Yet education
systems face constant economic and technological change, with attendant
issues of identity and power, community and culture. What are the
implications for language education of new 'semiotic economies' and
communications technologies? Of complex blendings of cultural and
linguistic diversity in communities and institutions? Of new cultural,
regional and national identities and practices? The New Perspectives
on Language and Education series will feature critical and interpretive,
disciplinary and multidisciplinary perspectives on teaching and learning,
language and literacy in new times. New proposals, particularly for edited
volumes, are expected to acknowledge and include perspectives from the
Global South. Contributions from scholars from the Global South will be
particularly sought out and welcomed, as well as those from marginalized
communities within the Global North.

All books in this series are externally peer-reviewed.

Full details of all the books in this series and of all our other publications
can be found on http://www.multilingual-matters.com, or by writing to
Multilingual Matters, St Nicholas House, 31-34 High Street, Bristol BS1
2AW, UK.

NEW PERSPECTIVES ON LANGUAGE AND EDUCATION: 90

Sociocultural and Power-Relational Dimensions of Multilingual Writing

Recommendations for Deindustrializing Writing Education

Amir Kalan

MULTILINGUAL MATTERS
Bristol • Blue Ridge Summit

DOI https://doi.org/10.21832/KALAN7802
Library of Congress Cataloging in Publication Data
A catalog record for this book is available from the Library of Congress.
Names: Kalan, Amir, author.
Title: Sociocultural and Power-Relational Dimensions of Multilingual
   Writing: Recommendations for Deindustrializing Writing Education/Amir Kalan.
Description: Bristol, UK; Blue Ridge Summit: Multilingual Matters, 2021.
   | Series: New Perspectives on Language and Education: 90 | Includes
   bibliographical references and index. | Summary: 'This book examines the
   writing practices of three adult multilingual writers through the prism
   of their writing in English as an additional language. It illustrates
   some of the social, cultural and political contexts of the writers'
   literacy activities and argues for a writing pedagogy that reflects the
   complexity of writing as a social practice' – Provided by publisher.
Identifiers: LCCN 2020056696 | ISBN 9781788926706 (paperback) | ISBN
   9781788927802 (hardback) | ISBN 9781788927819 (pdf) | ISBN 9781788927826
   (epub) | ISBN 9781788927833 (kindle edition)
Subjects: LCSH: English language – Study and teaching (Higher) – Foreign
   speakers. | English language – Rhetoric – Study and teaching
   (Higher) – Foreign speakers. | Written communication – Study and teaching
   (Higher) | Multilingualism. | Academic writing – Study and teaching
   (HIgher)
Classification: LCC PE1128.A2 K35 2021 | DDC 428.0071/1 – dc23
LC record available at https://lccn.loc.gov/2020056696

British Library Cataloguing in Publication Data
A catalogue entry for this book is available from the British Library.

ISBN-13: 978-1-78892-780-2 (hbk)
ISBN-13: 978-1-78892-670-6 (pbk)

Multilingual Matters
UK: St Nicholas House, 31-34 High Street, Bristol BS1 2AW, UK.
USA: NBN, Blue Ridge Summit, PA, USA.

Website: www.multilingual-matters.com
Twitter: Multi_Ling_Mat
Facebook: https://www.facebook.com/multilingualmatters
Blog: www.channelviewpublications.wordpress.com

The policy of Multilingual Matters/Channel View Publications is to use papers that are
natural, renewable and recyclable products, made from wood grown in sustainable forests.
In the manufacturing process of our books, and to further support our policy, preference
is given to printers that have FSC and PEFC Chain of Custody certification. The FSC and/
or PEFC logos will appear on those books where full certification has been granted to the
printer concerned.

Typeset by Riverside Publishing Solutions.
Printed and bound in the UK by the CPI Books Group Ltd.
Printed and bound in the US by NBN.

For Sayeh and Sam

Contents

Acknowledgments   ix

1   **Introduction**   1
   Prologue   1
   Description of the Book's Focus   3
   Significance of the Project   5
   Overview   9

2   **Conceptual and Empirical Background**   11
   Theoretical Backdrop   11
   Empirical Research   18

3   **Making Sense of Histories and Literate Legacies**   27
   Approach   27
   Evidence   29
   Making Sense of the Data   31
   Participants and Their Histories   32

4   **Literacy and Writing Discourses**   51
   Ontologies of Literacy   54
   Ontologies of Writing   66

5   **Writing as a Power Differential**   82
   Writing as Praxis and Claiming Agency   84
   Publishing and Dissemination as Inseparable from the Act of Writing   88
   Collaboration in Writing   93

6   **Written Texts as Organic Outgrowth of Complex Linguistic and Cultural Repertoires**   105
   A Philosophical Approach to Multitextuality   106

Multilingual Writing, Plurilingual Lives and Translingual
Practices   110
Non-Written Semiotic Engagement   117
Intercultural Competence   121

7 **Social and Institutional Lived Experiences**   **132**
'Good' Student, 'Bad' Student   132
Financial Resources and Education   136
Power Relations in Educational/Cultural Settings   139
Dominant and Canonical Curricula   142
Native vs. Non-Native English Users   146
Assimilation and Cultural Conformity   151
Immigration as an Intellectual Catalyst   156

8 **Mechanics and Practicalities**   **162**
Learning Writing Mechanics   163
From Paper to Digital Literacy Practices   166
Experiences with English Language Testing   168

9 **Implications, Recommendations and Potential
Further Directions**   **173**
Pedagogical Implications   175
Implications for Policy and Research   186
Epilogue   193

References   197

Index   214

Acknowledgments

This book is based on my doctoral research project, which was funded by the Social Sciences and Humanities Research Council of Canada (SSHRC) and conducted at the Ontario Institute for Studies in Education (OISE) of the University of Toronto. I am grateful for the support I received from these institutions. Without their generosity and trust, this project wouldn't have been completed. This research journey also facilitated my contact with great scholars and amazing individuals who shared their knowledge and experiences with me. Dr Rob Simon, my supervisor, offered his generous support all through the process of research and writing the project. Every conversation with Dr Simon about language and literacy education has helped me think of teaching and learning in new ways. Similarly, I was lucky to have the support of Dr Jim Cummins and Dr Julie Kerekes as members of my research committee. These scholars' work about minoritized language learners has impacted this book immensely. I am thankful to them for their generous support and valuable guidance. I would also like to thank Dr Antoinette Gagne and Dr Betsy Rymes for their feedback on my research. Additionally, I would like to thank the three writers who participated in the project and shared their histories with me. I am grateful for their trust and friendship. All through the project, I was touched and inspired by their passion, intelligence, resilience and humanity. I should also thank all the students who have attended my writing courses for everything that I learned from them. Without their engagement, open-mindedness and curiosity about new possibilities, I wouldn't have been able to advocate for alternative pedagogical practices in this book as confidently. Finally, I have to thank my wife and my son, to whom this book is dedicated, for all the love, care and kindness that they share with me in every step of my life, especially for their support during the writing of this book.

1 Introduction

Prologue

Today is a warm summer day in Dayton, Ohio in 2017. At my study desk, I am activating a laptop application to record my Skype interview with the writers who have participated in my research project investigating social, cultural and power-relational contexts of writing in English as an adopted language. Today's meeting, which is a follow-up group interview, is going be our last gathering, a few years after our initial interviews in Toronto, Canada. When I was designing the data collection process in Canada, I planned that for this final group interview I would invite the participants and their families to our apartment in Midtown Toronto for dinner as a gesture of gratitude. Life, however, took a different direction and one of the participants and I had to leave Canada, after our relatively recent arrival as immigrants, and re-start our lives in the United States. Choman's husband and my wife received job offers from the United States, and they could not reject the opportunity of having reliable full-time jobs. Choman's husband now has a high-level managerial position in California and my wife teaches philosophy at a private university in Ohio. Following this second immigration in a span shorter than a decade, Choman and I were also absorbed in the American job market: Choman started to work for a news outlet as a journalist, and at the time I finished my data collection, I was teaching academic writing to undergraduate students.

Our departure shattered my plans for an end-of-the-project thank-you party in Toronto, but it also raised important questions that related to the research project which you are going to read about in this book. What are some of the dynamics in the Canadian economy that have caused continual brain drain from Canada to the United States (Kesselman, 2001)? Why has ineffective human management of educated and skilled immigrants in Canada created a state of chronic frustration for newcomers in that they often have to fill jobs for which they are overqualified (Bauder, 2003)? Clarice, another participant in the study, was also considering applying for academic positions in the United States after completion of her PhD programme, indicating anxiety about the issue of immigrant employment in Canada. Among us – the participants and I – it was only Magda who felt settled enough in Canada, with a governmental job at a local ministry.

Consistent with these broader socioeconomic questions, there are also specific considerations about language and literary, which, for me as an educational researcher, are more appropriate to wrestle with. For instance, how much of the devaluation of immigrant talent in Canada – or what Bauder (2003) has named *brain abuse* – is imposed by Canadian educational structures through the numerous official and institutional linguistic interactions that newcomers have to engage with before and after they enter Canada? Such encounters include immigration and university admission language tests, devaluation of foreign academic qualifications, Anglo-Americentric curriculum, and centralized domi-nant pedagogies that are uninterested in youth and adult learners' intel-lectual, literate and linguistic backgrounds. Besides the socioeconomic problem of the invisibility of immigrants' skills, which leads to a great loss, a lack of vision and will to incorporate the experiences of pluric-ultural, plurilingual learners in everyday pedagogical practices renders Canadian language and literacy teaching questionable and disconnected from reality.

Although the trend is slowly changing, still many introductory linguistics textbooks describe Joseph Conrad's achievements, as a non-native speaker of English in the English literary scene, as an exception to the rule. The rule is, of course, the imaginary dominance of monolingualism, and hence the technical superiority of monolingual writers, while we know most people in the world are bi- or multilingual and many of those write effectively in their additional languages. If we zoom back away from the late colonial understanding of proper English and the literary canon, which 'honoured' Conrad to be a part of it, we could have a more realistic view of the presence of multilingual writers in our much more complex cosmopolitan societies than experienced in 19th and earlier 20th century with many respected multilingual writers such as Vladimir Nabokov, Joseph Brodsky, Ágota Kristóf, Anchee Min, Jack Kerouac, and so forth. With the same mentality but in a broader category, one could also easily identify thousands of multilinguals, like the participants of my study, who effectively engage with technical, academic, and literary writing in learned languages on a daily basis but do not appear much in our speculations and inquiries about writing.

In the same fashion, much second language research still feeds on quantitative textual and cognitive paradigms that fail to acknowledge the complex social, cultural, and political contexts of additional language learning and are often oblivious to language learners' complex discursive and cultural practices. Accordingly, these rich experiences, because of their invisibility, do not find a way into dominant pedagogical practices, which are often rubric-centred and drills-based activities inherited from industrial/colonial educational models.

Today – online and away from Toronto – my participants and I will have another conversation to continue our attempt to reveal some of their rich histories and intellectual practices, hoping to highlight the voices of immigrants as owners of knowledge rather than study subjects. We won't be able to solve the problem of the Canadian brain drain or brain abuse through this project, but we can construct notions that would add to the knowledge of language teachers by exposing complexities of writing in an additional language. With a focus on writing, this book, thus, is a contribution to the body of research concerned about the role of language in immigrants' experiences in Canada (for instance, Allan, 2016; Dagenais, 2013; Fleras, 2014; Miller, 2014; Simpson & Whiteside, 2015).

With the number of immigrants that English speaking countries have been receiving over the past decades, policymakers, academics and educators have sought ways to effectively teach English to newcomers for more comfortable integration, with recommendations ranging from assimilationist to more critical measures. Through this research project, my participants and I would like to invite North American policymakers and academics to pause from time to time and to listen to the immigrants themselves – who often speak more languages than most people involved in designing immigrant education in host countries – in order to learn from their intellectual and literate journeys. Those experiences can help illustrate strategies and approaches that mainstream educators in North American schools, who are typically brought up and trained in mono-cultural environments, might find inspirational and useful.

Description of the Book's Focus

This book is the outcome of an ethnographic multiple case study of the literate lives of three adult multilingual English writers conducted in order to describe how their socioculturally embedded literacy activities enriched their writing lives. Adopting sociocultural language and writing theories (Derrida, 1973; Dobrin et al., 2011; Kent, 1999; Wittgenstein, 1953), this project aimed to see what belief systems, discourses and power-relational contexts generated the literacy activities these multilingual writers engaged with and how these activities enriched their writing lives, particularly their English writing. From a poststructural sociolinguistic perspective, writing is neither an entirely individual activity nor the outcome of a cognitive process only. Every piece of writing, from this point of view, is a unit of discourse and an artefact carved by complicated sociocultural, sociopolitical and power-relational forces and dynamics. By means of this inquiry, I wished to see what literacy activities, social discourses and institutional interactions helped language learners create written texts in their additional languages in different contexts and for different purposes. Unveiling some of these complexities could inspire language teachers to regard writing more broadly as a social phenomenon and to devise their pedagogy accordingly. Through this inquiry, I studied the participants' literacy histories and writing trajectories in multiple languages in order to understand how their writing in English had evolved to the quality level that was appreciated by academic, literary, and professional circles that the participants joined as newcomers in Canada. I was also curious to learn if writing was a significant factor in the academic and professional success of immigrant adult professionals in Canada.

The participants are three women with different ethnic and linguistic backgrounds, one from Brazil, one from Hungary and the third from Iran's Kurdistan. Clarice, the Brazilian writer, is a graduate student who regularly engages with English academic writing and has published a number of articles in well-read high-profile journals. Magda, the Hungarian writer, is a textbook and technical writer. She also handles transactional and administerial correspondence on a daily basis as the coordinator of professional development programmes in a governmental institution. Choman, the Kurdish writer, is a novelist-journalist who publishes fiction in English and writes social and political analysis for a number of news outlets. I conducted this project to make sense of Clarice, Magda and Choman's lives between the texts they produced. I studied their literate lives in order to see what ideologies and sociocultural circumstances facilitated their writing practices, whose products were appreciated by Canadian English speaking readers in their corresponding academic, professional, and literary circles.

Over the past decades, there has been a shift from cognitive approaches in educational research to sociocultural inquiries about educational processes and phenomena (Barton & Hamilton, 2000; Gee, 1998; Heath, 1983; Heath & Street, 2008; New London Group, 1996; Street, 1993a). As will be explained in more detail, second language writing research, however, has been slow in adopting ethnographic research methods that highlight sociocultural dimensions of writing through critical lenses. Although much research has been conducted to examine the impact of gender, culture, race, and social status on multilingual writing (examples of which I discuss later), most of this research relies on textual analysis of language learners' final written products. There have been few attempts to move beyond textual analysis in order to explore literacy activities, discourses, and sociocultural contexts that help language learners write in additional languages. This project aimed to fill this gap.

The questions that guided this study were as follows:

(1) How do multilingual writers engage with literacy, especially with writing in English as an additional language?
(2) What are some of the sociocultural, discursive and power-relational contexts that shape multilinguals' experiences with literacy?
(3) What are some major examples of multilingual writers' intercultural and translingual practices?

(4) How can histories, experiences and perceptions of the writers who participated in my study inform pedagogy and practice?

Thus, in brief, this study was designed to explore (1) the participants' literacy practices, (2) the sociocultural circumstances and discourses that influence these activities, (3) how these activities have empowered the lives of these participants through their writing practices, especially writing in English, and (4) how the project's findings can be incorporated into everyday writing pedagogies and curricula.

Significance of the Project

This project is a response to the call of second language (L2) writing researchers who have been demanding more research on sociocultural, sociopolitical, and power-relational aspects of L2 writing. In an article in *Journal of Second Language*'s special edition on second language writing and postprocess theory – one of few concerted attempts among L2 writing scholars to focus on sociocultural approaches to L2 writing research – Leki (2003) invited L2 writing researchers to employ postpositivist, poststructural and postmodern paradigms in order to expand the horizons of the field:

> L2 writing research seems at times oddly insular, not even referencing work in second language acquisition much, not to mention other contemporary thinking that might help both to clarify and complexify our project. Are we in L2 writing missing out, being by-passed by the most interesting intellectual trends of our times ...? (Leki, 2003: 103)

Leki (2003) in the above passage is concerned about the slowness of L2 writing research to adopt postpositivist paradigms, which have been fruitfully used in educational research for quite a while, particularly in mainstream literacy studies. In a more recent assessment of empirical recent trends in second language writing, Riazi *et al.* (2018) concluded that among research projects reported in flagship *Journal of Second Language Writing* over 25 years, from 1992 to 2016, only less than 2% adopted a critical lens to study writing in additional languages. They defined 'critical' as research that 'primarily focused on political aspects of social contexts and their influence on individuals or groups and texts they produce, often highlighting the roles of power, race, gender, and/ or discourse' (Riazi *et al.*, 2018: 48), projects with the same focus as this book's.

What educators and policymakers in the United States and other Anglophone countries referred to as *reading* and *writing*, in the 1970s started to be called *literacy*, which was broadly intended to mean *situated reading and writing* or *reading and writing in context* (Barton *et al.*, 2000). This change of vocabulary is indicative of a shift of attitude as a result of more conscious attention to the sociocultural and sociopolitical circumstances under which the acts of reading and writing occur (Lankshear & Knobel, 2003) and to the societal and power-relational contexts that generate literacy activities (Freire, 1970; Freire & Macedo, 1987). The sociocultural nature of literacy teaching and learning has similarly been emphasized in the work of many other literacy researchers since the 1970s (Barton & Hamilton, 2000; Cummins, 1994, 2007; Cummins & Early, 2011; Gee, 1998; Heath, 1983; Heath & Street, 2008; New London Group, 1996; Simon, 2011; Street, 1993a).

One important consequence of viewing literacy as embedded in sociocultural contexts has been the emergence of new research tendencies towards ethnographic approaches in mainstream literacy research in order to observe, identify and describe learners' literacy activities within social, cultural and political contexts. However, the bulk of L2 writing research still focuses on the textual analysis of the final written products of language learners. Although there has been much research on sociolinguistic aspects of student L2 writing – such as the impact of gender on L2 writing (Belcher, 1997, 2001; Bermúdez & Prater, 1994; Breland & Lee, 2007; Johnson, 1992; Pavlenko, 2001) and the importance of culturally constructed rhetorical patterns in students' first languages (Connor, 2002; Connor *et al.*, 2008) – most of this research has mainly employed textual analysis of what students have written rather than the contexts where L2 writing occurs. In L2 writing research, unlike mainstream literacy studies, there has been much less reflection on multilingual writers' writing lives and their socioculturally embedded literate lives. This project targeted this gap.

Since Leki's (2003) invitation to adopt sociocultural approaches to multilingual writing – along with the impact of other socioculturally concerned views of writing in additional languages such as intercultural (contrastive) rhetoric (Connor, 1996; Connor *et al.*, 2008) and genre theory (Hyland, 2003, 2007); and with growing concerns about students' funds of knowledge (Moll *et al.*, 1992), multiliteracies (New London Group, 1996), and identities (Cummins, 2001; Cummins & Early, 2011) – some qualitative, ethnographic and narrative research on the writing lives of multilingual writers have been conducted (for instance, Belcher & Connor, 2001; Casanave & Vandrick, 2003; Lam, 2000; Prior, 1998; Skilton-Sylvester, 2002). This project aims to contribute to this new trend in multilingual writing research. At the same time, however, this research project differs from them in the following regards.

Qualitative research on the lives and experiences of multilingual writers has mostly focused on 'student L2 writers' or 'professional L2 writers' (Matsuda *et al.*, 2003: 157). Moving beyond this dichotomy, in this project I frame my study as an inquiry into the lives of *practicing multilingual English writers*. My participants were not student writers. I also did not find 'professional' a precise descriptor of the participants' writing existences (at least until this project was finalized). Although the participants were sometimes paid for their writing projects, writing was not a continual (or main) source of income for them but a skill that helped them strengthen their larger careers such as editing, teaching, consultancy and research. Stressing this fact can highlight the similarities of writing experiences between these writers and the general public, who have to constantly engage with writing for different reasons, rather than distinguish them as exceptional. Additionally, the label 'professional' might indicate that the writing skills of these writers are particularly more advanced than those of other 'practicing writers' who may not have been published but who have been, comfortably or with difficulty, functioning as dual or multilingual writers. The official and institutional borders of expertise between amateur and professional writers, or student and master writers, are often blurred. I rejected the 'student vs. professional' dichotomy because I regarded my research as interacting with *organic* writers outside compartmentalized educational settings in that it would allow me to see these writers in a frame that hosted many more members than 'professional writers': thousands of multilingual immigrants who write in learned languages in their everyday lives, yet their writing practices are often hidden. Hence, all through this book, I will refer to the participants as 'practicing' writers, emphasizing their organic and common experiences as opposed to exceptional or stellar.

The professional/student dichotomy discussed above has been mainly created as a result of the sites of research hitherto chosen for the projects interested to explore the lives of multilingual writers. Most of this kind of research has focused on writers within official educational settings. Some researchers have studied experiences of academic writers within academia and higher education – among both published university instructors (Belcher, 1997; Belcher & Connor, 2001) and university students (Canagarajah, 1997; Prior, 1998). On the other hand, there has been some research on the experiences of students within the K-12 school system (Matsuda *et al.*, 2003). In contrast with both of these trends, my research explores the writing lives of adult multilingual English writers beyond educational settings to create a more realistic understanding of what helps multilingual English writers function satisfactorily in their everyday lives in society. I interacted with the participants, through conversation and observation, in their everyday natural environments from home to work and also both in real and virtual worlds. Thus, this project, unlike previous research, did not focus on writing as a required skill within a particular educational setting (although one of the participants is a doctoral student); instead, this research studied writing as a hermeneutic tool for communication and power generation in everyday lives of adult multilingual English writers in English speaking environments.

Another factor illustrating the significance of this project is the geographical context of the project. Despite a growing international interest in exploring sociocultural approaches to multilingual writing, there have been no visible attempts to qualitatively describe the writing lives of multilingual English writers in Canada and in Toronto in particular. Over the past decades, Toronto has been the destination of large groups of newcomers to Canada, although recently Western Canada has also been attracting significant numbers of newcomers (Statistics Canada, 2011). Some of these new Torontonians struggle to effectively communicate with Canadian society through written language, which happens to be the main channel of academic, governmental, and business communication in Toronto. Some, on the other hand, successfully communicate in English and employ writing to empower their lives as immigrants. This project aims to understand what literate lifestyles enable these writers to effectively function in Canadian society. By learning from the experiences of these writers, we might be able to create pedagogical models that can help other adult English learners and immigrants' children in Canadian schools. At present, unfortunately, there is little awareness reflected in policies regarding the sociocultural and sociopolitical dimensions of teaching English writing to newcomers to Canada. In what follows, I will focus on one example of these policies, which will represent my last argument to illustrate the significance of this project, or the necessity of sensitizing Canadian educational policymakers and curriculum developers to the complexities of learning to write in additional languages.

Despite numerous scholarly conversations in literature regarding the significance of writers' literate lives and the sociocultural and sociopolitical circumstances that breed their literacy activities, most seminal official curricula of teaching English to newcomers to Canada show a lack of interest in these issues. For instance, the *Canadian Language Benchmarks: English as a Second Language for Adults* (Centre for Canadian Language Benchmarks, 2012) treats teaching writing as developing students' cognitive skills rather than helping students see writing as a hermeneutic and communicative practice, which involves intellectual collaborations, addressing authentic audiences, and writing for sociocultural change. *The Canadian Language Benchmarks* has a major impact on teaching adult English language learners in Canada. Independent language schools, Adult Education departments of school boards, and a variety of language assessment centres in Canada use this document as their main source of benchmarking reference. *The Canadian Language Benchmarks* is also the main foundation for all the curricula developed for courses offered in the Language Instruction for Newcomers to Canada (LINC) programme. LINC is an English programme funded by the Government, which helps newcomers to Ontario, Canada improve their knowledge of English in all four skills: listening, speaking, reading and writing.

The act of writing in English in *The Canadian Language Benchmarks* is treated as a cognitive skill which students should develop individually in a linear manner from grammatically simple forms of writing (Centre for Canadian Language Benchmarks, 2012: 109) to semantically complicated structures (Centre for Canadian Language Benchmarks, 2012: 133). A knowledge of writing in this document is defined as 'grammatical knowledge', 'textual knowledge', 'functional knowledge', 'sociolinguistic knowledge' and 'strategic competence' (Centre for Canadian Language Benchmarks, 2012: 135). *Grammatical knowledge* and *textual knowledge* are clearly technique oriented and are discussed as sets of skills that can be cognitively learned. However, although sections regarding *functional knowledge, sociolinguistic knowledge* and *strategic competence* in the document seem like appropriate spaces to emphasize the importance of multilingual writers' identities and the sociocultural circumstances under which multilingual writers produce texts in different languages, this *knowledge* is also treated as information about different English writing styles to be described and defined for the students. In this document, there is no emphasis on the social and collaborative nature of writing, nor is there any conversation about the power-relational dimensions of text creation, distribution and reception. This lack of interest in the sociocultural aspects of writing in a document as important as *The Canadian Language Benchmarks: English as a Second Language for Adults* in the Canadian context highlights the importance of the potential pedagogical implications of this project.

Overview

This book highlights the literate histories of three multilingual writers through the prism of their writing in English as their additional language. It illustrates some of the social, cultural and political contexts of the writers' literacy activities and discusses how those contexts impacted their literate and intellectual lives. It is important to reflect on para- and meta-textual dimensions of writing because organic writing practices are almost always performed within sociocultural and power-relational contexts. In our highly compartmentalized educational structures, writing education has been severed from those organic components, focusing mainly on writing stylistics. This book proposes creating space for organic writing practices in our everyday writing pedagogies. Such an attempt is especially important when learners write in additional languages inasmuch as cultural and linguistic differences make the social, emotional and identity-related layers of writing ever more complex. Effective writing pedagogies address that complexity.

In the opening chapters of this book, I introduce the theoretical frameworks that inform my analyses and arguments. These theoretical frameworks are postpositivist theories in philosophy of language, literacy studies, and composition theory that regard language as a societal and power-relational phenomenon. Then, I review instances of empirical research on L2 writing to show the gap that this book is meant to address. This gap, briefly, is ethnographic analysis of socioculturally embedded literacy activities that positively impact multilingual writing practices. Moreover, I share narratives that briefly sketch the lives of the writers whose writing practices are discussed as illustrations of the arguments of the book.

In the chapters that follow this introductory portion, I present the findings from studying the lives of the writers who participated in my research in five themes. First, I construct my participants' discourse practices based on their perceptions of what literacy is. Second, I share analyses of my conversations with the participants about writing as a power differential and exemplify those analyses with instances of the participants' lived experiences. Third, I explore the impact of the writers' multi-semiotic practices, pluriculturalism and plurilingualism on their writing practices. Fourth, I discuss some significant social contexts influencing the participants' learning trajectories. Fifth, I analyze highlights of my participants' interactions with technicalities of writing such as learning stylistics and taking standardized language tests. In the final chapter, I discuss the implications of my arguments for practice, policy and research.

2 Conceptual and Empirical Background

Theoretical Backdrop

> Language is a social art. In acquiring it we have to depend entirely on intersubjectively available cues as to what to say and when.
>
> Willard Van Orman Quine
> (2013, p. XXIV)

After centuries of philosophical speculation about ontology (what the world is) and epistemology (how we understand the world), Western philosophy in the early 20th century experienced a focused interest in philosophy of language. In this period, mainstream Western philosophers decided that any attempt to understand the world and our existence in it was informed by language because we could not think and talk about the world outside language. The study of language, accordingly, became the main priority of Western philosophy, a movement referred to as the *linguistic turn.*

The linguistic turn in philosophy created two waves one after another. First, there was an attempt to reduce language to logical statements separated from social, cultural, emotional and personal contexts in order to create a logico-linguistic medium that could reflect the 'truth' about the world objectively (Ayer, 1966; Carnap, 1937; Wittgenstein, 2004). Second, as a reaction to the first wave, postpositivist philosophical schools tried to show that language could never be reduced to symbols written on a page only. Language, from their perspective, was a form of life tightly bound to people's social, cultural, political, discursive and ideological existences. The dominance of postpositivist linguistic frameworks such as 'use theories' of linguistic meaning (Lycan, 2000), poststructuralism, and neopragmatism (linguistic pragmatism) would also impact the humanities and social sciences including educational research. In this section, first I discuss these developments in philosophy of language; next, I focus on the *social turn* in the New Literacy Studies and also in writing studies.

Language as an ideological hermeneutic tool

Early analytic philosophy (Kaplan, 1972; Russell, 1905) and logical positivism (Ayer, 1966; Blumberg & Feigl, 1931) attempted to reduce language to logical statements. They aimed to replace philosophy 'with the logical analysis of the concepts and sentences of the sciences, for [they believed] the logic of science is nothing other than the logical syntax of the language of science' (Carnap, 1937: xiii). This project, however, failed and opened the way for broader interpretations of what language is – interpretations that did not disregard the everyday contexts where language *occurs* as a complex hermeneutic tool for communication rather than a logical structure.

Among these interpretations, most importantly, Wittgenstein's (1953) *use theory of meaning*, allowed scholars to regard language use as 'one constituent' of 'a complex series of actions and practices' that humans, as social beings, partake in (Odell, 2006: 56). Wittgenstein (1953) wrote, 'Language is not a matter of marks on the blackboard bearing the expressing relation to abstract entities called "propositions"; language is something that people do' (Wittgenstein, 1953: 91). Based on this view of language, people not only speak and write their languages, but they *do* their languages. This definition of language will connect language use to humans' sociocultural beings and lives beyond the syntactic and morphological structure of language.

Wittgenstein (1958) used the concept 'language-games' to describe what *doing* one's language means:

> We can also think of the whole process of using words ... one of those games by means of which children learn their native language. I will call these games 'language-games' and will sometimes speak of a primitive language as a language-game. ... Here the term 'language-game' is meant to bring into prominence the fact that the speaking of language is part of an activity, or of a form of life. (Wittgenstein, 1958: 5, 11)

Poststructuralist philosophers also revealed more layers of the social cocoon that surrounded language. They argued that language was inherently ideological (Derrida, 1973, 1976, 2001) and power relations profoundly impacted text creation (Foucault, 2002).

By creating the concept of *différance*, Derrida (1973) showed language was innately ambiguous. Language, he held, constantly escapes meaning. What appears to us as the central meaning of a text is a perception fabricated by our ideological reading of the text, performed to ignore semantic ambiguities and confusions. Derrida coined *différance* by playing with the French word *différer*, meaning both 'to differ' and 'to defer'. Language, Derrida speculated, is immersed in *différance* because linguistic symbols do not mean anything by themselves and should endlessly refer to other words in a continual meaning-making mechanism, which keeps delaying the process of signification. Words might appear to be distinguishable from each other as unique entities because they 'differ' from one another, yet they fail to signify a fixed definition because they endlessly 'defer' meaning from word to word and from connotation to connotation. Language, thus, is too slippery to convey fixed meanings. The meaning of language is determined by the circumstances of the creation and distribution of the text, the ideologies at work within the text, and the interpretations of readers based on their perspectives.

Foucault (2002), furthermore, discussed how language was employed in ideological and power-relational battlegrounds. Power, he argued, constantly circulates in all directions to all social circles and layers. The network of the distribution and contraction of power is tied to innumerable social nodes, whose positions delicately but ceaselessly switch. Power is generated by three different means of exchange: first, exchange of material goods through bartering, buying, selling, gambling, stealing, charity and so on; second, exchange of people in different forms such as marriage, childbirth, employment, imprisonment, and so forth; and third, exchange of ideas or *discourses*, best recorded and represented in texts. Despite the claims that a certain discourse can offer the 'truth', discourses are merely means of aggression for more ground in power games. In the process of discourse construction linguistic texts are particularly instrumental. Every text is a part of the discursive battle that can knock one social level off balance or help the other find its ground in the entangled network of power. Therefore, the study of language should in fact be the study of sociocultural and sociopolitical circumstances in which language is used and texts are generated.

This dramatic shift in Western philosophy, sooner or later, would propel researchers and teachers into approaching literacy teaching and learning as a sociocultural phenomenon rather than the delivery of a number of techniques by an impartial teacher to be cognitively learned by students. In the next section, I will focus on this paradigm shift in literacy studies, which is usually referred to as the *social turn*.

Literacy studies and the *social turn*

Among the attempts to create a sociocultural research approach to literacy, the New Literacy Studies (NLS) can more conveniently exemplify the *social turn* in literacy studies. Street (2003) described what the New Literacy Studies represented as follows:

What has come to be termed the 'New Literacy Studies' (NLS) (Gee, 1991; Street, 1996) represents a new tradition in considering the nature of literacy, focusing not so much on acquisition of skills, as in dominant approaches, but rather on what it means to think of literacy as a social practice (Street, 1985). This entails the recognition of multiple literacies, varying according to time and space, but also contested in relations of power. NLS, then, takes nothing for granted with respect to literacy and the social practices with which it becomes associated, problematizing what counts as literacy at any time and place and asking 'whose literacies' are dominant and whose are marginalized or resistant. (Street, 2003: 77)

Briefly speaking, the characteristics that make NLS a suitable candidate for illustrating the character of the *social turn* in literacy studies are as follows. First, the scholars involved in NLS have approached literacy not only as physical acts of reading and writing but also as discursive practices, belief systems, and sociocultural norms that inform people's understandings of what literacy is and involves. Second, employing sociolinguistic and ethnographic methods, these researchers have tried to observe the literacy events that students engage in and the sociocultural circumstances that foster those literacy events. Third, NLS challenges dominant definitions of literacy that reduce literacy to classroom reading and writing; they regard literacy in broader terms to embrace students' native cultures, ideological tendencies, out-of-school literacies, mother tongues, and online reading and writing.

An early exemplar of NLS, Heath (1983) spent nine years performing a cross-cultural ethnographical comparison of literacy activities in two different communities: Trackton, a working-class white community, and Roadville, predominantly African-American with the same average income. Through comparisons of how students engaged with literacy in these two racially and culturally different communities, Heath (1983) highlighted the fact that *literacy events*, or students' reading and writing performances, were contextualized and should not be studied out of their contexts.

Street (1984), one of New Literacy Studies' leading theoreticians, similarly emphasized the context-dependent and power-laden nature of literacy teaching and learning by arguing against the *autonomous model of literacy* – which suggests literacy can be learned as a set of autonomous skills regardless of the social context – and in favour of the *ideological model of literacy* – in which literacy is considered as a social, cultural and power-relational phenomenon:

> I use the term 'ideological' to describe this approach, rather than less contentious or loaded terms such as 'cultural', 'sociological' or 'prag- matic' (see Hill and Parry 1988) because it signals quite explicitly that literacy practices are aspects not only of culture but also of power structures. ... Literacy can no longer be addressed as a neutral technol- ogy as in the reductionist 'autonomous' model but is already a social and ideological practice involving fundamental aspects of epistemology, power and politics. (Street, 1993b: 7, 19)

Barton and Hamilton (2000), also, held the same view that 'literacy is best understood as a set of social practices' (Barton & Hamilton,

2000: 9). This idea was central to the study on which this book is based in that it was conducted with the premise that successful multilingual writers not only possess certain linguistic and writing skills but might share social practices that impact their writing. Barton and Hamilton (2000) wrote, 'The notion of literacy practices offers a powerful way of conceptualising the link between the activities of reading and writing and the social structures in which they are embedded and which they help shape' (Barton & Hamilton, 2000: 7).

Similarly, the New London Group – another influential sociocultur-ally inclined literacy movement that followed NLS – in 'A Pedagogy of Multiliteracies: Designing Social Futures' (New London Group, 1996) warned that we needed to broaden our understanding of literacy particu-larly because of two developments. First, we are now living in an increas-ing diverse world with learners who come from a variety of cultures and thus perform diverse literacy practices. Second, cultural diversity and technological changes, particularly in the cyber world, have made us face new forms of text production and consumption in ways never experi-enced before. These considerations again show an emphasis on the social and historical contexts of literacy and education. One of the members of the New London Group, Gee (1986, 1998, 2008), for instance, wrote that literacy was tightly embedded in sociocultural contexts:

> The sociocultural approach to literacy overtly rejects the idea that textual practices are even largely, let alone solely, a matter of processes that 'go on in the head', or that essentially involve heads communicating with each other by means of graphic signs. From a sociocultural perspec-tive literacy is a matter of social practices. Literacies are bound up with social, institutional and cultural relationships, and can only be under-stood when they are situated within their social, cultural and historical contexts (Gee et al., 1996: xii)

This paradigm shift in literacy studies, from regarding literacy learning as a cognitive process to considering education as a sociocultural phenomenon, has had a major impact on educational research and studies in pedagogy. Methodologically, for instance, ethnographic approaches for studying socioculturally embedded literacy activities have claimed a considerable share in the realm of educational research; on the other hand, students' funds of knowledge (Moll et al., 1992), identities (Cummins, 2001; Cummins & Early, 2011), mother tongues (Baker & García, 2007; Cummins & Danesi, 1990; Schecter & Cummins, 2003; Skutnabb-Kangas & Cummins, 1988), and generally students' histories, legacies, and voices are paid closer attention to in pedagogical practices.

Also, relevant to this project, the social turn in language education has inspired multilingual approaches to education. This interest in multilingual education is referred to as the *multilingual turn* (Conteh

& Meier, 2014; Ortega, 2013; Sugiharto, 2015), which has also been repurposed in modified and complexified theoretical models such as plurilingualism (Piccardo, 2013) and translanguaging (Canagarajah, 2011; García & Li Wei, 2014). An emphasis on students' plurilingualism in these scholarly directions is often tied to notions such as intercultural practices, linguistic human rights, and pedagogical accommodation of diverse linguistic and literacy practices. The multilingual turn and its offspring, which more visibly connect with fields such as second language writing, also create new space for thinking about the sociocultural layers of reading and writing in and across multiple languages.

Writing theory and the *social turn*

The *social turn* has had a widespread impact on different fields in language and literacy studies and education. For instance, in composition studies different socioculturally informed teaching strategies have gained prominence and attracted attention. These pedagogical approaches include collaborative writing pedagogy (Howard, 2001), writing centre pedagogy (Hobson, 2001), community-service pedagogy (Julier, 2001), and cultural studies approaches to composition (George & Trimbur, 2001).

Among different attempts to highlight the metatextual dimensions of writing and its teaching and learning, the *postprocess writing theory* provides a more articulate explanation of what is means to teach writing while embracing its sociocultural and power-relational complexity. Postprocess writing theorists, in brief, hold that writing is neither an individual activity nor an entirely cognitive process. Written texts are the products of complicated semiotic, social, cultural, and political networks (Atkinson, 2003a, 2003b; Kent, 1993, 1999).

The word 'postprocess' as the label of a theoretical framework that could define the social turn in composition studies was first used by Trimbur (1994) in an article entitled 'Taking the Social Turn: Teaching Writing Post-Process':

> What is significant about these books [being reviewed in Trimbur's article]-and to my mind indicative of the current moment in rhetoric and composition studies-is that they make their arguments not so much in terms of students' reading and writing processes but rather in terms of the cultural politics of literacy. ... [These books] enact what has come to be called the 'social turn' of the 1980s, a post-process, post-cognitivist theory and pedagogy that represent literacy as an ideological arena and composing as a cultural activity by which writers position and reposition themselves in relation to their own and others' subjectivities, discourses, practices, and institutions. (Trimbur, 1994: 109)

This conversation in the field of composition studies has continued up to the present. In one of the last attempts made by postprocess scholars to define the sociocultural and sociopolitical aspects of writing, Kent (2011) wrote:

> Instead of understanding writing as primarily a thing-in-itself − such as a cognitive process or synchronic linguistic system or set of generic conventions − the postprocess mindset understands writing to be part and parcel of a larger semiotic activity that constitutes only one kind of human communicative interaction, albeit an incredibly important one. Understood from this perspective, writing, which always appears in the form of a text, must take its place among the heteroglossia of other signifying elements that give meaning to cultural life and that in a sense, enable us to triangulate and make sense of the world and the people who inhabit it. (Kent, 2011: xix)

A definition of postprocess L2 theory can be presented in two inter-related descriptive threads (Kalan, 2014). First, writing is not a single process that can be formulated and taught in a similar way in every classroom (Blyler, 1999; Pullman, 1999; Russell, 1999). The assumption that writing can be reduced to one single process has, in practice, resulted in the dominance of one particular genre that happens to fit that single process, namely Anglo-American essayist academic writing. In order to deal with the problems caused by this reductionism, 'essayist literacy' and the 'rhetoric of assertion' as dominant composition discourses should be challenged (Burnham, 2001; Couture, 2011; Root, 2003; Russell, 1999; Schilb, 1999) and writing teachers should broaden genre possibilities (Journet, 1999; Romano, 2000; Russell, 1999). An important consequence of challenging dominant genres would be providing students (particularly minoritized and marginalized students) with forms of expression that can more readily connect to their identities. Thus, moving beyond assertive and essayist discourses can also liberate students' agencies by connecting writing to their identities (Clifford & Ervin, 1999; Dobrin, 1999; Ewald, 1999).

Second, there is no simple pedagogy to be employed in the classroom in order to teach writing to students as an individual activity (Dobrin, 1999; Ewald, 1999; Pullman, 1999; Russell, 1999). Therefore, teachers need to move beyond the classroom as the only rhetorical situation (or writing context) and should question their role as the possessor of the *techne* of writing (Couture, 1999; Ewald, 1999; Petraglia, 1999). Contrary to the popular view of writing as a technique, written texts should be seen as products of complicated webs of cultural practices, social interactions, power differentials, and discursive conventions (Atkinson, 2003a; Casanave, 2003; Howard, 2001). Thus, from a post-process perspective, learning writing is basically learning knowledge design, rhetorical sensitivity, and hermeneutic guessing through a large number of literate activities (Casanave, 2003; Clifford & Ervin, 1999).

This brief theoretical introduction hopefully can represent the context and history available for alternative approaches to teaching and learning writing, approaches that treat writing as a societal interaction which involves communities and impacts power relations. In addition to theoretical conversations about sociocultural and political dimensions of writing, there has been a growing trend of empirical projects interested in metatextual dynamics that impact the process of writing in additional languages. The next section highlights examples of research with this tendency.

Empirical Research

This section provides examples of empirical studies that have examined the impact of (1) gender; (2) culture, race and ethnicity; (3) class; and (4) plurilingualism and multiliteracies on L2 writing. I chose this order for two reasons. First, this arrangement of topics broadly reflects what sociocultural areas have chronologically attracted the attention of L2 writing researchers. Second, this line of progression can illustrate the shift in L2 writing research from more quantitative textual analyses of written texts to more qualitative ethnographic approaches to multilingual writers' literacy practices, often presented as case studies. An emphasis on this methodological shift remains the focus of this section all through what follows inasmuch it can highlight the significance of the inquiry approach adopted for the research project which this book has been written about, namely an ethnographic multiple case study.

Gender

The emergence of the *social turn* in the field of literacy research occurred after women's studies – following the feminist movements of the first half of the 20th century – had formed a reliably solid body of literature and theoretical foundation. Thanks to the availability of polished feminist epistemologies, the question of gender quickly found its place in academic conversations about literacy, and in the same manner composition studies (Jarratt, 2001; Jarratt & Worsham, 1998; Phelps & Emig, 1995; Ritchie & Boardman, 1999).

Following the same trend, although with less momentum, L2 writing researchers have also felt the importance of studying the relationship between students' L2 writing and gender. They have theoretically speculated about such a relationship (Belcher, 1997, 2001; Pavlenko, 2001) and conducted empirical studies; for instance, Johnson (1992) examined a set of 35 papers written and reviewed by advanced female L2 writers. In this project, Johnson studied positive evaluation, intensifiers, and personal referencing – strategies believed to contribute to a feminine style of written communication. In a different project, Breland and Lee (2007), analyzing 632,246 essays written in response to 87 different prompts for the computer-based Test of English as a Foreign Language (TOEFL) examination, found that the scores of male and female examinees were almost the same, although the mean essay scores for female examinees were slightly higher than those for male examinees. Bermúdez and Prater (1994) also investigated how gender affected Hispanic writers' persuasive writing in English as an additional language. In this study, 37 elementary school students were asked to write essays in response to a prompt. The researchers observed that essays written by Hispanic women showed a greater degree of elaboration and a more discernible attempt to express the writers' points of view than those written by male Hispanic students.

As these examples show, from a methodological perspective, the bulk of the available research on the impact of gender on L2 writing has been conducted by means of textual analysis. Although these projects can give us an insight into the impact of gender on L2 writing, qualitative approaches that could shed more light on the experiences of female L2 writers are almost invisible in mainstream L2 writing literature and little attention seems to have been paid to the literate lives and writing practices of female L2 writers.

Nevertheless, the absence of qualitative inquiries into literacy experiences of women multilingual writers in mainstream L2 writing research does not mean that examples cannot be found in the margins of the field. Projects that have attempted to explore the relationship between writing and students' identities, backgrounds and multiliteracies tend to underline gender, to a greater or lesser degree. For instance, reports on identity texts (Cummins & Early, 2011) created by female students, including dual-lingual texts, discuss, although sometimes indirectly, the gender of the students involved in the projects. In another example, female multilingual writers such as Anzaldúa (2007) have published narratives of their experiences. Anzaldúa in *Borderlands/ La Frontera: The New Mestiza* used different written forms – including poetry – and dual-lingual passages in order to challenge Spanish/English, Latino/white, man/woman, heterosexual/homosexual and autobiography/ fiction dichotomies. If embraced by dominant pedagogies, identity texts and genre-flexible multilingual narratives can complexify dominant L2 writing teaching methods that mainly focus on teaching Anglo-American essay writing skills and thus create room for more gender expression and negotiation.

Similarly, in a more recent research trend, scholars have studied the challenges and experiences of women of colour in the process of migration in connection with L2 learning. For instance, Ennser-Kananen and Pettitt (2017) showed that, although counterintuitive, L2 proficiency does not guarantee social inclusion or socioeconomic advancement for migrant women. They state that:

> Racism, sexism, neoliberalism and other interacting systems of oppression can create dynamics that keep women out of classrooms, keep them from learning, and keep them from turning their linguistic gains into financial ones. Thus, any serious attempt at educating and empowering migrant women needs to also tackle these systems of oppression, as they exist within and beyond the receiving society and migrant communities. (Ennser-Kananen & Pettitt, 2017: 17)

In a different context but with a similar research mentality, Sandhu (2016) investigated the role of Hindi and English as the medium of education in urban North Indian women's existence in socioeconomic hierarchies. Emphasizing the role of labour in the migration of women in the neoliberal global market, Lorente (2017) and Vessey (2018) studied women of colour's involuntary domestic labour in the context of migration and the role of language in it.

Projects such as the ones described above are usually deemed to be connected to other research zones rather than mainstream L2 writing research. Thus, thinking about the place of qualitative studies of the relationship between gender and L2 writing, with a conscious attempt to highlight women L2 writers' sociocultural circumstances, literate lives, plurilingual identities, and multiliteracies would be a worthwhile endeavour.

Culture, race and ethnicity

In comparison with the fields of literacy studies, composition studies, and second language education in general – hosting a large number of projects on ethnic minorities such as students of colour or aboriginal students – there has been less attention to the cultural, racial and ethnic backgrounds of students in L2 writing research. The most noticeable body of research in L2 writing that specifically focuses on the impact of students' mother cultures is 'intercultural (contrastive) rhetoric' (Connor et al., 2008). This field of inquiry was born when (Kaplan, 1966) suggested that the problem of teaching ESL academic writing went beyond insufficient knowledge of vocabulary, grammar, and sentence structure. Kaplan urged ESL instructors to learn what sociologists and anthropologists had long known that language was a cultural phenomenon. Rhetorical rules, in the same manner, were cultural and historical constructs. In other words, different cultures produce different rhetorical traditions. As a result, in order to learn writing in a new language, one has to learn a new rhetorical/cultural convention as well as a new language.

All through the evolution of the field of intercultural (contrastive) rhetoric, L2 researchers have tried to compare and contrast rhetorical patterns employed in different cultures (read Connor (2002) for a review of the literature). Ventola and Mauranen (1991), for instance, compared Finnish academic writing and English scientific articles. Hatim (1997) analyzed Arabic-English discourse contrasts and differences in argumentation. Scollon and Scollon (1997), Zhu (1997), and Kong (1998) wrote about Asian-English contrasts. More recently, McKinley (2013) reported on Japanese to English contrastive rhetoric and Japanese university students' critical thinking in writing in English as an additional language. Exploring the rhetorical differences between Anglo-American journalistic writing and Iranian and Pakistani systems of newspaper article writing, Ansary and Babaii (2009) compared 90 editorials from *the Washington Times*, on the one hand, and *the Iran News* and *the Pakistan Today* on the other. With the similar textual approach, Nir and Berman (2010) examined complex syntactical structures in 64 narrative texts written by English, French, Hebrew and Spanish speakers (all graduate level university students) to shed more light on conversations about contrastive rhetoric. These are only some examples to illustrate the extent of work done in this area.

Similar to the main body of research interested in the impact of gender on L2 writing, most research on intercultural rhetoric has approached students' L2 writing through quantitative textual analysis. Although some qualitative research projects on contrastive rhetoric have been conducted (Benda, 1999), they have not attracted a lot of attention as key works and most of the research on the impact of students' cultures on their rhetorical tendencies is still very textual.

In the mother field of second language education, there has recently been a shift towards studying students' literacy engagements in relation to their culture, race and identity (Giroir, 2014; Golden & Lanza, 2013). This trend, however, is much less observable in L2 writing research. L2 writing researchers still prefer textual analysis to ethnographic descriptions of writers' literacy and writing practices informed by their cultures, races, and ethnicities.

Although qualitative research specifically interested in students' cultures, races, and ethnicities is not a prominent trend in L2 writing research, the impact of cultural and racial backgrounds of students on their writing – and sometimes specifically L2 writing – has not been ignored in research projects that highlight *class*, *multilingualism* and *multiliteracies*, which I discuss next.

Class (in association with ethnicity and language difference)

Quantitative projects that study the school performance of the children of immigrant low-income families, who use the languages of their hosts as additional languages, are not rare. One can find a large number of projects conducted by both large scale international research teams such as the Programme for International Student Assessment (PISA, 2012) and more local projects such as the research conducted by Shin and Otheguy (2013), which explored to what extent social class might have changed the Spanish spoken by Latin Americans in New York City. However, most of this kind of research comes from fields such as literacy studies or second language education in general rather than L2 writing research. The reports of these investigations usually focus on student literacy performances in general, yet if one probes them intentionally, one can find references to students' L2 writing as well.

Next to this body of quantitative research, there are examples of qualitative – mainly ethnographic – projects that discuss literacy and sometimes writing practices of the children of low-income bilingual or multilingual families. Nevertheless, similar to quantitative research concerned about the relationship between class and literacy learning, these projects hail from other areas of research – mainly literacy studies – rather than mainstream L2 writing research.

With the paradigm change in the field of literacy research following the emergence of the New Literacy Studies (Heath, 1983; Street, 1984), literacy researchers became interested in literacy activities of students, especially students that educational systems had failed. These students, not surprisingly, were usually financially and socially disadvantaged. Sociocultural descriptions of the literate lives of these students required a different set of research tools: qualitative ethnographic methods. As noted earlier, Heath (1983), in her *Ways with Words: Language, Life, And Work in Communities and Classrooms*, spent nine years performing a cross-cultural, ethnographical comparison of literacy practices between two small communities: Trackton, a working-class white community, and Roadville, predominantly African-American with the same average income. This study opened new methodological horizons that since then have been explored by many literacy researchers.

For instance, in *Immigrant Students and Literacy: Reading, Writing, and Remembering*, Campano (2007), a Filipino-American teacher researcher, described how he, along with his fifth-grade students, developed a language arts curriculum in a multilingual multiethnic school in the United States. The students, the children of immigrant families with more than 14 home languages, used their mother tongues, cultural practices and their own stories as the main components of the curriculum they created. In this research, Campano (2007) employed practitioner research paradigms to tell the story of his class. Blurring the border between research and practice, 'most versions of practitioner inquiry share a sense of the practitioner as knower and agent of educational and social change' (Cochran-Smith & Lytle, 2009: 37). Campano's ethnographic narrative is a good example of literacy research that also touches upon students' L2 writing.

Skilton-Sylvester (2002), in another practitioner led inquiry, gave a detailed qualitative description of her interactions with Nan, a primary school student who lived in a refugee Cambodian family of six in a one-bedroom apartment in a poor neighbourhood. Exploring Cambodian literacy practices in the form of a case study, she asked why Nan's literacy was deemed inadequate at school while she was such a prolific writer at home. Trying to answer this question, Skilton-Sylvester described how Nan, following Cambodian cultural norms, used oral expression and images alongside her English writing at home. These non-written forms of expression were usually ignored at school while rewarded at home.

Rather than presented as mainstream second language education research, the examples described above are associated with literacy research. This identification can highlight the fact that there seems to be more appetite and also comfort in the larger field of literacy research, in comparison with mainstream applied linguistics, to make sense of the experiences of multilingual learners ethnographically. The same methodological tools could be borrowed by L2 writing researchers interested in qualitative research on the literate lives and identity negotiations of L2 writers.

Multilingualism and multiliteracies

Over the past two decades, at least three influential academic conversations in education have pushed the field of literacy studies forward and helped combine discussions about gender, culture, race, ethnicity, and class into new packages such as *multiliteracies* and *multilingualism*: (1) the importance of students' literate legacies, for instance their 'funds of knowledge' (Barton & Tan, 2009; Moll *et al.*, 1992), (2) the importance of students' multiliteracies (Cummins, 2009a; New London Group, 1996), and (3) the availability of digital technology, which, by creating new semiotic possibilities, has driven the act of writing into a post-composition era (Dobrin, 2011). The above paradigms, among others, have enabled researchers to approach L2 writing through a lens that sees cultural, linguistic, and literate diversity of writers in ways that had not been discussed before. The research hailing from these theoretical frameworks has manifested itself in L2 writing research in two dominant trends: collections of (1) autoethnographic accounts and (2) case studies exploring the plurilingual, multicultural, and multiliterate lives of L2 writers.

Belcher and Connor (2001) in *Reflections on Multiliterate Lives* invited a group of multilingual scholars to share personal accounts (in narrative format) of their literacy engagements and practices and their challenges and experiences while learning an additional language. The writers involved in this project employed narrative research methods and autoethnographic reflections in order to display their literate lives as professional multilingual writers of English. Belcher and Connor found that although the scholars were challenged in different ways while writing across languages and cultures, they were not overcome by 'feelings of inadequacy, frustration and loss' (Belcher & Connor, 2001: 3); instead, they had clear visions of what they wanted to achieve and took control of their intellectual lives. The authors also regarded their book as contributing to the research trend that recognized the importance of narrative inquiry and autoethnography.

In the same manner, Casanave and Vandrick (2003), in a collection of first-person essays penned by published and established writers, illustrated how the process of publication involved shuttling between literate communities and literacies as a result of complex sociocultural and political negotiations. The accounts in the above collections are good examples of exploratory autoethnographic self-studies that illustrate the plurilingual, multicultural, and multiliterate lives of language learners and L2 writers.

Next to these collections of narratives, some case studies that followed more traditional empirical methods of qualitative inquiry have also been conducted. A focus on plurilingual, multicultural, and multi-literate identities of L2 writers requires qualitative reflections that can more comfortably occur in ethnographies and case studies. Among the ethnographies and case studies focusing on L2 writers, there are two projects that are frequently referenced in L2 writing research. Prior (1998), in *Writing/Disciplinarity: A Sociohistoric Account of Literate Activity in the Academy*, conducted ethnographic case studies of some graduate students' engagements with literacy in their academic disciplines. Prior conducted interviews, observed classroom activities, studied students' texts and analyzed teacher feedback on their texts in order to describe the students' writing processes. Through the ethnographic observations of these students' written and non-written commutation, Prior showed that literacy, rather than a fixed notion, was an open discourse constantly mediated by people, practices, artefacts, and institutions.

The second publication that has attracted the attention of L2 researchers is a case study of a Chinese teenager writing on the internet in English (Lam, 2000). Employing ethnographic methods and discourse analysis, Lam tracked the identity negotiations of an L2 writer through his online correspondence with a transnational group of peers. In order to map out the L2 literacy of this teenager, Lam employed participant observation, interviews, and textual analysis – a reminder of the shift in L2 research towards mixed and qualitative methodological approaches that can effectively reveal the multilingual and multiliterate lives of the students as well as the written texts they produce.

As these examples show, with the growth of the importance of sociocultural approaches to L2 writing research, there has been a shift from text-oriented quantitative analyses towards more qualitative research in the field. Also, with more awareness about the complexities of literacy learning and of language learners as plurilingual, multicultural and multiliterate people, boldly demarcated areas of inquiry in L2 writing research such as *gender, race* and *class* are discussed in more complex concepts such as *student identity* and *multiliteracies* along with other factors. This trend, however, seems to have been growing in the absence of engagement by mainstream L2 research in inquiries concerned about the impact of learners' lives on their writing. Most of the ethnographic qualitative projects described above were conducted in the larger field of literacy research, although the ones chosen happened to touch upon the lives of L2 writers. There is still much room for growth in mainstream L2 research for a serious focus on literacy practices and literate lives that can specifically impact student L2 writing. This book attempts to contribute to this area of inquiry.

Fortunately, as this chapter demonstrates, there is already a rich theoretical context and also enough empirical precedence for serious engagement with learners' literate, cultural, and intellectual lives and how those impact their multilingual writing. The slowness in L2 writing research in creating a holistic approach to students' writing events, more than a lack of knowledge or interest, is a result of our heavily industrialized and compartmentalized educational structures. In mainstream schools and universities, educators, following a Fordian conveyer belt mentality, are assigned, in different courses and levels, to only focus on certain regulated writing events. Students' writing practices are levelled in complicated categories according to streaming models such as academic-creative, academic-applied, native speaker-English learner, beginner-advanced, children-adult, and so on. Moreover, teaching writing is regarded as the job of general education programs and has thus been severed from organic contexts of specialized courses where writing should actually occur. Also, students' out-of-school writing practices are, typically, neither invited into the official classroom nor recognized as relevant to current genre-specific grade-earning writing assignments. Additionally, our rubrics, industrial assessment tools for mass evaluation, are not efficient enough to assess students' cultural and intellectual engagements that can significantly impact their writing practices. Our rubrics cannot make sense of students' cultural practices or their communities' beliefs about literacy. They do not reward students if they create artistic, activist, or entrepreneurial bonds with other students outside the classroom context or beyond the syllabus content.

The rubrics are also blind to the importance of students' mentors in their families, neighbourhoods, or online communities. Hence, our regimented writing curricula have not encouraged funding research that is interested in writing as a cultural practice connected with students' lives and their positions in the world. In this book, I try to highlight some less discussed dimensions of multilingual writing in order to demonstrate their significance and their pedagogical relevance.

3 Making Sense of Histories and Literate Legacies

Leaning against the literature outlined in the previous chapter, I studied the literate lives of three multilingual writers who successfully wrote in English. I approached these writers in Toronto, Canada after their immigration to the country. I was interested to learn how they understood and engaged with literacy, especially with writing in English during and in the wake of their migration. I was also curious about the social, cultural, and political contexts of their writing. Additionally, I wanted to learn about their intercultural and translingual practices. I intended to show that these writers' histories, perceptions and experiences could inform our everyday pedagogy and practice.

Inspired by the New Literacy Studies frameworks (Heath, 1983; Scollon & Scollon, 1981; Street, 1984), I thought of the concepts 'literacy' and 'literate lives' as *situated linguistic engagement* for the sake of having a conceptual launching pad to initiate the research project. However, these concepts were mobilized as open-ended constructs to be shaped during the course of my project by the participants' perceptions of and experiences with literacy.

Approach

I approached the project as a *case study* inasmuch as it followed these criteria for the qualitative case study design: (1) it addressed a *phenomenon*; (2) it explored a *bounded system*; and (3) it was intended to have a *descriptive* nature (Hatch, 2002: 30). The phenomenon that I studied in this project was the socioculturally embedded literate lives of three adult immigrant multilingual English writers and how their literacy activities, discursive lives, and social practices had informed their writing in English. I focused on the said phenomenon within a 'bounded system' (Creswell, 2007: 73) or in a 'natural context, bounded by space and time' (Hancock & Algozzine, 2006: 15). A bounded system, in other words, is a system 'in which the unit of analysis has fairly clear-cut boundaries in the eyes of the researcher' (Faltis, 1997: 145). Consistent with these definitions of a bounded system, the unit of analysis was the socioculturally embedded literate lives of three adult immigrant multilingual writers in Toronto, Canada from 2015 to 2018 and their recollections of their past literate histories in relation with their English writing. The design of this project, thus, was similar to that of a *multiple* (or *collective*) *case study* in that, by studying the literate lives of three participants, 'one issue or concern is ... selected, but the inquirer selects multiple case studies to illustrate the issue' (Creswell, 2007: 74). Accordingly, I also paid attention to individual differences between the participants as long as those shed light on the sociocultural circumstances of the participants' literate lives and histories. Finally, in harmony with the third criterion listed above, I aimed to provide a detailed description of the complexities of the literate, sociocultural and sociopolitical lives of the participants and the impact of their literate lives on their writing practices. This case study, thus, is more *descriptive* than *exploratory* or *explanatory* (Yin, 2009).

Case studies typically follow three main methodological orientations: *ethnographic*, *historical* or *psychological* (Merriam, 1998). This case study is an *ethnographic case study* for the following reasons. First, this study involved 'extended interaction with the group, during which the researcher [was] immersed in the day-to-day lives of group members' (Hancock & Algozzine, 2006: 31). I interacted with the three participants in this project – within and without this study – for years. I shared lived experiences with the participants as a 'skilled immigrant', in official terms, or a member of the community of educated international immigrants in Toronto. The immersion in the community thus preceded the choice and recruitment of the participants, and of course continued in a more systemic way after the official onset of this project. I regularly met the participants and observed their literacy practices at home, at work, and also online. I read the texts that the participants had written and discussed their content with them. I also met some of their family members and friends, and occasionally collaborated with them on other academic or cultural projects. Moreover, as a fellow immigrant, I frequently spoke with them about the discursive and hermeneutic possibilities that could help us communicate our skills and literacies in order to settle in Canada and navigate our future lives as adult professionals.

The phenomena studied in different traditions of case study research are usually 'events', 'situations', 'programs' and 'activities' (Hancock & Algozzine, 2006: 17). The phenomenon studied in this project – the participants' socioculturally embedded literate lives characterized by their literacy practices and literate histories – however, was more of a culture than the above cases, although I also explored the participants' activities and their life events and situations. The studied phenomenon was a *literate culture* shared by *practicing multilingual writers* in Toronto. A literate culture, in the context of this research, can be described as practices such as writing in English as an additional language, identifying Canadian writing genres, negotiating one's literate identity in the new context, joining writing communities, creating readerships in a learned language, navigating Canadian hermeneutic habits, and analyzing the dynamics of publishing and dissemination in Canada. Since I studied the dimensions of a literate culture experienced by all the participants as a *culture-sharing group* (Harris, 1968), this inquiry assumed an ethnographic character although it remained more of a case study than a classic ethnographic inquiry.

Evidence

Case study researchers make use of multiple sources of data including interviews, observations and documents (Creswell, 2007; Hancock & Algozzine, 2006; Hatch, 2002; Stake, 1995; Yin, 2009). Following the same tradition, I collected data for this study from the following sources: (1) interviews, (2) observations, (3) documents (including the participants' writings), and (4) literacy artefacts.

Interviews

Conducting interviews was the first step of the process of data collection. The interviews were a major source of information for this project. The interview data guided my observations and directed me to the documents that needed to be examined. I conducted three rounds of interviews. First, I spoke with each of the participants separately in a number of informal in-person interviews to discuss the context, design, and implications of this project. The first round of interviews allowed me and the participants to co-build a narrative about our shared experiences as multilingual writers. Due to the ethnographic nature of this study and my shared history with the participants as skilled immigrants, these preliminary interviews helped us generate a common understanding among us of the purposes of this project: exploring the literate culture that had helped us write in English (as well as in other languages that we knew) and be embraced by English readers and writers.

In the second round of the interviews, I conducted formal semi-structured open-ended individual interviews with participants to discuss their literate lives including the discourses through which they thought about literacy, the literacy events that they engaged in, the sites where their literacy activities occurred, the literacy artefacts that they used, and their multilingual writing histories, particularly their writing in English. Similar to the previous round of interviews, all the conversations in the second round were in person.

Finally, I invited all the participants to meet one another in a number of group interviews. The group interviews happened in three formats: face-to-face meetings, Skype conversations and email correspondence. Group interviews gave us the chance to share doubts, fill gaps, clarify thoughts, and follow up on new leads.

Observation

Guided by the interviews, I made observations of the participants' sites of literacy including their homes, workplaces and other literacy sites that they frequented such as libraries and even online spaces. As I will elaborate in the following pages, I had close relationships with the participants, and hence I had organic access to the sites mentioned. These observations helped me develop a more evidence-based understanding of the literacy events that the participants performed and the literacy habits that they had developed as a result of their literate histories. Observational data thus was used next to the participants' perceptions for a clearer picture of their literate lives with evidence of a different kind.

Documents

I gathered two groups of documents. First, I collected and perused all the writing samples that the participants could make available, including what they had written in English, in their mother tongues, and in other languages they knew. The texts that I prioritized for close reading were the participants' published writings; however, I also read their other writings that were available and shared with me. It should be noted that the latter body of text included the participants' writing on social media. Second, I gathered all accessible certificates, awards, letters to and from the participants, reviews and reports of their work, their multiple CVs at different points of their lives, and any other documented data that could inform me about the academic, professional, and intellectual communities that the participants had associations with.

For the analysis of the participants' written products, (a) I listed the topics each text focused on and categorized the foci in groups with relevant conceptual themes, (b) I identified the genre and the style of each piece, (c) I investigated the publishing and dissemination history of each publication, (d) I studied the purpose, the audience, and the reception of each text, (e) I extracted the major discourses that each text drew on, and (f) less systematically and more holistically, I looked for instances of intercultural rhetoric and translanguaging. This process of analysis would understandably become challenging when I dealt with texts written in languages that I did not know. In those cases, I discussed the same issues with the participants and recorded their thoughts.

For the analysis of the second group of documents such as CVs, certificates, awards, and reviews, I constructed the participants' professional histories based on significant progress and/or shifts in their careers and education reflected in these documents. Studying these documents, I specifically imagined what connections there could be between the participants' life histories and the writing they engaged with, examples of which you will see in the following chapters.

Literacy tools and artefacts

During the interviews and observations, I paid attention to the literacy tools and artefacts that the participants regularly used or had used in the past. I made lists of these artefacts and tools and archived pictures of them if they were available in the sites of literacy that I observed. These artefacts – which included books, dictionaries, newspapers, digital devices, applications, word processes, word games, puzzles, and so forth – were catalogued to help with analysis of the data for making sense of the sociocultural, financial and technological circumstances in which the participants' literacies were embedded.

Making Sense of the Data

All the data collected in the course of the study was pooled in a *case study database*. This database hosted all the field notes, transcribed interviews, memos, and detailed descriptions of photographs and pictures. Once all the data resided in the database, the data was coded. Significant words, expressions, and sentences were identified and coded by *vivo codes*, short descriptors, for survival and coping purposes. Next, the coded data were put back together in a variety of ways to let meanings, themes and categories develop. The analysis, thus, was a form of *categorical aggregation* (Stake, 1995), in which collections of instances in data, rather than single occurrences, are put together for relevant meanings and patterns to be developed. Categorical aggregation was particularly useful for this project – a multiple case study – since it allowed me to follow a replication logic and to conduct cross-case synthesis for comparison and contrast between the cases. The theories constructed in the course of the study were generated in a spiral rather than a linear fashion. In other words, data collection and analysis were mutually informed by one another along the way.

All through the process of analysis, I also used member checking to avoid misrepresentation of the participants' experiences. As stated previously, my participants and I used this project to make sense of our lives in North America as educated and skilled immigrants. Given this approach – as well as the impact of my close relationship with Magda, Choman and Clarice (personal and intellectual) on the process – more than participants, I saw these writers as co-researchers. The process of member checking for this project, thus, was not only a technical step for validation but an organic development for collective presentation of experiences and more meaningful theorization. An important outcome of this approach was the way this collective inquiry impacted the participants' comprehension of their own literate and writing lives. In our final group interview, I asked the three writers for reflections on our research process. Choman said, 'I don't usually look back at my life; I tend to look ahead. But because of these conversations, I feel I know much more about myself today. This can help me overcome some of my anxieties as a writer'. Magda added, 'The best part of this collaboration was creating a community, which reminded me of the significance of talking to each other … of the importance of conversation. This only makes us feel we're not alone'. Clarice also said, 'Listening to other members' experiences made aspects of my own writing visible for me that I had never noticed before'.

Participants and Their Histories

Following the norms of case study research, the three participants were selected by *purposive* (or *purposeful*) *sampling*. In *purposive sampling*, the researcher specifies the major characteristics of a population of interest and then tries to recruit individuals who have those characteristics. The criteria considered for inviting the participants to join this project were as follows. First, the three participants were adult multilingual writers whose writing in English – as an additional language – was received positively in their academic, literary, and/ or professional circles in Toronto after their immigration to Canada. Second, the participants represented three different ethnic backgrounds: Clarice: Brazilian, Magda: Hungarian and Choman: Kurdish. This variance in ethnicity would allow me to compare and contrast the experiences of writers with different linguistic backgrounds with writing in English while I was creating an account of their literate lives. Third, these writers were purposefully approached based on the writing genres that they principally focused on. Clarice regularly engaged with English academic writing; Magda did technical writing and business correspondence; and Choman was a creative writer who had published novels and short stories in English.

In the narratives that follow, I try to create some context for the readers to make better sense of the participants' literate histories. These histories have been constructed based on the participants' perceptions of their past as related to their literacy skills and writing lives. In each narrative, I highlight the participant's family and school circumstances, literacy and linguistic engagement, major political and historical events that impacted their literacy and writing lives, their experiences after arrival in Canada, and descriptions of their writing trajectories. Narratives in the study of migrants (De Fina & Tseng, 2017) matter because,

> Telling stories is a way of sharing and making sense of experiences in the recent or remote past, and of recounting important, emotional, or

traumatic events and the minutiae of everyday life. Stories ... are central to the construction of individual and collective identities and are used to index ways of being and social identifications. Furthermore, stories carry weight in important institutional encounters such as employment and immigration processes. (De Fina & Tseng, 2017: 381)

Choman

Choman (pseudonym chosen after Choman Hardi, the participant's favourite Kurdish writer) is a Kurdish novelist. She has published stories in English in Toronto and received some attention from Toronto literary circles. She also writes as a journalist and a literary critic. Choman is multilingual. Besides English and Kurdish (her mother tongue), she also knows Farsi and to a lesser degree, Arabic and French. She writes in English, Farsi, and occasionally in Kurdish. She started to learn English in secondary school, but she did not start writing stories in English until 2007, when she came to Canada. Choman left Canada to live in California in 2016.

I met Choman in Toronto in 2014. Through my connection with the Persian-Kurdish community, I heard about an Iranian-Canadian novelist called Choman, who wrote in English, and I started to follow her on Facebook. I met Choman after reading her first novel in English and a few years after I followed her social media activities. Our interests had a number of areas of overlap, which facilitated our connection. I read her fiction because of my curiosity about Canadian immigrant literature. An immigrant myself, I felt an urge to engage with Canadian literary works penned by other newcomers to Canada. Also, as an educator, I was eager to learn about ethnic minorities in Toronto and their experiences with migration; this knowledge, I believed, would help me interact with minoritized students in my classes more effectively. Following Choman's work, I became interested in her involvement in what she called the 'Kurdish cause'. I have been contributing to academic conversations regarding mother tongue-based multilingual education in Iran through a number of publications and presentations (Kalan, 2016). As an Iranian Kurdish activist, Choman wrote and was passionate about the state of the Kurdish language. Befriending her would allow me to learn more about her ideas and also the views of other mother tongue activists in her circle. Through Poets, Essayists and Novelists (PEN) Canada, she ran creative writing workshops and taught writing courses in a number of Toronto colleges, which facilitated our meeting through mutual educator/writer friends. Briefly after we first met, Choman decided to participate in my research project in response to my invitation.

Choman was born into a middle-class Kurdish family in Tehran in 1981. Her mother was a teacher from Sanandaj in Iranian Kurdistan. She had migrated to the capital for work and study. Her father was a journalist who worked for a TV station in Tehran while studying at university. After Choman's birth, however, the family did not stay in Tehran for much longer. Choman's father was arrested by the government for political activism. He was imprisoned; the family's apartment was confiscated; and Choman's mother returned to Kurdistan with Choman. With the assistance of Choman's aunts, all practicing teachers, Choman's mother resumed teaching in Sanandaj. The income of the family, though, was meagre – a reality of life for provincial Iranian teachers but perhaps a standard different from average North American teachers' income. As a result of this background, Choman's recollections of her past, including her literate life, were always tinted with memories of severe poverty.

This financial distress – which would not lose grip on the family even after the return of Choman's father after incarceration – informed most of Choman's descriptions of her literate activities, along with two other factors: the broken relationship between her parents and also her life as a girl in the traditional Kurdish society of the time. Shortage of money intensified the negative impact of the two other factors: it eroded the emotional bond between the family members, and it also targeted Choman's educational needs, some of which were deemed unnecessary luxury for a girl and thus a waste of money based on the traditional gender roles.

Despite all the socioeconomic odds against Choman, she not only survived but flourished educationally. Choman's descriptions of her literate activities in childhood indicate that the fact that Choman had educated parents (and aunts) saved her literacy life in different ways. Choman's father had received a master's degree when – as reported by Choman – 'at least half of the population of Kurdistan did not even achieve high school graduation'. Choman's mother also had a bachelor's degree, worked as a professional educator, and was the only breadwinner of the family when not many women worked outside their houses.

After his time in prison as a political dissident, the relationship of Choman's father with Choman and her mother was so problematic that Choman did not shy away from framing his behaviour towards them as 'misogynistic'. The resultant cold environment at home did not foster many occasions for oral exchange of thoughts and ideas. There was, however, an important literacy refuge: everybody read books together, although silently. What connected the family members were the written words quietly lying in Choman's parents' sizable library, which was her main source of solace at home. She learned the habit of reading from her parents as the only form of entertainment in her schooling years. Reading was an adventure that would lead to writing as the only form of expression accessible to Choman, although she was the only audience of her own work.

As a child, Choman wrote in response to the lack of communication at home and her vulnerable position as the family's daughter. She often read and wrote stealthily since engaging with any books other than school textbooks was not considered legitimate schoolwork. Choman described her act of writing in this period as speaking with pages when nobody listened and also a form of resistance. Although developed in the context of her childhood home, this view of writing would become the foundation of Choman's literate life at school and in society both before and after immigration to Canada. Choman told me she always felt an urge to stand up and speak out although there was a price to pay: rejections, dismissals, and exile.

At primary school, Choman wrote prolifically. She kept a diary, wrote reflections, recorded her philosophical speculations, and wrote stories with animal characters. She described what she wrote at the time as a mix of organizational, therapeutic, reflective and fictional. She wrote in Farsi, her second language and the compulsory language of instruction at school. She did not write in Kurdish, her mother tongue, because familial and societal discourses that she had access to did not encourage or value writing in Kurdish – a literacy practice she would adopt decades later on social media to reach out to a larger Kurdish audience beyond Iranian borders. Choman's need to write and her frequent engagement with Farsi helped her – unlike many of her classmates – to excel in the language to an extent that she at times corrected her Farsi teachers. She sometimes fell into trouble for the perceived academic irreverence, yet she welcomed the adventure as long as it helped her construct her identity as a just rebel who used language to challenge authority.

Choman added to her linguistic repertoire by majoring in English Literature in a university in Kurdistan. She completed her undergraduate education in her hometown, but graduate studies in 'foreign languages' – as it was called – was, at the time, only possible in the capital. As a result, she decided to move to Tehran. Receiving a master's degree, Choman started to work in a number of part-time college-level teaching positions away from the capital. Most notable among these positions is her job on an island, Qeshm, in the southernmost area in the country. Accepting a job in such a remote area was not what many young women in Iran would do. She, however, went to the island and became a source of inspiration for the local girls who became her students, an experience Choman called her 'sweetest memory in life'.

While studying in Tehran, Choman was still writing stories in Farsi. With state censorship controlling the literary scene in Iran, independent writers pursued their activities in underground writing circles, the most important of which were established and run by famous banned writers. Choman joined the Gol circle (pseudonym), a writing community named after a respected modernist novelist, now run by his students after his death. Choman wrote many stories in the Gol circle and established intellectual relationships that became important components of her identity as a writer and activist. With the exception of a few online publications, Choman never managed to publish a book in Tehran. It was impossible for her to acquire an official publishing permit for her stories, which focused on women's issues and the Kurds. The Gol circle years, however, were by no means futile. Choman had honed her creative writing skills, and more importantly she had earned the approval of an intellectual community who regarded her as a talented writer. When she was leaving for Canada, the manager of the Gol circle bid farewell to Choman with a final comment that Choman should not give up writing in Canada and that she had important stories that deserved to be heard, be it in a different language. He said she would be a great writer because she had a combination of talent and determination.

Choman learned English at secondary school. She was not exceptionally brilliant at English, yet she knew enough English to receive an admission to study English Literature at university. The university also did not particularly ignite her interest in English; Choman studied the required materials for her introductory English courses – with their focus on developing the four skills for non-native speakers – but did not passionately mix with the language as a source of intellectual inspiration. Farsi was still her main literary fuel. Choman's relationship with English changed when she started to read English fiction and poetry. *Animal Farm* and Langston Hughes' 'Theme for English B' and also women writers such as Emily Dickinson and Sylvia Plath were among her favourite English works and figures initiating her tight connection with intellectual thought expressed in English.

Once in Canada, Choman's linguistic landscape changed dramatically. In Iran's Kurdistan, Choman's dominant language for writing was Farsi. Writing in Kurdish was a skill she had never developed, and English was a new language, whose literature only marginally added to her literary life, which basically occurred in Farsi. In Canada's Ontario, Choman re-prioritized her linguistic life. She learned French, started to write fiction in English for the first time, and embarked upon seriously engaging with her mother tongue, Kurdish, by writing the language and reading its classical texts.

Choman had entered Canada with a student visa for a graduate Creative Writing programme in a reputable college in Toronto. Application to such a programme was partly a conscious decision for a change in Choman's life to focus entirely on writing fiction, but it was also an attempt to receive a university admission to enable her to experience living in a different country. The Creative Writing programme – along with a number of other writing-related courses and workshops including a two-year programme in editing – created important networking possibilities for Choman. On the one hand, she managed to enter communities of emerging writers in Toronto; on the other hand, she landed editing and writing teaching jobs as her main source of income.

Transition to a new life after immigration was not an easy process. Choman had to come to terms with her hyphenated identity, which she considered as a double-edged sword: a hindrance and, at the same time, a source of empowerment. She faced discrimination because she was not 'Canadian Canadian' – and she felt she would never be. On the other hand, however, she had access to Kurdish-Iranian cultural practices – such as daily interaction with song and poetry, as she exemplified – which for Choman was a source of peace of mind, satisfaction, and an antidote to the alienation and depression caused by life in a consumerist society. As a Kurdish-Iranian, Choman had already practiced living a hyphenated life and adding another hyphen to make space for her new 'Canadian' identity, although difficult, was not an impossible challenge.

A more complex cultural negotiation was language, the very tool of Choman's craft as a story writer. Unlike Magda and Clarice, who – as academic and technical writers – used language to mainly report and communicate, Choman, in addition, used language aesthetically. Choman told me she always felt vulnerable as an 'accented writer'. Choman's mastery and command of the Farsi language would not easily translate into English: the lexical control, tone consciousness, colloquialism, and so forth. Choman described herself as an energetic runner whose feet were chained. Despite this challenge, Choman wrote stories in English and, perhaps more importantly, published them. She ironically was first published in this learned language.

Choman published her first book only a few years after her arrival in Canada in 2010. The book, Choman's first attempt in writing in English, is a collection of short stories. Each story focuses on the life of an Iranian woman. The women of her stories live in a variety of settings from urban neighbourhoods in the Iranian capital to remote villages in Kurdistan. The theme that connects the stories is the struggles of Iranian (mainly Kurdish) women to fight back patriarchal societal forces that surround them. The resistance is portrayed in a variety of manifestations: in the state's treatment of women, in women's relationships with their partners and families, and in different forms of sisterhood. Choman's first book was published by a publisher who was interested in dissemination of the voices of non-white Canadian writers. Choman's book, and the readings and speeches which followed the publication, consolidated her position in the Canadian community of writers with an international background, which, it should be stressed, was – and still is – a precarious marginalized circle, often critical of privileged mainstream Canadian literature.

Choman's second book was published in 2013. The book relates the final days of the life of a Kurdish village teacher in prison. The primary school teacher has been imprisoned because of alleged involvement in separatist attempts for an independent Kurdistan, a charge he denies but for which he is punished by death. While in prison, he writes letters to his students and to his family and friends. Choman's book is a poetic representation of these letters, reflecting the teacher's thoughts, beliefs, and hopes. Choman published this book in England with another non-mainstream publishing house, which specifically supported books focusing on human rights issues. In addition to these two main books, Choman has published a number of short stories with similar themes in literary magazines in and outside Canada.

The media attention that Choman received after the publication of her literary work resulted in a number of awards, scholarships and invited council memberships (which I cannot list to protect Choman's anonymity). Additionally, in the wake of publication, Choman gave a number of speeches, interviews and readings (in Kurdish, Farsi and English). She also actively engaged with social media to reach and expand her readership. This body of written and oral text – which included much sociopolitical commentary – practically became a significant component of Choman's writing trajectory, and to the extent that it created a turn in her career by pushing her towards journalism.

In the midst of political developments in the Middle-East when we were conducting the research – especially with the visibility that the Kurds found in the wake of the decentralization of Iraq and Syria – Choman became heavily involved in writing about the Kurdish cause as a journalist. The result of this phase of Choman's life was tens of articles in English explaining issues regarding the Kurds, their challenges, and their visions for the future. While writing for news media outlets, Choman continued working on her fiction in the United States, to which she moved in 2016, following her husband's acceptance of a job offer. She is currently seeking ways to enter the mainstream literary scene in the United States, mainly in order to reach a larger audience. She has become an active member of a number of literary circles in the United States, exchanging experiences with American writers. Choman is critical of the commercialization of literature in the United States, yet at the same time she tries to break into the system while maintaining her literary, intellectual and ideological integrity.

Clarice

Clarice (pseudonym chosen after Clarice Lispector, the participant's favourite Brazilian writer) is a Brazilian PhD candidate at a prestigious university in Canada. She is a teacher and a researcher. She teaches groups of adult English learners at college level. She also occasionally teaches sessional courses at university level. She was selected for this project as the participant whose academic writing in English was received on a par with native writers of English by editors, peers, and professors. Although not a native speaker of English, not only was she able to comfortably deal with her university assignments as a student, she had also published some English academic articles as well as a few in Portuguese, her mother tongue. In addition to English and Portuguese (her mother tongue), she also knows Italian and Spanish. She wrote in Portuguese, in English, and, much less frequently, in elementary Spanish. She started to learn English at the age of 13. She has been actively writing in English since 1994, when she went to university to study English literature. She moved to Canada in 2008.

Clarice is a PhD student in language education in a respected university in Toronto. She is a graduate researcher, already emerging in her field as an important academic voice because of her scholarly contributions. I first met Clarice in 2013 in a Critical Pedagogy course, and we almost immediately became intellectually intimate thanks to our shared interested in exploring what critical pedagogy meant in additional language education. We collaborated on different projects and formed an informal academic circle consisting of the department's international students interested in multilingual education. Next to academic interests, what had brought Clarice and me (and other students in the circle) together was a need to share our struggles and experiences as international professionals. We exchanged information about our research projects, the university's structural and procedural dynamics, conferences, journals, employment opportunities, and so forth. We regularly met on and off campus and collaboratively navigated our way through our journeys as immigrant academics. I invited Clarice to join the project as an academic writer after the publication of her first few English articles.

Clarice was born in 1976 in Brazil in a small city in the state of São Paulo. She was born into a working-class family tense with relationship problems. Clarice was the family's third daughter. Her father, the child of Italian immigrants, suffered from lack of job security compounded with an alcohol problem. The father's situation corroded his relationship with Clarice's mother to a degree that the couple had to separate. Clarice's parents divorced when she was 12. Clarice's mother had little formal education (up to grade 5) and no source of income. Now a single mother, with three young daughters, she had to steer the family through a precarious financial situation – a taxing job that she would successfully handle by bringing up educated daughters, two currently teaching in Brazil and Clarice pursuing an academic life in Canada.

The family's financial struggles loomed significantly large in Clarice's recollections of her childhood and her literacy engagement in that period. Clarice's mother weathered the situation and generated hope in the family by creating the discourse that education was the only solution to the problems that the children had. Clarice and her sisters had access to public education, which removed a concern for making enough money for tuition. The girls believed that as long as there was peace at home and enough money to get by, education could transform their life if they studied hard. Clarice's mother did not merely preach the value of education but guided her daughters by example. Despite all the restrictions caused by running the family single-handedly, she went back to school to complete her primary and secondary education. Meanwhile, she actively engaged with her daughters' schooling by creating a safe space at home, providing constant supportive supervision, and giving priority to the girls' educational needs in the family budget. After graduating from high school, Clarice's mother decided to attend college also. In fact, she graduated from college the same year as Clarice did. Her passion for learning was contagious and created a consciousness about the impact of education among the girls that would remain with them for the rest of their lives.

The emphasis on education at home created an urge in the girls to study. Clarice – as she remembered – became 'addicted to studying'. She at times refused to play on the street with her friends – a cultural norm in their neighbourhood – to stay at home and study. There was always schoolwork, and there were also books, although not many. Because of their socioeconomic status, the family could not buy many books and there was not an established reading culture. Clarice did not remember her parents ever reading to her. They were too busy working and had no time for activities of this nature. Thus, unlike the other two participants, Clarice did not enjoy the luxury of easy access to written print. Nevertheless, Clarice had her own creative ways to get her hands on printed words. She read her older sisters' books and asked them questions about the content that she did not understand. The sisters – who would both become teachers – soon became Clarice's academic references, the role her parents never played. Clarice read her sisters' books, and when there were not new books, she re-read them. She even once attempted to memorize a dictionary. Clarice described this period in her life as a time of heavy engagement with learning, which was initially motivated as a solution for financial problems but gradually evolved into a form of love for learning and a thirst for knowledge.

Although print literacy was not the family's strongest tradition, oracy was. Clarice, her mother, her sisters, and sometimes also members of the extended family, like her aunts, constantly exchanged thoughts orally. If studying dutifully was deemed as a family mission to guarantee a better future for the daughters, dinner table conversations were a more organic literacy event functioning effectively in parallel with formal learning. The dinner table gatherings prepared a safe space for the children to express, listen, and develop a sense of belonging. Clarice recalled the family's dinner table exchanges as the backbone of her literate life – a foundational blueprint for her comprehension of the world, communication of perceptions, and dissemination of knowledge. The dinner table conversations – which could take up to five hours – were free-flowing oral texts that would embrace different subjects based on the circumstances, the family members' interests, and the family's emergencies. Clarice left the childhood house many years ago, but still whenever the family re-unites – in Canada or Brazil – the dinner conversations resume. Interestingly, thanks to digital technology, even when the members are separated, they seek each other's advice through groups they have created on mobile applications. Clarice could receive up to 100 messages a day.

The pro-education context in which Clarice grew up created a fertile ground for her multiple literacy activities. Next to school academic involvements, she wrote plays and directed small theatrical productions. She also developed a passion for indie rock and later became the lead vocalist in the rock band that she created with her friends and led.

Another major literacy event was language learning, most importantly engagement with English. Clarice's interest in English started with pop culture and American music. As a child, she memorized the lyrics that she heard on the family radio, especially the words sung by the members of her favourite band New Kids on the Block. Clarice's older sister – who had learned English at school – gave her elementary lessons and taught her how to use an English-Portuguese dictionary to decode the American pop lyrics. At school, English became one of her favourite subjects. Yearning to learn more English than regularly taught at the public school where she was attending, she decided to enrol in a private language school. At home, the debate over the tuition fee for Clarice's new extracurricular activity did not take much time: there was no extra money for English. There was only one possibility: Clarice would have to negotiate with her departed father for financial help. He agreed to pay the fees, which was the only financial contribution to the family since his divorce. After a few months, however, he ran out of money and Clarice stopped going to the language school. Nevertheless, Clarice's English teacher would not lose one of her best students. She knew of an institutional grant for underprivileged students who were interested in learning languages and guided Clarice's mother to apply for the grant. Clarice learned English in the same language school for free until she was accepted at university to study English Literature.

Clarice's passion for English did not make her oblivious to the colonial and imperial nature of the spread of the English language and its expanding hegemony in the world. Clarice regretted not spending more time on Spanish. She believed it was stunning how little Spanish she was exposed to in a continent where almost everyone but Brazilians spoke Spanish. While the Brazilian radio stations that Clarice listened to gave generous amounts of airtime to English songs, there was little interest in Spanish content. This issue was never a passing concern in Clarice's house. One of Clarice's sisters has always refused to speak English, although she knows the language. In a contrasting path – in comparison with Clarice's choice to devote her time to English – Clarice's sister embarked on learning a Brazilian indigenous language as a form of resistance against linguistic imperialism imposed by the dominance of English and also Spanish and Portuguese. Clarice's love affair with English thus has never been free from rough patches.

Clarice studied English Literature at Universidade de São Paulo (USP), the most prestigious higher education institution in the country. Entering the university, however, was not easy. Clarice never thought of applying to USP because she imagined a student with her economic background would never be admitted into the institution. She instead started studying Translation in a small university in São Paulo. In that college, through her newly established network of friends who were involved in language teaching, she took advantage of an inter-institutional undergraduate programme to take an examination which if passed, would enable her to study English Literature at USP. She comfortably passed the exam thanks to her command of English, a skill much sought after at the USP's English department.

Clarice's choice to study English literature was not accidental. While exploring English pop lyrics, Clarice also read her first English novel at the age of 14: George Orwell's 1984. Clarice regretfully remembered her lack of interest in the Portuguese literature taught at school, caused by pedagogical practices that obsessed over presenting the official canon and disregarded student engagement – a problem which often becomes more acute when students are from marginalized populations with little connection with 'official' literature. Through English, thus, Clarice saved her love for reading literature, but in a language different from her mother tongue. At university, she continued her engagement with literature, but in a more systematic fashion and with a critical edge. Clarice's professors shared an inclination to approach literature through critical theory, which for Clarice was a bridge between literature and social justice.

Clarice's BA in English Literature (with a minor in Linguistics) was only the beginning of a long scholastic journey in Brazil. By the time she moved to Ontario to study in Canadian higher education, she received an acting certificate from Senac São Paulo; also, she completed a Bachelor of Education at University of São Paulo. Additionally, she received a Certificate in English Language Teaching to Adults from the University of Cambridge. These qualifications solidified Clarice's career as an EFL teacher in São Paulo, Brazil's financial capital. Having come from a humble background, Clarice, now in her early twenties, had her own apartment in downtown São Paulo, a car, and enough money to enjoy a comfortable middle-class life. Nevertheless, after a while, Clarice decided to leave her life in Brazil to learn more about the world. Clarice used migration as an epistemological tool to quench her curiosity about what was happening beyond Brazilian borders.

She flew to Canada through an admission from a university in Ontario to do her third degree: Master of Arts in Applied Linguistics. Similar to the other participants, Clarice had to re-do graduate studies in Canadian institutions in order to penetrate the Canadian academic and professional structures. She, for instance, would not be able to teach English as an additional language – what she successfully did in Brazil – without receiving a certificate such as TESL Ontario. Even after graduating from lengthy TESL Ontario programmes, there was no guarantee that she would be given a job in the highly saturated teaching market in Ontario without the right connections. This phenomenon is often explained as lacking 'Canadian experience'. The term, however, has less euphemistic equivalents such as 'devaluation of foreign-acquired qualifications and credentials', or 'brain abuse' as labelled by Bauder (2003).

Going through the obligatory Canadian re-certification, more than learning academics, Clarice used her time to navigate major discourses in Canadian educational research. She also developed a network of scholars who appreciated her Brazilian experiences and helped her translate those into cultural codes understandable for Canadian academics. In a sense, Clarice used her time in graduate school as a space for intercultural negotiations.

Writing the Canadian way was among those negotiations. The Canadian instructors' perception of 'good' academic writing and their requirements were different from those of Clarice's Brazilian teachers. Clarice identified the differences, but she debated if she should conform to the new writing style. In our conversations, Clarice explained that she had to wrestle with two major rhetorical challenges when shifting to Anglo-American academic writing rhetoric. First, she had to come to terms with using the oversimplified 'thesis-support-conclusion' template since in Portuguese there was much more room in the structure of an article for manoeuvre. Second, South American argumentation and analysis had a more critical (if not radical) nature that Clarice saw missing in her classmates' writings. After a period of negotiation and experimentation, Clarice decided that she could make some formalistic compromise, but she would still make use of the Brazilian rhetoric by adding rich analyses to her pieces instead of mere illustration of facts. Clarice's style became her strength and was appreciated by graduate-level professors who expected to read deep analyses with a strong authorial voice. Clarice successfully developed a hybrid style which became the foundation of her academic writing all through her master's programme and also her doctoral studies in Language and Literacy Education, which she immediately started after her graduation from her master's programme.

Up to the moment of writing these lines, Clarice has published eight major academic papers and is working on six other pieces. Clarice published her first two articles immediately after starting her PhD programme. Clarice's first English article is a piece published in Brazil. The article reports how Clarice and her colleague incorporated drama activities into teaching English as an additional language in their language school in São Paulo. The second article – authored by Clarice only – focuses on ESL teaching methodology. Clarice published this piece in a Toronto professional magazine, which targets local ESL teachers. The first two publications were strategic choices for an international junior graduate researcher: with the first article, she flaunted her international experiences to an English-speaking audience; and with the second, she started to carve out her image as an emerging scholar in Toronto.

Clarice's next five publications solidified her academic position in terms of scholarship expected from a graduate researcher. By publishing in a number of prestigious journals – as a PhD student – Clarice contributed significantly to her field. She published an article about teaching intercultural competence in language classes in an important Canadian journal. She also published another article in one of the most reputed journals in her field internationally. This paper highlighted her experiences as a dramatist by making recommendations for teaching ESL through drama. In addition to publishing in these well-read and referenced journals, she also published a book chapter about linguistic and cultural diversity in a handbook on research and practice in heritage language education.

Clarice's last two publications were the result of her conscious attempt to re-connect with Brazilian educators and academics. She published an English article in a Brazilian journal and also a paper in Portuguese, a self-imposed challenge to share her research in her mother tongue.

Clarice shared with me her reflections on the process of writing and publishing academic papers. While Clarice was fulfilling her career requirements by writing and publishing, she developed deep philosophical rationales for her act of writing. Clarice regarded academic writing as practicing citizenship. She said she was writing because she felt she had something to say and what she said could have tangible impacts. Another important component of writing for Clarice was intercultural and interlingual communication, which would enable newcomers like Clarice to give to and take from the society they joined. By writing academically, Clarice said, she was conversing with Canadian society and making sense of it as her new home.

Magda

Magda (pseudonym chosen after Magda Szabo, the participant's favourite Hungarian writer) is Hungarian. She works as a learning consultant in a governmental organization in Toronto. She is involved in professional development and organizes workshops for government employees. Her work requires a great deal of letter writing, emailing, note sharing, memo writing and creating handouts and guidelines. She also has experience in creating educational textbooks. Magda is multilingual. Next to English and Hungarian (her mother tongue), she speaks German, Russian and Dutch. She writes in Hungarian, English and German. She started to learn English in secondary school and to write in English actively in 1999. She moved to Canada in 2012.

Magda works in a provincial ministry as a learning consultant. She is a staff trainer, project manager, executive consultant, and relationship advisor. She develops talent programmes for senior managers, facilitates career development panels and workshops, and develops communication, promotional and marketing strategies and materials (such as brochures and videos). Landing this consultant position in the tough Canadian job market – for a newcomer in particular – has been mainly the result of Magda's creative identity negotiation as an international professional with a rich background in human resources management, publishing, marketing and adult education. By adding a Canadian Public Administration degree to her previous qualifications, Magda successfully bridged her experiences into the Canadian job scene. Thinking about genre as a criterion for participant recruitment, next to Choman as a novelist and Clarice as an academic writer, Magda joined us as a technical writer. Magda has written a variety of language learning textbooks. Moreover, in her current position as a learning consultant, she engages with different forms of professional writing and writes letters, memos, briefing notes, presentation materials and speaking notes in English on a daily basis.

Magda and I were neighbours. We lived in the same apartment block and first engaged in conversation when picking up our children from the primary school in our neighbourhood. Magda and I (and our families) had just landed in Toronto. We were both navigating our ways through the maze of the employment process in Canada. We frequently met and talked about our struggles with university application and job search. Through these conversations, we discovered new areas of common interest such as literature, philosophy and art. We realized that employment was not the only challenge that we were facing as newcomers. Our expectations about artistic and literary engagement in everyday life also did not necessarily match the realities of mainstream Canadian culture industry, which, we found, was more commercial than intellectual. Magda – and also her husband, who was an accomplished artist – gradually filled the place of the intellectual friends that I had left behind as a result of immigration. After a break, I could again talk to some people about literature and philosophy in ways that felt more familiar for me.

Magda was born into an educated middle-class family in Budapest in 1972 and received schooling in Hungary's Communist era. Magda described her engagement with reading in the house as the main foundation of her literate life, a 'family tradition' – in her words – which she thought was established mainly because of her mother's career as a teacher. All the family members read a lot and read together. Some of the gaps between the reading spells also were filled with conversational exchanges about the books that they read. Magda's description of this ambiance almost perfectly matches the reading practices in Magda's own household today, with her husband and her daughter and also long periods of the presence of Magda's mother when she comes to Canada to see the family.

Similar to Clarice and Choman, Magda experienced parental disaccord. Magda's parents separated when she was 14. However, unlike Clarice and Choman's cases, my pool of data did not contain information about the impact of the divorce on her life or intense interactions between Magda and her father. One likely explanation based on Magda's statements might be that the vacuum caused by the absence of her father was immediately filled by Magda's two supportive brothers and her early marriage only a few years after the divorce. The next man in Magda's life also came quickly: her son, born when Magda was 19.

Among the three participants, Magda was the only one with children. It was interesting to be reminded by Magda that we often forget that motherhood (and parenthood in general) is also an important factor in one's intellectual and literate life. Magda had her son when she was young and her involvement in her son's education took the form of co-learning. They, for instance, learned new languages together. The parent-child collaborative learning continued with Magda's second child, although she was older when she had her. In Canada, Magda closely followed her daughter's education to learn about Canadian perceptions of quality literature and writing. Magda and her daughter navigated Canadian textual practices together by comparing them with Hungarian traditions.

In addition to the imprint of family literacy practices, Magda also regarded her experiences with official schooling as significant, although in her descriptions the latter often sounded like a secondary influence. A typical K-12 school in Budapest – like the one Magda attended as a child – offered rigorous traditional training (an approach shared by many other European educational structures). Although Magda felt things were changing now, she remembered the Hungarian pedagogical and curricular approach as extremely strict – a judgment that Magda made more confidently now that she could compare it with the Canadian approach. Hungarian primary school students were expected to read and write almost perfectly in grade one. In secondary school, the students were exposed to a lot of European literary classics, especially poetry. The materials were not levelled or watered down and there was no demand or desire to reform the dominant banking teaching model. Nor was the content watched for age appropriateness: Magda read a lot of 'dark, tragic, depressing' literature. Nevertheless, she enjoyed reading at school. It helped her relate with a range of human experiences, and the difficult language made reading an easy skill for her in her later life.

Despite the comfort that she felt dealing with the 'strict' Hungarian way of teaching reading and writing, Magda was by no means an obedient student. She frequently argued with her literature teachers and challenged dominant interpretations of the texts they read, a habit she even had at kindergarten. She only received one prize sticker at kindergarten, and it was because she had not argued with the teacher on that exceptional day. On the way back home, she debated whether it would be wise to share the news about the only honour sticker that she had been given, or if she should take the sticker off her uniform since it was more of a confirmation of her unruliness.

Magda went to school when Hungary was run by a communist system. I asked Magda how she remembered the effects of the system on her literacy practices. Magda shared a few thoughts. Education was free for the public. The schools were not always perfect and up-to-date, but Magda as the daughter of a middle-class family in the capital had constant access to publicly funded schools. Books were also affordable. Moreover, higher education – which was free also – was not regarded as a means to find higher paying jobs. Most people went to university simply to learn more and meet like-minded people, especially in the humanities. The flip side of the system was, however, the ideological hegemony reflected in the curriculum. The top-down curriculum interestingly included learning Russian, a demand whose rationale was not always clear to the students. Although Magda learned the language as a child, she never met a Russian until she came to Canada.

Magda's higher education qualifications are numerous, multi-disciplinary, and from multiple countries. When she was 21, she received a Bachelor of Education from a university in Budapest in 1993. Following that, she continued her studies in Austria in Language Education and also Educational Integration, both completed in 1999. Starting a career in textbook writing, she came to Canada to study Publication in a university in Toronto. After graduation, she went back to Hungary and studied a Bachelor of Pedagogy and Master of Adult Education. After her immigration to Canada she did yet another degree and studied Public Administration in Toronto.

Magda's time in Austria was very fruitful both linguistically and career-wise. Magda had learned some English at school (mainly in high school), but it was not until she started to study Language Education in English in Austria that she seriously engaged with learning English. At the same time, she had to learn German for everyday life and business connections. Despite the fact that her command of English and German was still far from advanced levels, she approached a prestigious Austrian publisher with ideas about multilingual books for language education. To her surprise, the publisher loved the idea and immediately employed Magda. An extension of the 1957 European Economic Community (EEC), the European Union (EU) was founded in 1993, only a few years before Magda found her job in Austria. Not surprisingly at the time in Europe, there was a lot of interest about education methods that could help Europeans communicate effectively despite language differences. In this atmosphere, Magda found herself in the middle of a community of European educators, administrators and policymakers who wrote textbooks in multiple languages. Magda gradually focused on producing textbooks that helped teachers teach language across the curriculum as opposed to offering languages in core subjects.

Whereas in Austria Magda mainly wrote textbooks, as a consultant in Canada she mostly engaged with transactional writing and preparation of training content. Once in Canada, Magda had to wait a while to find her way into the job market, dealing with the usual devaluation of foreign credentials. Despite the challenges, with her Canadian degree in Public Administration, she found a job in a provincial ministry as a learning consultant. Magda described her role as a staff trainer, project manager, executive consultant, and relationship advisor. She developed talent programmes for senior managers, facilitated career development panels and workshops, and created communication, promotional, and marketing strategies and materials.

In addition to numerous technical obstacles that hinder the progress of immigrants in Canada – most importantly the systematic devaluation of their education and professional knowledge – Magda, similar to Clarice and Choman, underwent different forms of identity negotiation to navigate cultural, communicative, and – as far as writing is concerned – rhetorical differences. Magda's sharing of such experiences was thought provoking since – unlike the other two participants – Magda could be categorized as white and Western. Despite the stereotypes regarding the monolithic nature of Western culture, Magda had to frequently adjust and compromise in order to culturally feel at home in Canada. Magda and her family were conscious of this reductionism regarding 'European whites'. Complaining about the invisibility of Hungarian culture under the large umbrella of 'white European', Magda's husband said that Hungarian identity had faded in grand cultural and historical narratives. Despite distinct characteristics and cultural practices, the Hungarians were naively pigeonholed as Western by non-Western people and broadly looked at as Eastern European by Americans and Western Europeans.

Magda, thus, had her own share of identity negotiation in Canada despite her 'whiteness'. Magda understood that the Canadians might do things differently and looking for ways for easier integration was helpful, but she believed there had to be some kind of third space (Bhabha, 1990) where newcomers and Canadians could have an intercultural dialogue with the immigrants offering their voices and views. Among the cultural challenges that Magda faced, she, for instance, was shocked at the amount of everyday writing people engaged with in Canada: emails, letters, applications, even school and university assignments. It is important to stress again that this cultural shock hit Magda despite her background as a highly educated European and also a technical writer constantly performing different forms of functional writing. As a newcomer, Magda also realized that Canada had a presentation culture where more than hard skills one needed the soft art of marketing oneself. A desire to share this knowledge with other newcomers directed Magda to form her current professional image as a consultant.

Such negotiations were difficult but advantageous. Magda believed her multilingualism and living in multiple cultures had enriched her life. Reading and writing in different languages had changed Magda's worldview in ways she could have never imagined. As much as her history was dear to her, she felt happy to have left behind a number of discourses that previously felt unquestionable. She did not give me particular examples of such discourses but told me that she now had fundamental ideological disagreements with her close friends who had continued to live in a mono-cultural monolingual mode.

Magda's writing trajectory can be divided to two major phases: before and after immigration to Canada. Before immigration Magda wrote and produced language learning textbooks, and after immigration she mainly engaged with transactional and technical writing. I approached Magda for the latter, for the writing genre which is often broadly labelled as 'business correspondence'; nevertheless, through this project I discovered that Magda had a fascinating history in her pre-immigration writing life – which was entirely hidden to me despite our close relationship and my general interest in her intellectual life.

Magda wrote 19 language teaching textbooks in Hungarian, German and English from 1999 to 2002. The books basically belonged to three language courses which she developed while working in Austria and Germany. The first course was a content area-based English Language curriculum, which was designed to teach English while students engaged with subjects such as mathematics, geography, history, music, art, and physical education. The second series was a course to make teaching and learning English as enjoyable as possible with thematic activities for the classroom. The third was a beginner English-German integrated curriculum that covered all subjects of the school curriculum.

Although Magda was working on a few textbooks when I was conducting this study, she had not published any textbooks in Canada yet. Instead, in her new job as a consultant in the ministry, she engaged with different forms of professional writing including: briefing notes for ministry's senior administrators; programme and project proposals; speaking notes for guest speakers at learning events; curriculum and programme guides for executive learning programmes; PowerPoint presentations; email and letter writing; and marketing statements.

Magda's writing trajectory could be better understood in the backdrop of her philosophical view of literacy, traces of which are visible all through her life. During our interviews, Magda enthusiastically spoke about self-awareness, grassroots leadership and mobilizing agency for change. Magda's writing has always been a means at the service of the actualization of the said concepts to lead her life into meaningful directions by exploring one's self, tapping into others' potentials and creating collaborative possibilities to bring about change.

***

The above narratives do not reflect the participants' complete histories. They are phenomenological reconstructions of the participants' pasts as relevant to their literate lives. These narratives are meant to highlight major events in the participants' lives that somehow influenced their writing trajectories. These stories hopefully can help readers contextualize the analyses and arguments that will be offered in the following chapters. My conceptualizations will be illustrated by Magda, Clarice and Choman's perceptions and experiences, and these broad sketches of their lives can help readers make better sense of those illustrations. In the following analysis chapters, these writers' life stories, perspectives, and experiences will be re-visited in connection with theories and concepts that shed light on sociocultural and power-relational layers of writing.

Furthermore, these narratives might include experiences that are shared by the students of educators who happen to read this book. In the introduction, I emphasized that although accomplished writers, the participants would not be treated as exceptional in this project but representatives of a large number of multilingual writers who on a daily basis engage with adopted languages in different contexts. This view convinced me to think about the participants as *practicing* writers as opposed to *professional* or *exceptional* writers. These brief narrative representations of the participants' lives, I hope, can help readers see that many of our students' experiences are similar to those of Magda, Clarice and Choman. Despite the participants' current positions with degrees of power, confidence, and influence, like many of our younger students, they had to struggle with issues such as family problems, financial shortages, concerns about identity, complex political contexts, and so on. These narratives thus can help contextualize the participants' experiences for easier identification and hence accessible inspiration.

4 Literacy and Writing Discourses

A significant consequence of the *social turn* in literacy studies – and accordingly in second language writing – has been the realization that in the process of learning languages and literacies, students' beliefs regarding literacy, the cultural values that they attach to reading and writing, and their ontological views of language learning matter immensely. This knowledge requires that educators, researchers, and curriculum developers proactively engage with learners' belief systems and find ways to navigate students' 'awareness of literacy, constructions of literacy and discourses of literacy, [and] how [they] talk about and make sense of literacy' (Barton & Hamilton, 2000: 7). This chapter offers arguments about the significance of writing and literacy discourses based on Clarice, Magda and Choman's statements; literacy and writing behaviours; social practices; and cultural backgrounds that can explain (a) what the participants regarded as 'literacy' and (b) what 'writing' meant to them. In my interactions with the writers who participated in my inquiry, I intended to address a number of questions regarding the participants' literate lives. Here are the questions that guided our conversations: What were the participants' major current and past literacy practices? What were some of the sociocultural, discursive and power-relational contexts of the participants' experiences with literacy? And how did those experiences impact their writing practices? This chapter specifically responds to the notion of discursive practices or the participants' perceptions of literacy and writing.

Before sharing descriptions of the participants' ontologies of literacy and writing, I provide a basic definition for the concept *discourses of literacy*, which inspired the title of this chapter. In order to show the complexities of the process of *language learning* – a term which rather inaccurately connotes languages are learned like other skills and techniques – language education scholars had to construct new concepts that would illustrate languages were not learned merely cognitively but languages *were lived* in actual sociocultural and power-relational contexts. These concepts entail a long range of endeavours to capture the multilayered nature of language. Among more established notions in the field of second language education, Swain (2006), for instance, offered *languaging*: 'a process of making meaning and shaping knowledge and experience through language' (Swain, 2006: 98); or in literacy research there were conceptualizations such as *literacy practices*, which Barton and Hamilton (2000) defined as 'the general cultural ways of utilising written language which people draw upon in their lives. In the simplest sense literacy practices are what people do with literacy' (Barton & Hamilton, 2000: 7). Similarly, from different academic quarters, scholars attempted to broaden our view of literacy by illustrating identity-based (Cummins, 2001; Cummins & Early, 2011), multiliterate (New London Group, 1996), plurisemiotic (Jewitt & Kress, 2003), and power-relational (Freire, 1970; Freire & Macedo, 1987; Janks, 2010) layers of language and literacy learning – on some of which I focus in the next chapters. This chapter hinges upon another important concept from the same trend: discourses of literacy.

Educators and learners walk into educational settings with discursive legacies that help them understand what literacy involves, why they should engage with reading and writing, and how they can teach and learn new languages. Educational institutions, similarly, are structured and run according to certain literacy discourses, or philosophies of teaching and learning. The same is also true about educational policies and curricula, which are designed in accordance with particular understandings of literacy. All these stake holders can only engage with literacy when they are situated within sociocultural discourses that facilitate their perceptions of reading and writing.

Being conscious of the discursive nature of literacy can help us see that teaching and learning are not only offering and receiving linguistic components of a language; language education is also an exchange of discourses of literacy between educators and language learners. Language learners – especially youth and adult skilled immigrants who are the main focus of this book – while reading and writing in a new language, experience living in new sociocultural existences. Language users in new cultures not only learn linguistically, they also have to navigate new belief systems about literacy, unfamiliar pedagogical practices, and discourses of literacy which are often different from their understandings of literacy in their own belief systems or what Gee (1986) called their 'discourse practices':

> Literacy is seen as a set of discourse practices, that is, as ways of using language and making sense both in speech and writing. These discourse practices are tied to the particular world views (beliefs and values) of particular social or cultural groups. Such discourse practices are integrally connected with the identity or sense of self of the people who practice them; a change of discourse practices is a change of identity. (Gee, 1986: 719–720)

Literacy discourse practices, thus, are *forms of consciousness* (Scollon & Scollon, 1981) regarding norms for text generation, distribution, preservation and semiotic consumption, which are formed and reformed as a result of our interactions with different *discourse communities* (Borg, 2003).

The construction of the concept discourse practices has been particularly instrumental in distinguishing between minoritized learners' native discourse practices and the literacy discourses practiced in dominant educational settings. It has, in other words, made the frictions between *primary* and *secondary discourses* (Gee, 1998, 1989) – or individual vs. social; and home vs. institutional discourses – visible. Over the past decades, the gap (and/or overlap) between these primary and secondary discourses has occupied much of Anglo-American literacy research, having to deal with the legacy of colonial literacy discourses that deemed the colonized as 'primitive', 'under-civilized' and 'illiterate' (Gee, 1986). For instance, the earlier New Literacy Studies (NLS) research (Heath, 1983; Scollon & Scollon, 1981; Street, 1984) aimed at deconstructing the 'literate-illiterate' dichotomy (Ong, 2013) by showing that the 'illiterate' had indeed sophisticated literacy lives that happened to be different from mainstream European literacy practices.

Since these earlier conceptualizations, the notion 'discourse practices' has been revisited in more complex theorizations than employed by NLS. Scholars, for instance, have suggested more attention to hybrid discourse practices (Kamberelis, 2001), alteration of discourse practices to blur demarcations between cultural categorizations (Barr, 1998), reflection on discourse practices in regard with multimodality by moving beyond a question of written word only (Prior & Hengst, 2010), and speculations about the differences between discourse practices in real and virtual learning environments (Blanchette, 2001). In the same manner, the findings of my inquiry – as will be unpacked in this chapter – show that the discourse practices of skilled and educated youth and adult immigrants in today's cosmopolitan large cities have much more complicated patterns than illustrated in earlier NLS projects.

The sizable amount of data hosting my participants' perceptions and understandings of literacy shows their eagerness to talk about the discourses through which they regarded literacy, and thus the significance of their discursive engagements. Magda, Choman and Clarice – all practicing multilingual writers – did not show a great interest in talking about their literacy achievements (written products) and even their practical methods of text generation without highlighting their philosophies of literacy. Their ontological ownership of their literacy narratives, I learned in the course of the project, had empowered the participants – all through their schooling years and writing lives – to be influential actors in power relations between them and their teachers, editors, publishers, and also society at large.

In what follows, I share aspects of the participants' discourse practices. In order to map out Choman, Clarice and Magda's discursive behaviours, I analyzed their words from our conversations and their writings (and in some cases their interviews with other people available online or in print). Moreover, I used my observation memos of the participants' textual production and consumption patterns and their give and take with societal discourses, particularly the participants' interactions with Canadian social discourses – as skilled immigrants – as was the main focus of my research.

In this chapter, I first highlight the most important themes that can describe Clarice, Choman and Magda's ontologies of 'literacy'; and second, I write about their understandings of the phenomenon of 'writing' with a particular attention to the impact of the participants' discourse practices on their writing in English as an additional language. When concluding the presentation of each theme, I briefly discuss possible pedagogical implications and, when suitable, propose recommendations for educational policy. These implications and recommendations will be fully fleshed out and revisited with more detail in the final chapter of the book.

It should be explained that in this chapter – as in some other parts of the book – readers will feel delays in focusing on the participants' English writing as a result of my interest in illustrating that writing in a learned language is inseparably embedded in writers' literate lives in general and that it subtly entangles with other semiotic and discursive activities. This extra attention to what happens beyond the act of writing in English as a dominant language is intentional. As detailed previously, if language use (Wittgenstein, 1953) is 'one constituent' of 'a complex series of actions and practices' that humans, as social beings, partake in (Odell, 2006: 56), in order to understand an individual's writing in one language, we must explore their engagements with other semiotic systems, their behaviour in social situations, and also their belief sets. From another theoretical angle, if linguistic signification occurs in a state of *différance* (Derrida, 1973) – which delays immediate meaning making by constantly adding new hermeneutic layers to language – in order to understand an individual's writing, we also need a method of analysis resembling *différance* – or as practiced in writing this book, deferring a focus on the ultimate written products in English by making the chain of literacies and discourses leading to those products visible.

Ontologies of Literacy

In this section, I share Clarice, Choman and Magda's understandings of what literacy is and their perceptions of the forms in which literacy engagement occurs. Dominant curricula often fail to highlight the importance of creating room for learners to discuss their discourse practices. Nor are current educational structures designed to provide time, space, and training for teachers to creatively tap into learners' native literacy discourses. Established assessment and evaluation methods, similarly, lack attention to students' discourse practices. It is significant to highlight the literacy discourses of practicing multilingual writers in order to create awareness about the importance of engaging with learners' philosophies of reading and writing, and of education in general. It also provides an opportunity for educators and curriculum developers to learn from successful multilingual writers' perceptions of what literate engagement means. In this section, I frame my participants' ontologies of literacy in the following themes: (a) literacy as cultural collage, (b) literacy as engagement with metamorphic semiotic media, (c) texts as ideological bundles, and (d) literacy discourse formation as a fluid practice.

In the passages that you are going to read, I try to show that despite the impact of more visible discourse practices such as those we inherit from our ethnic, family and school cultures, discourse practices are fluid concepts that are hard to identify and define. Nevertheless, I will argue that this abstractness will provide space for teachers and leaners to (re)construct discourse practices in shapes and forms that best fit students' lives and their envisagements of their future intellectual directions.

Literacy as cultural collage

Magda, Choman and Clarice described literacy, first and foremost, as culture. What they meant by 'literacy as culture' was their native literacy discourse practices, which they had inherited as a result of living in certain geographical, ethnic, and linguistic contexts prior to their immigration to Canada. In our conversations, these writers specified three cultural contexts with significant impact on their literate lives: their ethnic cultures, their family cultures, and their school cultures. Choman, Clarice and Magda held that the literacy practices that those contexts equipped them with had helped them write effectively in English. They saw their literate lives mainly as products of the said cultures and less of formal education aiming to teach them English or writing. I found their attachment to their native cultures for making sense of literacy very important. This attachment will remain the core of the arguments presented in this section, however, with two additional layers.

The participants engaged and talked about the discourses they had received from their mother cultures with admiration – as a source of empowerment – and at the same time with some critical distance. They regarded their cultural baggage as extremely crucial in their success as multilingual writers but emphasized that they were flexible in reforming their discourse practices as they crossed cultures. I am intentionally inserting the idea of 'critical distance' here because the data I present below reflect the participants' complex understandings of their cultures including the inspirational cores and some rough edges. Choman, Clarice and Magda felt they were indebted to their cultural backgrounds because of the way those impacted their intellectual formation. They, nevertheless, shared stories about borrowing from other cultures and learning from other traditions.

It should, also, be noted that remembering the past can never be entirely objective. In the course of this project, Clarice, Magda and Choman reconstructed their histories through recollections of their past by arranging their literate and intellectual experiences in formats that represented their legacies in most empowering interpretations. The narratives that Magda, Choman and Clarice constructed in order to make sense of their lives, and the ownership that they claimed over their literacy narratives and discourse networks that surrounded them, were as significant as the experiences they actually had.

Having highlighted some complexities involved in discussing the participants' views of literacy as culture, I first start with the impact of ethnic/national culture on the participants' literacy practices, a theme which ran across most of my conversations with the participants regarding literacy discourses. Magda, to exemplify the theme, believed that her 'Hungarian cultural and literary background' (her words) significantly impacted her writing in multiple languages. Magda understood Hungarian intellectual traditions as those welcoming multilingualism and offering access to rich European traditions of art and literature. Magda, thus, regarded Hungarian culture as connected with linguistic and literacy practices that encouraged acts of reading and writing in the context of established traditions of schooling and education consistently observed over several centuries in Europe. She felt that, as a child, she was deeply embedded in those cultural traditions. Magda was particularly proud of the large amount of textual performance that her native culture required her to engage with, while she also tried alternative approaches to textual engagement in order to mitigate the strictness of the literacy discourses which she was brought up with in Hungary:

> The Hungarian approach towards literacy is a very strict one. Although it has changed a bit now, Hungarian kids are required to read and write almost perfectly in grade one. Similarly, throughout high school and university students are required to read a lot of literature. We were exposed to a lot of literature, a lot of novels and especially poetry. I personally enjoyed reading. I liked it, but I see now how little I understood what we had to read.

In her early forties now, Magda was born in Hungary's communist era into a middle class educated Hungarian family. A combination of rich and dynamic European-Hungarian literary world; family values regarding reading as the main form of entertainment at home; and societal discourses that placed education above monetary success formed Magda's intellectual life as inseparable from literature and art. The impact is still vivid not only in Magda's work and writings, but in everyday lives of all her family members. Over the past seven years, I frequently met Magda, her husband, her daughter, and her mother (who stayed with Magda's family in Canada half of the year). I met them on many occasions in everyday family settings. I do not recall one single encounter when the family's conversations did not include references to literature, art and music.

Choman, in the same manner, thought that Persian-Kurdish traditions of heavy engagement with poetry and song formed her verbal and textual tendencies and created a space for her as a child to verbalize her imagination, a blessing for which she was ironically punished from time to time, being a girl. When Choman's family faced serious financial problems — which were not rare occasions in her life — her father considered preventing her (and not her brothers) from going to school to reduce expenses, the reasoning being Choman 'was a girl and could help with the housework'. 'So I had to do all the house chores in the evening so that I could go to school in the morning. This way the family would have no excuses to stop me'. Despite unfavourable cultural gender roles regarding schooling, the deeper ethnic legacies of linguistic expression encouraged her to heavily engage with language both orally and in written form.

In a different cultural context in Brazil, Clarice also underlined the imprint of societal literacy practices on her life. In disadvantaged sections of Brazil — as described by Clarice — oracy functions as a significant addition, and sometimes an alternative, to engagement with written language for expression and exchange of knowledge and experience. Clarice was brought up by a single mother with little formal education who, despite financial obstacles, orchestrated a home culture that bred three highly educated children: Clarice and her sisters. Clarice spoke with me about the function of oracy in her community:

> We very often had family dinner conversations, my mom, my two sisters, and I. We talked about what we learned at school during the day. Even nowadays if I go back to visit my family, we are going to sit at the table — and it's always during and after a meal — for hours: two, three, four even five hours. It never ends.

Clarice's verbal virtuosity and her social comfort would provide her with many venues for collaboration in different forms of text generation. She became a singer-songwriter in a Brazilian rock band and wrote and directed theatrical performances when younger. As an academic writer, on the other hand, she successfully communicated and collaborated with scholars in different circles and assumed numerous unofficial leadership roles to build writing and research communities. I met Clarice frequently in her department and I witnessed how she – thanks to her oral and social skills – shared her research with her colleagues in informal dissemination spaces such as corridors or class breaks, stirred interest in them, and initiated collaborations for writing projects.

As these examples of participants' cultural discourses show, national, ethnic, communal, and societal discourses are often handed down through family literacy traditions. Magda, as I underlined earlier, engaged with reading as it 'was just part of everyday life. My mom cannot go to sleep without reading. It's absolutely a family tradition'. Choman, in the same manner, was exposed to family discourse practices that would impact her literate life immensely:

> We had a huge library in our house. When you're a kid, your parents are your heroes. When you see them reading books, reading becomes second nature to you. Then when you're bored as a kid, you always have this option: reading.

Next to ethnic and family cultures, Magda, Choman, and Clarice made frequent references to their school cultures while recalling their intellectual pasts and discourse practices. Although the participants were at times critical of official schooling and none identified as a 'top student' in K-12, the participants stressed the impact of the literacy practices they inherited from their non-English speaking schools and universities. Clarice, for instance, said:

> In Brazil I had to write a lot at school and at university. I mean different kinds of essay. In Portuguese you can be more flowery, more creative. If you do the introduction-body-conclusion, it's extremely boring and you won't get the grade. ... We are a product of the system too.

Choman and Magda also seemed to share the attitude that their native schooling experiences – despite their imperfections – provided them with profound literacy practices that became solid grounding for their future academic and professional success in Canada. In our interactions, I found, that this appreciation of non-Anglo-American literacy practices assisted these immigrants in their identity negotiation with Canadian educational and professional structures, which sometimes treated their academic backgrounds as inadequate (Schellenberg & Maheux, 2007). Magda, Choman and Clarice did not glorify their schooling experiences before arriving Canada; however, they rejected naive and simplistic – and often power-inflected – interpretations of their academic and professional legacies as having lower standards by providing complex and nuanced narratives that highlighted the strengths of their school cultures (Guo, 2009). The Canadian tendency to undervalue immigrants' qualifications, which is rooted in its colonial and imperial history, is a major contributor to the phenomenon called *brain abuse* (Bauder, 2003), suffering caused by devaluation of foreign credentials and expertise.

The participants' cultural, family, and school traditions were not the same; nor were the socioeconomic circumstances that they grew up under: Magda came from an educated middle-class Hungarian family with modest but reliable financial resources; Choman from an educated family in an underprivileged community with serious economic issues; and Clarice was brought up with two other siblings by a single mother who had no formal schooling and was often financially challenged. Nevertheless, all three participants were exposed to (and chose to report from their reflections) discourse practices that enriched their literate lives in different ways. I intentionally wrote 'chose to report' in the previous sentence to acknowledge the fact that as much as the findings presented above reflect what formed the participants' discursive behaviours, they also reveal the participants' active involvement in creating their *literacy narratives*, or the ability to marshal the discourses surrounding them in arrangements that would enrich their literate lives. In other words, what they said were accounts of what happened but also of how the participants understood what happened and how they thought what happened impacted them over time.

I have listed that the participants perceived 'literacy culture' as (a) ethnic/national, (b) family, and (c) school literacy traditions. Educators who teach youth and adult learners have little control over the formation of such discourses because most of those solidify in their students' pasts. They, however, could impact students' remembrances and interpretations of their literate backgrounds and intellectual potentials. Literacy teachers can enable language learners to create flexible forms of discursive collages or discourse maps – of past and present discourses – that can enrich their literate lives. All through the analysis of the data associated with this section, the theme that loomed larger than the actual discourse practices that the participants engaged with was the discursive consciousness by which the participants picked, highlighted, and packaged discourses within their sociocultural orbits to enrich their intellectual lives and support their literacy activities. In other words, although partaking in empowering discourse practices is important, the narratives that explain discourse practices are also as (if not more) important.

It is essential that writing teachers reflect on the importance of students' active involvement in creating their discourse narratives. Positive discourse narratives help students successfully negotiate their writing identities and enable them to regard their writing activities as important textual contributions. Educators should create activities that support students' creation of discursive collages and discourse maps that foster the emergence of positive academic and professional identities. Curriculum developers also should devise curricular substance that encourages such discursive consciousness. Building on the shared quotations from the participants, I can exemplify this process by highlighting how the participants gave more colour to the experiences that fostered their literacy against serious social obstacles: Magda by giving more weight to exposure to good quality literature over inflexible traditional pedagogy; Choman by highlighting the family's library as a solace away from the presence of active patriarchy; and Clarice by putting the impact of her home's oral culture over the influence of poverty.

In order to comprehend the significance of active construction of positive literacy narratives, one can think of colonial experiences to create a high contrast context where such practice has been part and parcel of cultural revival and anti-colonial resistance. Literacy discourses are various and function organically in their own cultural contexts. Ranking literacy practices or judging their values, thus, is often the result of wishful interpretations motivated based on the power relations between the observer and the local population. For instance, Western colonial narratives painted other cultures' literacy practices as inferior. They labelled oracy as illiteracy, literary mythology as superstition, and out-of-school literacy practices such as engagement with native religious songs, prayers, and art as barbaric. In response to such destructive narrative building, there have been postcolonial attempts to reconstruct literacy narratives in whose frames the value of native literacy practices can be regained (Battiste, 2017; Battiste & Youngblood, 2000). Today's educational contexts might be considered different, yet no classroom is free of power relations, especially in those hosting multilingual leaners such as refugees and immigrants. Teachers should be reminded that judgments of literacy practices are not objective but power-relationally loaded. Cultural differences are complex and teachers' views of their students' academic backgrounds are hardly objective. This subjectivity, however, should not be necessarily seen as a hindrance. It in fact could provide space for educators to collaborate with their students to construct literacy narratives that highlight the strengths of their students. In this manner, teachers can help students take control of describing their discourse practices.

The findings of my inquiry corroborate the significance of discourse practices, contextualized by early NLS researchers, yet in the light of the data from my research context – multilingual educated youth and adult immigrants – I believe the concept needs to be complexified to properly respond to today's new demographic, cultural, and economic circumstances. Unlike what Gee (1998) maintained, *discourse practices* cannot be always simplified as *primary discourse* and *secondary discourse*. In practice, literacy learning involves *sets* of *discourse narratives* (ways of arranging primary discourses) and *sets* of *discourse additives* (secondary, tertiary, and so on that can be added to discourse narratives, get omitted, or be replaced). Although many of the issues in the earlier chapters of postcolonial agendas remain unsolved – such as the aboriginal issues in Canada and the black and white racial divide in the United States – a new demography of immigrants is growing in North America, whose members are often more educated and skilled than average North American citizens. In Canada, this has happened mainly as a result of immigration policies that reward educated applicants and in the United States because of the large intake of highly competitive international graduate students. In order to make sense of this populations' discourse practices – like those of my participants – we need more nuanced theoretical frameworks than the primary and secondary discourse theory. One alternative could be what I just described as 'creative discourse narrative formation'.

The developments of discourse narratives are complex, messy and amorphous, and the participants displayed different approaches to (re)constructing their discourse narratives. They possessed great flexibility in framing and reframing their literate lives to produce healthy, balanced, and harmonious discourse narratives that highlighted the value of their literate pasts in order to successfully interact with the new discourses they encountered in the wake of their immigration. The same ontological flexibility was also evident in the participants' other conceptualizations of literacy, which I discuss next.

Literacy as engagement with ever-metamorphosing semiotic media

Magda, Clarice and Choman saw literacy as tightly connected to physical manifestations of language in a variety of different media. Literacy for them was a phenomenon that grew and spread through different semiotic systems. This notion of literacy is inclusive and embraces all forms of text generation from writing one's opinions in traditional essays to reposting multimodal content online. Clarice, for instance, explained how her view of literacy grew with new technological possibilities:

> I think my understanding of literacy has gone through changes over the years just because we have a larger number of mediums. We have mediums that we didn't have before. Literacy involves so much: artistic, oral, visual, and kinesthetic experiences. There is way more than reading and writing for me.

Such conceptualization of literacy has two important consequences. First, consciousness about the ever-growing variety of linguistic manifestations, made possible by new semiotic media, requires semiotic agility: 'shifting ... rapidly and fluently between and among semiotic worlds' (Prior, 2010: 233). From this point of view, learning literacy is understood as broader than reading and writing; it is, instead, mastering semiotic meaning making in its different forms. In other words, teaching literacy is not only teaching reading and writing, but also reading and writing in different media. Second, regarding literacy as a concept growing in accordance with the emergence of new semiotic possibilities challenges literacy hierarchies and hence creates more room for alternative literacies in educational settings, including those practiced by minoritized and marginalized populations.

This view of literacy, framed above in Clarice's words, is in line with the New London Group's multiliteracies manifesto (New London Group, 1996) and also other projects that followed the same trend (Coiro, 2008; Cope & Kalantzis, 2000; Gee *et al.*, 1996; Yelland *et al.*, 2008). I, however, would like to add to this research thread by highlighting that when we are discussing the experiences of multilingual writers in terms of media and technology, we should pay attention to the fact that physical migration in the world, say from one country to another, is also a form of semiotic migration between media and technologies used in different geographical and cultural contexts. While the proposals of the London Group, and the subsequent research, often framed multiliteracies as a contemporary need in order to respond to the then emerging 'variety of text forms associated with information and multimedia technologies' (New London Group, 1996: 61), my participants' life histories show that if you migrate from culture to culture, you will encounter new modes of textual interaction regardless of the technological history of the host culture. Technological development is not linear unless you have a static positionality in the world. My participants' literate lives show that although they were born into certain sets of semiotic media, they comfortably adopted new semiotic forms of expression in their new contexts.

Choman, Magda and Clarice effectively handled semiotic migrations mainly because of the discursive creativity by which the participants had to redefine themselves in the world. Part of this discourse negotiation was modifying media practices. For instance, despite coming from a country where social media platforms were banned and a heavy dose of censorship undermined textual representation and dissemination, Choman's semiotic flexibility in her new context in Canada was remarkable. Although officially a novelist, Choman was actively involved in other written genres; she wrote newspaper articles, essays and poetry. Choman shared what she wrote with me on a regular basis, and it was interesting to see how her writing style switched from that of a poetic storyteller in the morning to a dry hard-hitting journalist at night. She was also impressively fluent in using social media, which she used both to share news about her publications and to post opinions. She was active on all main social media platforms. She had almost 8000 followers on Facebook and close to 2000 followers on Twitter. Moreover, she produced audio and video texts (in multiple languages) and shared them on YouTube. Her one Kurdish dance YouTube video was viewed almost 4000 times.

More than technological adaptability, this semiotic involvement was a result of discursive consciousness about the impact of available media and genres for most effective forms of communication. That is why, Magda, in contrast with Choman, had zero presence on social media despite her good command of digital text making. She believed her active involvement in social media might damage her career as an education consultant interacting with ministry officials. Hence, literacy for the participants was ever-evolving semiotic possibilities but with less emphasis on the technological side and more on the communicative potentials in different sociocultural situations. To connect the content of this section with our previous conversation about literacy narratives, the notion of literacy as constantly branching into new semiotic media can also be described in the light of the idea of discursive agility needed for (re)creating variant collages of literacy narratives. In brief, discursive agility paves the way for semiotic agility. Although it is tempting to discuss technological development as following a linear pattern of progress, the same line of development does not occur across all cultures and countries, nor do effective learners decide to engage with a new medium only because it is 'new'. Successful learners pick media that enrich their literate lives in their specific contexts.

This view of the role of technology in education has important pedagogical implications, especially as education is becoming increasingly more digitized. Educators and policymakers need to decide if they employ technology to improve the quality of teaching and learning, or use educational settings to display technology. In case of online education, the question might be: are institutional decisions to create more online courses and programs made based on a desire to enrich teaching and learning, or, as can be witnessed in many places, according to a strategy to make traditional classrooms disappear for more profit?

Texts as sources of literacy discourses

Next to defining literacy as culture and multiplying forms of semiotic representation, the participants also discussed how textual products themselves hosted discourses that informed their understandings of literacy. When consumed, texts form our view of the world and thus impact the way we think of culture, expression, and imagination – all of which connect to literacy in one way or another. Texts (including textbooks and readings that teachers opt to use in the classroom) are not ideology-free training equipment. They, in contrast, host ideas and perspectives that shape their consumers' minds – a view which highlights the importance of conversations about critical literacy, critical curriculum, and the literary canon.

Magda said, 'In all of the examples that we were exposed to – in history or literature – we were always told that great people don't focus on money but focus on art and expression'. Magda's stance on the ideological load hidden in texts can complexify our understanding of the sources of discourse practices and literacy beliefs. Although mother culture is the seedbed of literacy, it is neither fixed nor unchangeable. New forms of linguistic interactions and intertextual references can multiply literacy practices and events. Literacy breeds literacy and facilitates cultural interaction as an important channel of peaceful intellectual exchange and a reciprocal venue for understanding and appreciation. Accordingly, our discourse practices are constantly shaped and reshaped by the texts we read (films we watch, songs we listen to, and so forth), what their characters do, and how their authors/creators picture the world.

Choman's background also indicated a pattern of selecting and absorbing discourses from the texts she read in Kurdish, Farsi, and English. In Kurdish, for instance, she read the Kurdish poet Choman Hardi (whose name I borrowed for Choman's pseudonym), who is a university instructor in Iraqi Kurdistan, contributing to the Kurdish feminist movement. As for Farsi text, she told me, she had grown up with Ahmad Shamlou and Forough Farrokhzad's poetry, the former one of the founders of socially committed contemporary Persian poetry and the latter one of the most taboo-breaking modern female Iranian poets. Among her favourites from English literature, she taught George Orwell's *Animal Farm* and *1984* to discuss politics internationally and in the Iranian context. Choman's favourite writers shared discursive foundations such as social justice and women's issues with Choman's own writing – with both her fiction and news articles. While I was writing this paragraph, I checked Choman's last Facebook post and was struck by the discursive echo of the same mentality about literature in the quotation she had shared about a poetry book that centred around the experiences of the Kurds as its subject matter: 'The poetry is praised because it "simultaneously explores hope and horror while documenting the transformative processes of coping"'.

Discourses of literacy, thus, can be adopted in complicated and often invisible dynamics of textual consumption. As far as everyday pedagogy is concerned, this finding underlies the significance of literacy teachers' textual choices for their students. It also reveals the complex relationship between educators and the canon: whether they decide to replicate the dominant canon in their classes or attempt to alter it and invite their students to reconstruct the curriculum in order to make empowering literacy discourses accessible to students through the texts that they share with their classes.

Literacy practices as fluid discourses

As the above phenomena, discussed as ontological representations of literacy, show, discourse practices are hard to identify because they are not solid entities readily accessible to learners and teachers of reading and writing, or researchers for that matter. Literacy discourses are multiple, multiplying and metamorphic. More importantly, in every attempt to identify discourse practices, the process of remembrance, reflection on, and selection of discourses renders any act of inquiry more creative that objective. This precarious epistemological situation is not only the result of the inevitable subjectivity of the observer, but the fluidity of discourses and their constant changes in adapting to new literacy and textual contexts. I opened this chapter with highlighting the collage nature and complexity of our discourse maps. This final theme, which could also be read as a conclusion to the section, stresses the fluid nature of each discourse in our already complex literacy narratives.

Choman, Magda and Clarice showed awareness of the fluidity of discourse and literacy practices and were conscious that over years they had developed the ability to navigate and negotiate literacy discourses, as evident in these words by Carice: 'I think my understanding of literacy has gone through changes over the years'. I initiated this inquiry by the intention to highlight discourses that the participants practiced as effective models of thinking about literacy. However, I learned from the participants' complex experiences that there are no exemplary discourse practices that would universality lead to academic success. Effective discourse practices differ from society to society and from community to community. Successful learners know this fact and learn to negotiate discourses. Magda, for instance, described the impact of Hungarian pedagogical traditions on her literate life in a positive light generally; however, when encountering different literacy practices in Canada, she embarked upon reviewing and rearranging her discursive legacy to find the best possible points of connection with Canadian literacy discourses. Magda was proud of the European literary tradition and the Hungarian cultural practice of exposing children to literary classics from an early age. She held that this cultural tendency had helped the average European remain intellectually connected with the cultural elite. In North America, she initially found it strange that young children – including her daughter – were provided with simplified kids-specific books:

> I'm kind of debating between these two versions. ... [As a kid,] I did not understand [everything] when I was reading those books. But when I'm reading poetry now, I think 'oh, wow this is what it is really about'. But I think *interest* is coming from that time because we were required to read. Do you have to make kids read literature that is not written for them but that somehow puts something in their mind that later it can come out and flourish? ... When I saw kids' books in Canadian libraries,

I was shocked: 'What is going on? These are not books. This is a joke'. But it was very interesting how I experienced my daughter's school. She writes stories at school from time to time. The stories are the genre that she is reading in Canadian books, much simpler than what I read as a kid. I think those books made her realize, 'Okay, I can write a story like this with a lot of pictures'. Kind of thing I never considered literature. But no, this is what made her think 'I can do the same' and the story she wrote was really amazing. What I want to say with this is that I kind of embrace now both cultures and both environments.

I intentionally focused on Magda here in order to highlight the fact that even immigrants who are perceived to culturally function under the shared umbrella of 'Western tradition' would also have to go through complicated forms of discourse negotiation, let alone learners with stronger cultural contrasts. Creating enough room for minoritized and racialized learners' native discourse practices thus is an important pedagogical consideration. It also benefits other students by creating access to more discourse possibilities. If discourse practices are fluid, our pedagogies should also be flexible and facilitate learners' discursive journeys in the wake of their physical migration.

Discourse practices are rooted in students' pasts, which are not readily accessible to educators. This poses some challenges in the classroom in terms of recognition of students' native discourse practices as well as filling the gaps for smoother interactions with the host society's discourses. For instance, students' perceptions of textual engagement are deeply connected to their ethnic, family, and school cultures that may or may not have been nurturing. Or as educators with a certain positionality in the world, we may or may not be able to easily see how learners' home literacy practices connect with their current classroom and school culture. Also, students may or may not have had access to various semiotic and textual sources. The fluidity of discourse practices and the open-ended nature of our literacy narratives, however, create a wonderful opportunity for educators to actively help students in constructing their current and future literacy directions. Discursive vagueness, which might appear as an undermining factor in the process of teaching and learning, is ironically a potential space for growth as long as teachers create space for their students, their peers, and their communities to negotiate and reconstruct their discourses in shapes that best help them commutate with others in their new contexts. In other words, this space activates the agency of the student and the teacher to determine positive discourses that represent the student as able to succeed.

Ontologies of Writing

With the backdrop of what literacy meant to the writers who participated in my inquiry, here I zoom in on the participants' perceptions of the act of writing, specifically. It is important to crystalize multilingual writers' ontological views of writing since those understandings constantly impact their writing lives and written products. Choman, Magda and Clarice, in short, saw writing as *hermeneutic design*, facilitating their participation in societal communication and assisting them in playing stronger roles in power relations. They, accordingly, regarded text generation as *life events* as opposed to self-contained written products with objectively testable aesthetic or technical qualities. The participants also spoke about writing as an *epistemological medium* for exploring the world and the self. This exploration, their writing lives showed, required *genre flexibility* and *genre agility*.

The question 'what is writing' has been asked and answered by a number of different scholarly communities. In educational research, there has been a lengthy conversation over the past decades describing writing as a product, then a process, and finally through postprocess paradigms. This conversation, rather than a philosophical debate about the nature of 'writing', has mainly aimed at improving writing pedagogy. The prospects created by the process theorists' critiques of product-oriented approaches have had an enormous impact on classroom practice and curriculum development particularly in North America. There has been much less postprocess influence when it comes to mainstream writing pedagogy – and especially second language writing – although not for want of theoretical speculations that regard 'writing' as more than skill-based craftsmanship: See for instance: expressive pedagogy (Burnham, 2001), lifespan development of writing abilities (Bazerman *et al.*, 2017) rhetorical pedagogy (Covino, 2001), genre pedagogy (Hyland, 2007), cultural studies pedagogy (George & Trimbur, 2001), feminist pedagogy (Jarratt, 2001), queer composition (Alexander & Gibson, 2004), and identity text generation (Cummins & Early, 2011).

On a different front, writing has also been discussed in different forms in critical pedagogy and literacy studies. Paulo Freire (1970), among the classic references, did not think 'writing' as separable from *conscientization (conscientização)* or *critical consciousness*. Writing, in Freirean terms, is a vehicle for transformation through problematizing the *status quo* by (re)naming it: 'To exist, humanly, is to name the world, to change it. Once named, the world reappears to the namers as a problem and requires of them a new naming' (Freire, 1970: 69). Hilary Janks (2013) also – as an example of a more current version of the same philosophy – defined writing as (re)designing text with considerations about power, access, and identity. This conceptual trend in literacy research is consistent with postprocess theory in that it focuses on societal and power-relational aspects of writing. The potentials of these two trends, however, have not been fully employed in second language writing.

In philosophy, also, there has been a long tradition of speculating about 'writing' from Plato's 'Phaedrus' – which is contemptuous of writing – to Derrida's *Of Grammatology* (1976), *Writing and Difference* (2001), and *Speech and Phenomena* (1973) – which oppose Plato's distrust of writing, holding 'writing and grammatology are more important and even "older" than the supposedly pure structure of presence-to-self that is characterised as typical of speech' (Reynolds, 2018: para. 21). Philosophy of literature (Carroll & Gibson, 2015; Lamarque, 2008) also specifically focuses on what literature is and hence speculates about the nature of creative writing.

More than the listed scholarly trends, literary theory has been a significant source of inspiration for North American literacy and English teachers over the past decades through two different channels: first, Anglo-American New Criticism (Ogden & Richards, 1946; Ransome, 1941; Richards, 2014) with a formalist approach resulting in pedagogies of *close reading*; second, through continental and Russian thinkers such as Mikhail Bakhtin (2010) and Gérard Genette (1992, 1997), who, unlike the New Critics, had a broader view of textuality, manifesting itself in writing studies mainly in conversations about genre. Genre pedagogy has also managed to creep into the field of second language education (Hyland, 2007).

My interactions with the participants regarding multilingual writing underline the importance of viewing multilingual learners' writing in the less utilized post and critical frameworks discussed above. As well as sensitivity about the mechanics and architecture of the text, post and critical theories of writing invite more attention to larger sociocultural and sociopolitical circumstances in which written communication occurs. Magda, Clarice and Choman's thoughts on the nature of writing were in line with this understanding of writing.

Writing as hermeneutic design

Studying the lives of multilingual writers is a valuable opportunity for writing studies (in North America with a total focus on English) to study the act of writing across languages and cultures. I learned from my conversations with Choman, Clarice and Magda, from observations of their writing practices, and from analyses of their writing trajectories that notions of 'great writing' are often tribal beliefs despite claims to universality. The participants in my study maintained that the criteria for 'good writing' changed from language to language, culture to culture, institution to institution, and from writing community to writing community. Even within each writing community, they thought, standards for 'quality writing' changed based on the then current positionality of the community, their sociocultural purposes, their audiences, and the alterations of the discourses within the community over time. In accordance with this view, writing for the writers involved in this project was first and foremost a means for communication with members of some specific communities. Stylistics, mechanics and aesthetics, they thought, were important, but were determined only when the communication mode was set and communication channels were established and started to function. Writing, in this sense, is mainly about navigating the addressees' communicative expectations, their cultures, their ideological stances, and their positionalities. This ontological view of writing is similar to what postprocess theorists' have described as 'hermeneutic guessing':

> When we produce and analyze discourse ... we engage the other in a dialogic way; we move back and forth, shifting ground, in an attempt to align our hermeneutic strategy with the other's, and in so doing, we continuously create tenuous resolutions to this dialogic interaction. These open-ended resolutions or momentary herme-neutic pauses never represent, however, a precise alignment of our hermeneutic with another's; that is, they never represent the end of guessing. (Kent, 1993: 43)

The participants challenged the notion that teachers, editors, or publishers possess objective criteria for 'great writing'. They believed when gatekeepers offer judgment for writing quality, more than impartial evaluation, they engage with power-relational and discursive dealings inherent in teacher-student and editor-writer relationships. Effective writers see navigating these relationships as an important component of their writing practices, which go well beyond the physical act of writing and formalistic performance. These notions were frequently discussed in my conversations with the participants, particularly with Clarice and Choman, who – as an academic writer and a novelist – regularly struggled to engage with the paradigms that informed reviewers, publishers, journal editors, and also teachers' readings of others' writings, paradigms that were typically more ideological than objective. Clarice, for instance, said:

> Many teachers impose their own perspective of writing as great writing. I am working at a student success centre where I help students with their academic writing. Students come because they are suffering. They come because somebody has said that there is something wrong with their writing, and most of the time they don't even know what is actually wrong. ... We take a look at the syllabus, and usually profes-sors' syllabi don't clarify those expectations. It is a hidden agenda. It's what they expect in their minds.

As a doctoral student dealing with scholarly journals – which often have different (if not contradictory) views of academic rigour in research writing – Clarice emphasized the significance of regarding writing as paradigmatic engagement with one's readership:

> That's important because when you are writing, you have to know where your readers are coming from and what academic legacies they have. Who is your audience? Which journal are you going to be sending this to? How much rigour do you have to have in this part or that part, because that is what they would want to see? You need to find out about the paradigms they come from.

This discursive and paradigmatic communication is often much more complicated when multilingual writers migrate from one language/culture to another. In this case, writers not only need to navigate personal and institutional ideologies; they should do so in the context of a new language and a new culture. Choman recalled her hermeneutic journey from Kurdish culture with rich oral communicative practices to North American writing-centred social life:

> The shift from an oral to a written communication culture was an interesting experience. If you are after funding to make a film, as a few of my friends and I intend to do, you should prepare an application package including letters, proposals, histories, but if you want to deal with a Kurdish TV station, there is no written application; it's all oral interaction.

After immigration to Canada, Choman managed to learn the Canadian art of writing applications. She effectively communicated with writing agents and publishers. She also became an active member of half a dozen of writers' associations and councils, performing different forms of correspondence. Besides, she successfully applied for a number of jobs including teaching and editing. This everyday written communication included what had to be said and how, but also ideological redlines that could not be crossed: 'You should know who has what redlines. I know I can say things in what I write for this newspaper that I cannot say when I write for that one. I play with redlines'.

Writing for Choman, Magda and Clarice was mainly constant hermeneutic interpretation, adjustment, and – at times – resistance. Writing in this sense is not an isolated skill but one component of a writer's communicative repertoire (Rymes, 2014) and rhetoric only a tool at the service of a communitive purpose (Fields & Matsuda, 2018). This perspective on writing challenges pedagogical practices that ignore the momentary and slippery nature of hermeneutic engagement and reduce writing to content and style and by consequence restrict students' involvement in the process of meaning making. As Jakobson (1960) held, communication is complex and includes numerous features: on the one hand, the addresser and the addressee with different emotive, conative and ideological backgrounds; and on the other, the sociocultural context, phatic interaction, and metalingual codes.

Gadamer (1975) offered a nuanced interpretation of the process of meaning making in reading, which could also be adopted to better understand the nature of writing:

> A person who is trying to understand a text is always performing an act of projecting. He projects before himself a meaning for the text as a whole as soon as some initial meaning emerges in the text. Again, the latter emerges only because he is reading the text with particular expectations in regard to a certain meaning. The working out of this fore-project, which is constantly revised in terms of what emerges as he penetrates into the meaning, is understanding what is there. (Gadamer, 1975: 36)

Hermeneutic design for writers involves the same constant adjustment of meaning making based on readers' expectations and writers' interpretations of the communication context. Because this semantic relationship is based on interpretation rather than an ultimate understanding of form and content, it always occurs in the discursive culture which informs readers' and writers' meaning making – or sociocultural horizons that make interpretation possible. Gadamer (1975) described the process using the concept *hermeneutic horizon*:

> The horizon is the range of vision that includes everything that can be seen from a particular vantage point. Applying this thinking to mind, we speak of narrowness of horizon, of the possibility of expansion of horizon, or the opening of new horizons, and so forth. ... A person who has no horizon does not see far enough and hence overvalues what is nearest him. On the other hand, 'to have a horizon' means to not be limited to what is nearby but to be able to see beyond it. A person who has a horizon knows the relative significance of everything within this horizon, whether it is near or far, great or small. Similarly, working out the hermeneutical situation means acquiring the right horizon of inquiry for the questions evoked by the encounter. (Gadamer, 1975: 269)

Inspired by Gadamer's *hermeneutic horizon*, one could read my participants' words as evidence for their cognizance of the presence of horizons of interpretation, where readers' and writers' discourses attract each other, merge, and also conflict. 'All texts and all individuals possess a horizon of understanding, which Gadamer defines as culturally and historically situated vantage points from which meaning is projected or ascertained' (Simon & Campano, 2015: 474).

Potential interpretation horizons understandably multiply when writers live and write across cultures and languages. Multilingual learners often face systems of rhetorical judgment that make little sense to them because, unlike native speakers, they were not born into those paradigms. It is important that writing instructors highlight the existence of hermeneutic horizons which might shape readers' interpretations of their students' writings. Such a move, first and foremost, involves a switch from a deficit mentality, which regards students as lacking rhetorical competence, to a perspective of hermeneutic sensitivity to the diversity of rhetorical expectations. A pedagogy of hermeneutic sensitivity sheds light on the cultural, ideological and power-relational layers of assessment of writing and avoids creating a veneer of objectivity. Such a pedagogy, for instance, invites self and peer assessment to create space for conversations that can help reveal instructors' biases and perspectives. Moreover, it opens up limited classroom readership to new target populations for the students to engage with hermeneutic horizons that they are not familiar with. This move involves serious reflection on the role of publishing and dissemination in writing classes, about which I will write later in detail.

Written products and writing processes as life events

If writing, as concluded above, involves encounters between writers' and readers' interpretive horizons, ideological worlds, and cultural beliefs, every piece of writing is a *life event* that contributes some quality to our social existence. In my conversations with Magda, Choman and Clarice, I was interested to learn about what writing was beyond a technical process that resulted in producing a written product, typically required by a teacher or editor. While writing, my participants did focus on their final products and the dynamics that guided the process of production as one might understandably expect, yet they also saw each written product as an event that defined their life in a certain way. Magda, Choman and Clarice believed that there was often more to the act of writing than the completion of a writing task because not all the writing events that they enjoyed engaging with created polished products, including those they held dear and thought impactful despite their stylistic imperfections. On the other hand, not all the polished products that they produced were received well or empowered them in a meaningful way. For these writers, a writing project, more than a finalized product, was an event for which they wrote or which impacted their lives. For Choman, for instance, the publication of her first novel in English was a turning point in her life, but as significant (if not more) were her childhood scribbles, which gave her solace in a home tense with parental conflict. Some of Choman's short stories in English though – although literarily wrought well – attracted less attention than her online interviews in Farsi about women's issues or about the struggles of the Kurds. In the same manner, there was no trace left of the plays that Clarice co-wrote with her students in her drama classes in Brazil, but the impact of the experience was so fresh that it became the foundation of some of her academic work about drama in language education. Measuring the quality of the act of writing based on the impact that it could potentiality have on one's life would significantly change our view of effective writing curriculum design and writing assessment.

Book and journal publishers are often interested in written products that they can easily market and sell and that, at the same time, strengthen their editors' ideological and professional agendas. They, for instance, look for polished finalized products of regulated lengths focusing on a niche theme. Educational centres, also, favour some written products over others. Schools and universities prefer writing that they can easily evaluate and also record and present as proof of effective teaching or performance. They also look for comfort in smooth administration of examinations and writing assignments; they tend to assign shorter single-authored report formats that students can mass-produce by use of rubrics. Although Magda, Clarice and Choman – sometimes gladly and sometimes unwillingly – converged with the above agendas and formed their products accordingly, their polished finalized products were merely tips of the icebergs of their writing lives – although those products were indeed highlighted in their resumes in the job market. Choman, Clarice and Magda had left many writing projects unfinished at different points in their lives. Choman, for instance, had numerous unpublished short stories in Farsi and English, some aborted in initial stages yet inspiring new projects. Next to much raw, untrimmed, and unfinished writing, the participants also engaged with alternative forms of text production that, although deemed less prestigious than more orthodox writing formats, had significant impact. Clarice, for instance, summarized her research projects in YouTube animation videos viewed by thousands. Clarice believed her YouTube animations might have a larger audience than her academic papers which had undergone rigorous reviews.

Choman, Clarice and Magda used writing to connect with new communities; they experienced new cultures and languages through text; they wrote as a form of resistance; and they wrote to enter new realms of knowledge and join new intellectual circles. Workplaces and educational centres, however, are not always interested in such experiences because they occur beyond engaging with writing as a product formatted according to certain formalistic traditions. In contrast, the writers involved in this project perceived their writing activities mainly as social practices that formed their lives. For instance, Choman, as a creative writer, perceived her engagements with writing as philosophical and social as well as literary:

> Writing for me has been everything, many things. It's been very personal, very literary, very social, very philosophical. I never started writing because I thought it was an intellectual skill and I had to learn it.

In addition to challenging a product mentality about writing, the participants' understanding of writing also was broader than the frame offered by classic versions of process theory. None of the participants led the conversation towards defining their typical writing process because each writer's writing process changed constantly depending on the writing project and writing circumstances. In other words, what generated their textual products was not a particular process. In contrast, their writing process regularly took new forms based on the task in hand. Here is how Clarice recalled her struggles with process pedagogy:

> I remember one of the writing assignments I had during my master's programme ... the first assignment was an outline of your essay, the second assignment was only a three-page paper based on your outline, and then we wrote the final essay. I hated it. I did not see the point and I even asked the prof 'why do I have to do this, if that's what I want to get done? Can I just do the essay and give it to you two months in advance?' He said, 'No. It's going to help you with the process'. I said, 'It's not going to help me'.

Clarice's issue with the approach was mainly with 'process' taught and evaluated as a set sequence rather than a space for developing ideas. Postprocess theorists have been sceptical of reducing writing events to a single formula for the writing process (Blyler, 1999; Olson, 1999; Pullman, 1999; Russell, 1999). In this scenario, Clarice intuitively challenges the same notion and desires the process flexibility that has always empowered her writing life. In my observations of the writing processes performed by the participants, I failed to capture one single process shared by all the participants, and even employed by a single participant at all times. The participants were thoughtful and strategic about the processes that generated their texts (brainstorming, literature review, outlining, seeking feedback, and so forth); these processes, however, varied based on the projects they engaged with, their interest in the projects, and their life circumstances – which provided them with time, space, and resources to write. Rather than a certain process formula, the participants claimed strong ownership of their own writing processes, which varied in form. Clarice's resistance against the manner in which the assignment was designed should not be interpreted as rebellion against process pedagogy but should be read as a student's desire to co-construct the process with her teacher.

In another observation, the participants' most fruitful writing processes were not those happening in the classroom, but were often the products of out-of-school projects that created genuine interest in them. Most important of these events were artistic, literary, and academic projects which Magda, Clarice and Choman participated in along with their family members, neighbourhood friends, and school peers in extracurricular activities. These events included complex dynamics such as learning new languages, attending illustration workshops, typing training, calligraphy, working with musical instruments and travelling around the city – steps hardly included in traditional process-based writing curricula. At some point in her college life, Magda had been invited to write a textbook in English and German. Although confidant about her English, Magda had to rapidly improve her elementary German to handle the project. In another example, when I last talked to Choman, she was attending a MOOC (Massive Open Online Courses) course claiming to teach how to write a bestseller in North America. Before giving her latest novel a final edit, Choman had decided to learn from people involved in commercial literature – which had never appealed to her literary taste – to see if there was room for tweaking her novel to attract the attention of American literary agents. Formulized writing processes in dominant writing pedagogies do not often include such experiences.

Magda, Clarice and Choman thought their written products and writing processes were important; however, they were deliberate in speaking about their products and processes in the context of the life events that motivated them to embark on different writing projects. This finding can help us imagine writing pedagogies with assignments that resemble life events. Such assignments can be projects that connect with ongoing sociopolitical issues or involve students' communities in response to the issues the community members are struggling with. Also, those assignments could be designed to scaffold students' academic and professional lives by connecting to other activities that students are involved in. Writing projects that are treated as important events in one's intellectual life often end in some form of public display and dissemination. They also connect students with different artistic and intellectual circles in partnerships that typically outlive the writing project in hand. Those projects become important components of students' intertextual identities and become significant additions to their writing trajectories.

Writing as a tool of inquiry

One method of turning a writing assignment into a life event is employing writing as a tool of inquiry, or an epistemological medium, in order to understand the world instead of asserting opinions about it. If writing is basically hermeneutic design, then it is, by character, always exploratory. As I previously discussed in my explanations about the hermeneutic nature of writing, when writing, as in other forms of communication, we constantly explore *more* effective ways of communication, as communication is never smooth, complete, and perfect. Product and process approaches to writing do not tend to see writing as an open-ended and dynamic practice; they typically fail to appreciate writing as a vehicle for inquiry and exploration: an epistemological medium for learning as well as reporting information and expressing fully formed opinions.

Writing as a vehicle for exploration involves two different layers; first, writing for learning, reflection, imagining new possibilities and also healing. Choman, Clarice and Magda shared experiences that corroborated scholarly conversations about 'writing for learning' (Emig, 1971; Rivard, 1994) and 'writing as therapy' (Feldman, 2011; Prior, 2019; Sampson, 2007). Choman for instance said:

> When I reached puberty, I wrote poetic prose about the issues that were on my mind; for instance, 'what is childhood?', 'what is adulthood?', 'what is life?' And there were some reflections: 'who am I?', 'where am I?', 'what am I going to do?' and some were remedial pieces I wrote when I felt sad. And the next category was daily memoirs: 'What happened today'. 'My dad said this or that'. So my writings were a mix of therapeutic, reflective, organizational, and fictional. 'Writing' was my best friend.

The second layer, which more specifically relates to the lives of multilingual immigrants, is writing as a creative inquiry into one's position in the world. I am intentionally using the adjective 'creative' to emphasize that while immigrants write to understand who they are in their new society, they at the same time *create* new academic and professional identities in the host country by communicating and connecting through writing. I interacted with Magda, Clarice and Choman for years and witnessed how they wrote to create and make sense of their identities in Canada. They used writing to present themselves, to navigate, to negotiate, to test the waters, to examine prejudices, and to challenge dominant discourses. Meanwhile, they used the feedback they received to comprehend and further shape the kind of person they were perceived to be.

Clarice's academic writing, for instance, involved much more than reporting her research findings; it, also, helped her create her image as an emerging scholar in a highly competitive environment. When I invited Clarice to this project and told her that I wanted to study the life of an academic writer and she was a good candidate, she doubted if she should be called an academic writer because 'I have only few publications'. Years after that initial encounter, Clarice's impact as a scholar has grown by each new publication. This interpretation of the impact of writing is not a surprising finding when we think of professional growth, yet it has interesting pedagogical implications. If writing is so closely (and obviously) connected to one's image, identity, and positionality, why do dominant curricula not approach writing as a tool for identity negotiation? What are the causes of our obsession with the quality of writing assignments that are typically written for an audience of one, the teacher, when writing can also be used as a tool for inquiry? What are some different ways in which learners can use writing to explore the world and themselves rather than assert opinions or report facts and findings? Facts and opinions are important to be shared and discussed, but are they not presented best in a writing trajectory with space for reflection and modification instead of single products that are often judged based on their formats rather than the intellectual substance?

Genre fluidity and flexibility

Writing genres can be conceptualized by two different approaches (Chandler, 1997): first, genres can be treated as autonomous forms with fixed defining elements; second, genres can be regarded as dynamic systems or living texts which loosely resemble genre families but keep altering. Many instances of classroom practice – mainly influenced by centralized curricula and standardized test preparation syllabi – reflect the first approach, treating genres as closed and autonomous. Most editing and publishing practices also pressure writers to shape their pieces according to the genre moulds that publishers have a market for, or imagine that it is the case. Job application, grant writing and business correspondence in the English language, also, have strict rules – at least when taught to English learners as manifested in textbooks and dominant pedagogies.

The alternative view, in contrast, regards genres as dynamic textual systems (re)formed by communicative circumstances, sociocultural contexts, and technological possibilities (Swales, 1990). From this perspective, clear-cut borders between fiction and non-fiction, academic and creative, and compositional and technical frequently blur. The writing lives of the practicing writers who participated in my study hosted genre experiences with the fluidity and flexibility highlighted in this latter view. Nevertheless, the participants' multi and transgenre writing practices had often been reduced and presented as their expertise in one particular genre for employment, publication, or assessment purposes.

Considering genres as closed systems has had two major pedagogical consequences. First, drawing thick borders between genres has created a genre hierarchy in educational centres, dominated by essayist literacy. Second – even within the current hierarchy with academic writing at the top – it has hindered pedagogical creativity in teaching essay and report writing since the features, qualities, and characteristics of Anglo-American academic genres are typically treated as fixed, comfortably identifiable, and universally replicable.

As I previously explained, one important criterion for recruiting participants for my study was diversity of genres they engaged with:

Choman: fiction; Clarice: academic writing; and Magda: technical and transactional writing. I adopted this criterion to see if the writers' writing practices significantly differed from genre to genre. In the course of the study, I learned that despite the current genre hierarchies and the genre specialties highlighted in Magda, Clarice and Choman's CVs, the participants heavily interacted with a variety of genres as learners. Similarly, as writers, they produced texts in multiple genres. I, for instance, chose to recruit Clarice for this project because she had concentrated on academic writing, and, as an aspiring non-Anglo-American academic who published in English, she was a suitable participant for my study. Although we were close friends and met frequently, I was never aware that Clarice had also been a poet and playwright until I systematically studied her literate history, and I was shocked to see how societal and academic practices narrowed down presentation of our genre practices and rendered large proportions of our genre experiences invisible and even irrelevant. When younger in Brazil, Clarice wrote songs for a rock band that she was a member of. She also wrote plays in different contexts:

> I have written scripts. I was a drama teacher before I came to Canada. So I co-wrote with my students. I also rewrote and modified classical plays for my students. And, of course, I wrote plays in Portuguese in Theatre School – after my undergrad studies in English Literature.

It is almost impossible to quantify the impact of Clarice's literary past in Portuguese on her English academic writing but much less difficult to see that Clarice, as a writer, was comfortable migrating between genres, although some of those genres might remain hidden in professional and educational settings.

I approached Choman as a novelist, but my initial perception that she mainly engaged with fiction was later challenged. Like Clarice, Choman experimented with different genres. Despite the image reflected on her Facebook page as a novelist in the initial years of my study, we were both conscious that in the later period of our collaboration she was mainly writing as a journalist:

> The current situation in the Middle East has activated journalism about Kurdistan. And since I have been given this chance to write the stories of the Iranian Kurds, I have become more interested in journalistic writing. I feel when my writing is connected to a cause and when I value this cause, it really helps my writing. It's very complex. My writing is also the same: a combination of art, literary form, society, and politics.

Choman's emphasis on her transgenre writing practices reminds me that her fiction also – perhaps reminiscent of the major contribution of Iranian cinema to the art-world: mixing fictional and documentary elements – in many ways has been journalistically realistic. Choman in her first novel in English documents short sections of the lives of Iranian women. In another novella building on the remaining letters of an executed Kurdish teacher/activist, she records his last days in prison.

The belief in fluidity of genres as their usual state requires writing pedagogies to develop students' genre agility. When discussing Magda, Clarice and Choman's ontologies of literacy, we focused on the notions 'discursive agility' (flexibility in thinking about literacy) and 'semiotic agility' (comfort in interacting with different semiotic systems including language). The concept 'genre agility' (the ability to write in multiple and between genres) is the natural extension of those concepts. 'Genre agility' is, also, inherently connected to the previous three themes in this section: hermeneutic design, writing products and process as life events, and writing as a tool of inquiry. Genre agility is best developed in response to life events that motivate individuals to write. Also, employing different genres helps us explore and understand different aspects of life and horizons of meaning. On the other hand, effective hermeneutic design requires genre agility inasmuch as successful communication is not possible without constant genre guessing.

Summary

In this chapter, I shared my analyses of the literacy and writing discourses that informed Clarice, Choman and Magda's literate and writing lives. I sought to learn about these practicing writers' perceptions of what literary and writing are. It is important to discuss how multilingual writers think about literacy because literate activities do not occur in a vacuum, but within a discursive context. We work with language based on our understandings of what the nature of language is and what its uses are.

Literacy is, first and foremost, a cultural collage of philosophies and practices that we inherit from society, family, and school. Educators interacting with migrant populations, who often have to perform in learned languages, must meet the challenge of making language learners' discursive backgrounds visible in order to organically add new discourse practices to learners' beliefs about literacy. Moreover, the nature of literacy also transforms as more media are available for linguistic exchange. This observation is particularly significant amidst the current digital developments challenging dominant print-based views of literacy. This shift has pedagogical implications since it raises questions about the use of multimodal media in the classroom. The next theme highlighted that literacy breeds literacy and that many of the participants' perceptions of literacy were inspired and influenced by the contents of the books that they had read. If texts themselves are important sources of literacy discourses, educators should be conscious about the texts they choose for students to read. Part of this consciousness is reflections on diversifying canonical curriculum in order to undermine the dominance of certain discourses and the omission of others.

The underlying concept that connected the above themes was the fluidity of literacy discourses and the open enededness of the narratives that describe our literate pasts. Some literacy discourses are easier to identify than others such as core cultural practices like the status of poetry in Kurdish culture or the significance of oracy in Brazilian culture. Nevertheless, some literacy discourses are abstract, vague, and difficult to identify particularly when it comes to individuals who experience translingual and cross-cultural lives, where discourses merge and diverge and where beliefs about literacy frequently contradict and complement one another. Any attempt to reflect upon and present one's discourse practices is subjective and selective. The writers who participated in my inquiry had the ability to frame and describe their discourse practices in a manner that presented powerful and empowering narratives of their literate lives. It is crucial to develop curricula that make space for nurturing such an ability: for multilingual students to reflect on their literate legacies and current literacy engagements in order to create literacy narratives that allow them to see their intellectual lives in a positive light.

Writing for the participants was essentially a form of hermeneutic design, involving complex communication dynamics such as the positionalities of the addresser and the addressee and the power relations between them, and also the sociocultural contexts of communication and interpretative paradigms that the writer and the reader employ to understand each other. If writing is hermeneutic design, 'great' writing is not wrought according to fixed objective formulas. Effective writing happens in a communitive context between the sender of the message and the receiver, the two sides who possess varying rhetorical legacies. The necessity of a meaningful communitive context for writing had convinced the participants to remember their writing practices as life events that strengthened their social positions. Teaching writing should include highlighting the significance of hermeneutic guessing, which can be best achieved by encouraging genre agility and also by recognizing writing as an inquiry tool to understand the self and the world. Pedagogically, the laid out understanding of writing would require a transition from traditional composition classes to genre-flexible translingual multimodal writing communities. In such communities, writing teachers should facilitate writing practices that (1) target audiences beyond the classroom, (2) include much more than essayist literacy, (3) reconstruct curricula with the students in response to their current issues, (4) expose students to a variety of genres, (5) blend genres, (6) create multimodal texts, (7) create texts in multiple languages. These pedagogies, instead of being preoccupied with the *techne* of essay writing, will mainly focus on genre understanding, the hermeneutics of communication, students' literate histories, the discursive nature of text production, the collaborative aspects of writing and the power-laden character of dissemination of text.

One important theme that could have been inserted in this chapter is: writing as a *power differential*. My observations of Choman, Magda and Clarice's writing lives and my conversations with them show that writing in English as a learned language for the participants (and also writing in general) was a determining factor in the power relations these writers found themselves in all through their lives. The large number of themes regarding the participants' perceptions of and experiences with power-relational aspects of writing made me specify one whole chapter to this issue. In the next chapter, I focus on power and writing.

5 Writing as a Power Differential

In the inquiry which this book is based on, I was interested to learn about the discursive and power-relational contexts of multilingual writers' engagement with literacy. I wondered how those contexts impacted their writing practices, particularly when they wrote in English as an additional language. In the previous chapter, I discussed themes such as literacy as an evolving cultural collage and writing as hermeneutic design. Here, I describe how relations of power, whether in society, community, or classroom, impacted the literate and intellectual lives of the practicing writers who participated in my inquiry.

Despite occasional scepticism about transformative pedagogies that suggest approaching teaching and learning writing as praxis (Fulkerson, 2005), in disciplines such as history, literary criticism, anthropology, and especially philosophy, the bond between writing and power has always been in the forefront of conversations about writing. For instance, Derrida (1979) deconstructed the old questions: 'Who can write?' and 'What can writing do?' revealing that they merely suggest writing and power are *related*, whereas writing *is* power and power *is* writing. He regarded those questions misleading for:

> Fostering the belief that writing *befalls* power ... that it can ally itself to power, can prolong it by complementing it, or can serve it, the question suggests that writing can *come* to power or power to writing. It excludes in advance the identification of writing *as* power or the recognition of power from the onset of writing ... Writing does not come to power. It is there beforehand, it partakes of and is made of it. (Derrida, 1979: 117)

Derrida's writing-as-power theory is not an isolated proposition. Decades after the publication of the above passage, the same message is heard in different academic, artistic, and activist quarters. Grada Kilomba is a Portuguese scholar-writer-artist of colour, whose work aims at decolonizing knowledge drawing on race, gender and class relations. In the video installation 'While I Write' from her *Decolonizing Knowledge: Performing Knowledge project*, Kilomba (2015) askes:

> So, why do I write?
> I write, almost as an obligation,

to find myself.
While I write,
I am not the 'Other',
but the self,
not the object,
but the subject.
I become the describer,
and not the described.
I become the author,
and the authority[.]

Similarly, there have been other power-conscious approaches to teaching writing, and more broadly teaching language and literacy: for instance, cultural studies pedagogy (George & Trimbur, 2001), feminist pedagogy (Jarratt, 2001), queer composition (Alexander & Gibson, 2004), activist literacies (Simon & Campano, 2013), and in second language education identity-text creation (Cummins & Early, 2011). To unpack one example in this trend, Blommaert (2010) used the concept of *literacy regimes* to show how different norms of textual production compete in a hierarchical system by attempting to control production and reception:

> Literacy regimes, for Blommaert, are hierarchical (2010). Those regimes belonging to geopolitically dominant communities with elite languages and material resources have the power to insist on their norms in translocal contexts. ... Blommaert's orientation builds on the tradition of situated literacy (Heath 1983; Street 1984) to consider each text in its settings of reception and production. (Canagarajah & Matsumoto, 2017: 2)

The contributions of critical theorists, gender scholars, and post-colonial thinkers to writing studies has created some awareness about writing and power particularly in composition classes at college level (Lea & Street, 1998; Tate *et al.*, 2001) – and to some but lesser degree in K-12 education (see for instance, Christensen, 1999, 2000, 2009) and in English as an additional language classes (for instance, Cummins & Early, 2011). This awareness has manifested itself in questioning the dominance of the essayist literacy in most professional and academic structures in the West, especially the Anglo-American West. Essayist literacy has been deconstructed as a male European capitalist literacy practice (Farr, 1993; Trimbur, 1990): male because the Anglo-American essay is assertive and not explorative or expressive; European because it regards poetic and non-written modes of communication – common among non-Europeans – as inferior; and capitalist because it awards report writing, which lubricates the movement of capital, labour and goods in complex business structures.

The rhetoric of assertiveness, whose promotion has caused the dominance of argumentative/persuasive essay writing in educational centres, in everyday functional writing – such as resume, cover letter, and grant writing – has also shaped values and practices that work against multilingual learners, immigrants, and refuges, especially in the job market. In Canada and the United States, for instance, job application and proposal writing are mainly a form of self-promotion, self-marketing and personal branding. Such concepts are often frowned upon in many non-Western cultures that value professional humility. Moreover, learning the complex rules of CV, cover letter, and proposal writing in a new language is difficult and time consuming. These complexities, among other reasons, put newcomers to North America at a disadvantage in job search and application writing (Cervatiuc, 2009; Guo, 2009; Kerekes, 2005, 2007, 2018; Krahn *et al.*, 2000). The problem, of course, should not be reduced to lack of technical or cultural knowledge of the rules and dynamics of job application. Linguistic difference often becomes an excuse for racial and ethnic discrimination and turns application writing into hurtful power games (Carlsson & Rooth, 2007; Kaas & Manger, 2012; Pager & Shepherd, 2008). It has been studied and reported that in addition to language skills, adult immigrants 'should develop the 'soft skills' they need to find employment and integrate successfully into the workplace' (Derwing & Waugh, 2012: 1), part of the 'soft skills' being developing the ability to navigate societal power relations.

Texts are material products that can be sold, so they are attractive for their financial potentials. Texts also influence thought and can impact society and thus their distribution raises sensitivity and triggers action for control of textual expression. Considering the intricate networks of power surrounding writing, it is important to ask how conscious literacy and language teachers and learners are of the power-laden nature of writing. In this chapter, I attempt to explain some of the power-related dimensions of writing in multiple languages in connection with the experiences of the writers who participated in my research. First, I report how Choman, Magda and Clarice saw writing as a form of praxis, aimed to impact lives, communities, or society. Second, I illustrate power-relational aspects of writing by examining the dynamics of publishing and dissemination. Third, I write about writing as a catalyst for community building and for forging cultural and political collaborations. In this third section, I focus on the often-unseen collaborative side of writing: the invisibility which allows dominant curricula to reduce writing to individual contextless assignments.

Writing as Praxis and Claiming Agency

Praxis for Freire (1970) was 'reflection and action upon the world in order to transform it' (Freire, 1970: 36) and literacy an essential component of this transformation. Rooted in this conceptualization – amidst the growth of the popularity of critical pedagogy in North America – there has been much written about 'writing as praxis' (see for instance, Kitchin, 2014; Lysaker, 2014; Yagelski, 2012). Yagelski (2012), as a token of this scholarly trend, wrote about the transformational potentials of writing when the act of writing is viewed as sociocultural and political action:

> Writing instruction at all levels of education continues to be informed by a narrow conception of writing as procedure and by persistent misconceptions about writing. ... In general, we simply don't teach writing in ways that give students access to its transformative power; we don't allow them to experience writing as a way of making sense of themselves and the world around them. (Yagelski, 2012: 189)

Comprehending and transforming the world also requires making sense of ourselves and our place in the world so that we can claim agency to create change. Awareness of one's positionality and claiming agency through writing has also been discussed in composition and writing studies – especially in postprocess theory with an emphasis on 'creat[ing] new possibilities for epistemological and discursive agency' (Clifford & Ervin, 1999: 188).

The experiences of the participants in this study stress the significance of praxis and agency in relation to writing. Even a very quick skim of the lists of Choman, Clarice and Magda's publications would show their writing almost always aimed at transformation of some type. Choman's stories (in her fiction and journalistic writing) often document voices of the Kurds, minoritized in Turkey, Iran, Syria and Iraq. In her fictional work, her characters are mainly women and her main subject matter women's issues. Her writings as a journalist also reflected the same social commitment. She, for instance, wrote about women Kurdish fighters, domestic violence, language rights, and racism. Clarice's academic writing, similarly, had a discernible critical substance. Clarice was particularly interested in students' plurilingualism and advocated recognition of minority languages at schools. Magda's textbook writing also was basically educational and thus intended to help learners. I spoke with these women to learn about how conscious they were of socially sensitive topics that they chose to write about. I also asked whether writing helped them summon their agency for change. Choman shared with me her reflections about the mentality behind her socially concerned fiction and journalism:

> I wrote as a form of rebellion and resistance. I was even punished for writing at home [since it wasn't considered genuine schoolwork]. My mom would find my writing pad in my physics book and get angry because I wasn't 'studying'. My engagement with poetry and literature

was considered some kind of perversion. Half of my intellectual life was not considered *legit* because I was a girl. ... Sex-based discrimination has always been on my mind – long before I knew there was a word such as feminism.

Choman's writing, hence, does not hail from a vacuum and involves lived experiences and important forms of identity construction. In my conversations with Magda about this topic, the term 'to do a crazy thing' became a code between us, denoting: to write – or to initiate a project – in order to address a social issue or solve a problem (with or without any academic or professional rewards). When I asked her if she 'did crazy projects' beyond her 'official' writing funded by organizations she worked for, she told me about a series of educational videos that she wrote and directed:

I sometimes do things that you might call 'crazy'. For example, I realized that parents in the Hungarian community in Toronto had problems with providing meaningful alternatives for their kids not to play on iPad all the time. So I approached the Canadian Hungarian TV here in Toronto and said, 'Let's do something about this'. I produced a series of TV shows about this issue. I invited three, four families, kids and parents together in the media room [of the apartment we lived in and filmed the videos].

This desire to act (through textual/cultural production) is tied to trust in one's abilities and to an understanding of the potential outcomes of activating one's agency. See how Choman took ownership of the impact of her life as a writer/activist:

I have learned that I have to stand up and speak up, and I have faced a lot of trouble for that. I have even been fired. In Iran, I was interrogated because I was involved in the fight for women's rights.

Magda also echoed the same consciousness: 'I shouldn't rely that much on that [others' judgments about my writing]. I should have more confidence in myself, in whatever I do'.

An important area of research with a focus on the role of culture on second language writing is intercultural (contrastive) rhetoric (Connor, 1996; Connor *et al.*, 2008; Kaplan, 1966; Kubota & Lehner, 2004). 'Contrastive rhetoric is an area of research in second language acquisition that identifies problems in composition encountered by second language writers and, by referring to the rhetorical strategies of the first language, attempts to explain them' (Connor, 1996: 5). Clarice shared with me how, when writing up her master's thesis, she had to resist her supervisor's request to 'soften' her Brazilian writing rhetoric, which – as Clarice described – was denser and more abstract than typical Anglo-American college writing. She did not change her style entirely and started to negotiate with her supervisor about her rhetorical approach. Clarice's rhetorical resistance eventually led to the acceptance and even admiration of her writing style by her mentor because of the analytic possibilities that her 'complex' Brazilian rhetoric permitted:

> When I first started writing – you know for real – in a North American context, I was pretty much trying to assimilate my writing [into Anglo-American norms]. My supervisor was always asking me, 'Try to do this, to do that'. And I replied, 'But that's very restrictive. I don't want to do this'. I started using all my criticality into my writing and all of a sudden people started to like it. And I was like, 'Oh, okay, awesome'. Then I continued. I don't think it's an accident. It is also a matter of being confident enough to know who you are and to know that there is value in it. It's not easy though.

Writing is a form of being in that it helps one define oneself and insert one's identity in power networks to create change. It is difficult to imagine writing as a meaningful event without considerations for agency and praxis (Miller, 2014). This proposition is basically a reminder that amidst the dictates, restrictions, and occasional irrationalities of our complicated academic and professional structures, we should pause and ask why students should be interested in writing a piece that bears no relevance to their lives or the society in which they live their lives. The pedagogical implications of such a view are profound. How can teachers design assignments that are praxis oriented (Christensen, 2000)? How much of our students' lives, concerns, and interests can we see in their writing? Which audiences are learners' written assignments targeting in addition to their teachers? The same questions should also be asked about writing in a learned language. What kind of writing curricula could we construct for additional language learners in order to enable them to feel empowered and impactful in their newly adopted languages? Although these questions might appear as suggesting challenging directions, educators in different contexts have actually tried to approach teaching writing with an eye on its power-relational dimensions in creative ways. For instance, learners have been invited to participate in different forms of community service writing (Julier, 2001), emerging writers have been encouraged to adopt oral history (Montero & Rossi, 2012) and ethnographic methods (Sinor & Huston, 2004). Also, different types of project-based approaches (see for instance, Levis & Levis, 2003) have been mobilized to inspire student writing at the service of larger social and academic visions than the completion of a course assignment.

The writing practices of Choman, Magda and Clarice were tightly interwoven with questions about their social impact. They also wrote as a form of intellectual existence that would help them construct their identity and present it publicly. The act of writing for Clarice, Magda and Choman often activated their agency in their interactions with society and in the process of identity negotiation. From this perspective, it is interesting to ask if writing assignments in schools and colleges are designed to allow students to engage with writing as a form of praxis. Do our students' writings connect with societal discourses? Do our assignments help students feel that they are part of ongoing cultural, intellectual, academic and political debates? In second language writing, in particular, what are some assessment strategies that help teachers value intellectual and discursive substance of students' writings as much as, if nor more than, their linguistic performance. One significant strategy to help teachers move towards such a direction in writing classes is creating possibilities for publishing student work, which I discuss next.

Publishing and Dissemination as Inseparable from the Act of Writing

> Publication is inseparable from writing. I have a finished novel on my table now, and I am looking for an agent. Does this novel really exist unless it is published and read? How much does it exist? Even if it is published but not read, what's the point? (Choman)

Writing classes would benefit from including publishing in mainstream writing syllabi and from sharing the texts that learners construct with audiences larger than the writing teacher. In reading studies, there has always been a significant theoretical trend – best represented by reader-response theorists (Fish, 1976; Iser, 1980; Rosenblatt, 1994) – proposing that 'text' comes into existence only when it is read by the 'reader'. If we adopt the same concept in writing studies, it will help clarify that the act of writing is hardly complete before a readership interacts with what we write. In order to reach an audience though, we need access to technology for publishing and to distribution channels. Publishing and distribution structures are often surrounded by complicated networks of power nodes. Who funds the publishing technology? Who has the know-how? Who controls communication networks? Who benefits from current policies and laws regarding publishing and dissemination? Who pays writers, buys their writings and sells them? What apparatus has the authority to quality check, reward, or omit texts?

I opened this chapter with a citation from Derrida (1979) stating that it is misleading to ask how power and writing are *related* because writing is not separate from power to be somehow related to it: writing *is* power. Right after this argument, he writes, 'What is astonishing is not writing as power but what comes, as if from within a structure, to limit it by a powerlessness or an effacement' (Derrida, 1979: 117). There is an invisible will in power structures to block dissemination by controlling the publishing and distribution apparatus as if it knows that text is, indeed, a source of empowerment.

In his 'institutional theory of art', Danto (1964) defined art – and by extension creative writing – as:

> X is an artwork in a classificatory sense if and only if (1) x is an arti-fact (2) upon which someone acting on behalf of a certain institution (the artworld) confers the status of being a candidate for appreciation. (Carroll, 2003: 227)

In a possible *institutional theory of writing* inspired by Danto's theory, the act of writing would be recognized as satisfying two conditions: (1) the production of written texts and (2) the willingness of the members of the *writingworld* to display the written products for public consumption. In practical terms and for the purposes of this book, in such a theory of writing, the process of writing in a learned language cannot be comprehended fully if we do not think about the editors and publishers who accept and reject submissions by multilingual writers. While judging the quality of submissions, those gatekeepers in practice sustain or terminate the existence of a writer's work because texts do not come to be without an active readership. Teachers, similarly, can foster or abort the writing process depending whether or not they consciously attempt to develop pedagogies that can connect students with readers beyond the classroom and that promote interacting with the writingworld as part and parcel of the writing process.

As I explained previously, Choman, Clarice and Magda regarded writing as hermeneutic agility developed in response to their life events: to join professional communities, to make their voices heard, to resist oppression, and to reconstruct their identities as immigrants in Canada. Through the lens of my proposed 'institutional theory of writing', life events that are entangled with writing experiences would involve power-laden scrutiny of gatekeepers (of institutions, associations, professions, the press and media) typically from the dominant racial and linguistic populations. Too often we fail to reveal this very important dimension of writing to our students. When we teach writing to speakers of other languages, we need to employ pedagogies that expose students to experiences that show that the academic journal industry favours native speakers of English (Lillis & Curry, 2006; Paasi, 2005); that the literary scene is dominated by white writers and – in Canada for instance – 'indigenous writers and writers of color ... lack ... representation within the publishing industry' (Edwards, 2017: para. 14); and that professional structures frequently reject job applications with non-Anglo-American names on them (King *et al.*, 2006).

The multilingual writers who participated in my research were conscious of biases involved in the dynamics of publishing and professional application and the importance of navigating corridors of power after they had the finalized written products in their hands. Clarice, for instance, said:

> I agree writing involves more than a skill or an intellectual ability; literacy is action and includes active dissemination. As for publishing, I am an academic, so one of my duties as a citizen is to publish. ... And isn't that why a lot of people don't write? Because they don't have an audience? For instance, at school who is the audience? The teacher. ... I write academic articles and publish them because right now I feel I have something to say. And I think there are some people who can learn from some perspective of what I have to say. I navigate institutional requirements and distribution systems because I feel that if I write something and if I don't get it published, it's meaningless. I don't write for my PhD courses just to pass the course; that's cruel, empty, extremely boring. I could but I don't because I feel you can go beyond.

Over years, I observed Clarice's attempts to learn about research publication and dissemination in North America. As an international graduate student, Clarice had to go through an intensified version of the usually uncomfortable dynamics of academic publication: constant rejections, lack of access to established writing communities, having to deal with reviewers who did not know much about her speciality, and the occasional comment about her being a non-native writer of English.

Most academics experience at least some of these obstacles and develop an awareness of the inner-workings of the journal industry to maintain their writing careers successfully. Clarice's dissemination practices, while showing some of the same trends, included elements that were particularly noteworthy. While playing by the rules of the academic writingworld in order to get published as a junior researcher, Clarice displayed much professional courage and dignity. In the first year of our doctoral studies, Clarice and I published articles in a prestigious journal in the same issue. Both of our submissions were accepted on condition of numerous revisions. I rapidly applied the suggestions in excitement for the prospect of being published in an important journal for the first time. Clarice was not convinced that the reviewers' recommendations for her article were helpful. She believed that some of the changes might compromise her findings or alter the theoretical paradigms based on which she had written the article. She argued back against some of the reviewers' views and published the piece only when she believed it truly reflected her thoughts. This process at times threatened the possibility of her being published, but Clarice remained resolute. Clarice married this academic integrity with active learning about the workings of the journal industry. Meanwhile, she also helped her colleagues and aspiring academic writers by sharing her experiences with them. She worked in one of her university's writing centres to support international students with their academic papers. Moreover, she organized academic writing workshops conducted by students for students so that, in Clarice's words, 'they can talk about what often remains veiled by editors and professors'. Clarice's approach to navigating the writingworld, while trying to remain true to her thoughts and writing vision was an inspirational model for interacting with the gatekeepers of the journal and academic publishing industry.

In the literary world also the challenges of publishing and distribution are taxing. Although today there are more technological possibilities for self-publication, distribution is typically the point where power, politics, and money control voices. Choman shared with me some of her experiences with book distribution in Canada:

> When my first book came out, I was really excited. I arrived in Canada in 2007 and published my first book in 2010. It was unbelievable. But when it was done, when the book was physically out, I was really shocked. I soon realized what a dirty world the literature industry was. The experience was entirely different from what I'd expected. Big newspapers wouldn't review my book. Why? Because my publisher wasn't Penguin, or another big name. Although my publisher is the most multicultural publisher in one of the most multicultural cities in the world [Toronto], its books are entirely ignored. Gradually things became clearer and clearer for me, things like who decides what books to be reviewed and where. And all the publicity really badly written books get. Now, having published a few books, I am just trying to see how I can navigate the system like finding a really good agent. Or I'm thinking about reframing my style of writing in North America, where everyone is obsessed with thrillers. Can I borrow a few of their techniques to communicate with a larger audience? Can I make my books more marketable?

Effective writers do much more than crafting formalistically well-wrought (Brooks, 1947) products: they deeply reflect on power-relational aspects of writing, including the micropolitics of publishing and dissemination. I started this section by coining the term the writingworld after Danto's the artworld. To conclude this section, I try to answer the question, 'What does the writingworld (or writingworlds) involve?' in the light of the data I collected during my interactions with Magda, Clarice and Choman.

I learned from these writers that, when thinking about publishing and dissemination, one should not forget that the writingworld is (a) hierarchal and (b) tribal. The writingworld is hierarchal; as a result, what determines dissemination possibilities for writers is not only the quality of their writing but their position in the pecking order. The writingworld is also tribal, so despite claims on objective assessment through blind peer review and similar methods, writing circles tend to publish their own members more often (Hill & Provost, 2003; Wenneras & Wold, 1997). The participants in my study doubted unconditional belief in the veneer of rigour and professionalism typically displayed by journal and publishing industries and advised better understanding of the impact of ideological and financial aspects of publishing.

Describing dissemination channels as hierarchical and tribal might appear to be a bleak view of the publishing world – especially with its challenges multiplied for multilingual immigrants who have very little access to circles of power. Nevertheless, the very tribal nature of publishing, ironically, could open the doors for emerging writers. I learnt from Clarice, Choman and Magda's experiences that in a highly compartmentalized publishing scene, where different groups of writers have their own small niches, it is likely that if emerging writers find a tribe with whose members they share interests, they would receive support for dissemination. I am using the word 'tribe' intentionally to deconstruct discourses of objectivity that hide the power-relational aspects of publishing writing. Academic publication, for instance, often occurs as a result of different forms of discursive allegiance. Publishing in academic journals involves participating in academic conversations, necessitating certain choices of form, content, considerations for audience, style, and even specific citations, which would help you to be recognized by others as working within similar discourses.

In a casual conversation with Magda, I was lamenting about the rejections that I faced years ago as a young poet by the publishing industry. Magda asked me, 'How many publishers did you approach?' I had to pause and think to remember: '... Two or three'. She smiled and said I was not 'rejected'; I did not 'find the person who appreciated my poetic style', and I should have tried more publishers. Magda then said when she was with like-minded people, she always felt there was a lot of thirst for new projects even within rigid 'prestigious' publishing houses:

> When we arrived in Canada, I started to work for Oxford University Press Canada. At that time they only sold textbooks from the US and the UK. I kind of started something new there and told them, 'Why don't we publish Canadian content books by Canadian textbook writers?' Now they actually have a lot of books by Canadian authors for the Canadian market.

Magda's view of how philosophical alliances can work as a positive force in the power relations involved in textual generation and dissemination connects well with the next section, which focuses on the role of collaboration in the writing process, but before that, I conclude the current section with a few lines about publication-centred writing pedagogy.

Although there have been reports of educators who consciously included publishing in the process of teaching wring (see for instance,

Bloom, 1990; Frater, 2004; Robillard, 2006; Woodin, 2008), dominant pedagogies often skip emphasis on dissemination and the power relations it involves. It is essential that we think about learning writing as a process that includes dissemination and interaction with authentic readerships. Such an approach will often include explicit conversations about ideological, political, and financial dimensions of writing, which more often surface in the publication process. Developing ways to publicly share and display student writing, in particular, will impact students who are writing in additional languages. The quality of emerging multilingual writers' work is often judged harshly in assessment systems mainly interested in formalistic dimensions of writing. Writing assignments designed to encourage English learners to publish their work, even with limited circulation, will boost students' confidence by allowing them to look at themselves as the owners of their adopted language.

Collaboration in Writing

Collaborative writing has long been an area of attention in writing studies in general (Howard, 2001) and in the same vein in second language writing (Storch, 2005). Much has been written about student collaboration in the process of writing from brainstorming and co-writing to peer assessment (Falchikov, 1986; Keh, 1990; Storch, 2005). There is a growing body of research on online collaborative writing tools and wiki writing (Barton & Cummings, 2009; Chao & Lo, 2011; Passig & Schwartz, 2007; Tharp, 2010). In academic writing, scholars have advocated collaborative writing as a component of participatory research in that it gives voice to research participants, allows a multiplicity of perspectives, and makes contributors' positionalities visible (see these examples, Simon *et al.*, 2014; Simon *et al.*, 2016). Other forms of cooperation in writing have also been reported; for instance, writing centre and student success support (Bawarshi & Pelkowski, 2008; Hobson, 2001; Shafer, 2012).

Collaboration in writing can be understood as two different phenomena. First, collaborative writing can be seen as a pedagogical tool to invite students to physically write together, to edit each other, provide peer feedback, and co-author text. Second, collaborative writing could be regarded as formation of writing communities often motivated by certain social, cultural and political agendas. Whereas in the former approach what is stressed is the physical act of co-writing, in the latter the focus is on building a writing community that aims to support its members discursively as well as technically. Thus, although in most forms of writing collaborations discursive and technical interactions are indistinguishably interwoven, a change in emphasis can create writing groups with different characteristics. The findings from my research highlight the significance of discursive collaborations formed in writing communities. Choman, Magda and Clarice remembered intellectual partnerships as more significant than physical co-writing. They joined and also initiated a variety of writing circles and intellectual relationships to produce writing. By exemplifying those collaborations, here I highlight the power-relational aspects of writing latent in cooperative textual performances.

Critical collaborations

Educational research which has its roots in psychology is interested to study writing as an individual cognitive performance (Zuengler & Miller, 2006), and thus as a product crafted or a process performed by an individual writer. This interest is understandable once literate practices are viewed as generated by dynamics at work in the brain mainly. The social turn in education, however, allowed us to think of writing as a cultural and communal phenomenon and to think about texts as artefacts produced and processed as a result of social relationships, discursive interactions, and also exchanges between the members of intellectual, literary, and professional communities.

Despite the valuable attempts reflected in the research listed in the introduction, pedagogies that overtly nurture collaboration in writing classes are not still the norm but considered alternative approaches. Rather than teachers' personal decisions, the dominance of traditional writing pedagogies can be a result of departmental and assessment practices used to recruit, admit and evaluate students as single individuals for pragmatic administerial and financial purposes. The same phenomenon occurs in the market-oriented publishing world also. 'The market exerts its power by insisting on a single, preferably recognizable, authorial name' (York, 2002: 14). This is also true in academic settings. For instance, in doctoral research and tenure processes, sole-authored publications are appreciated, but collaborative writing is viewed as beneath pieces with single authors.

It makes sense for profit-oriented organizations to approach writing as an individual performance, yet the question is, what is the impact of ignoring the collaborative aspects of writing (both physical and discursive) on student performance? The literate lives of the participants in my research show that the absence of collaboration from the writing process would hinder effective writing practices. Here, as an example, I discuss Magda's writing trajectory as a technical and textbook writer to illustrate collaborative aspects of her writing. The educational materials that Magda prepared for workshops and meetings were often peer-checked before the events or were edited after them for future use in response to audience feedback. It should also be noted that much professional writing is often modelled on written traditions customary in professional and administerial organizations, which makes writing of this kind highly collaborative but in a rather invisible way. My analysis of Magda's technical writing showed her experiences were no exception and she constructed her writing in sync with formats that she inherited from previous department of office members.

At a more visible level, Magda's textbooks were collaborations between her and her publishers based on the ideas Magda developed and shared with them. Magda did not make a living as a professional textbook writer only. She wrote textbooks mainly for educational purposes in parallel with her jobs as, for instance, a consultant or a staff member. As a result, the ideas for most of the textbooks that Magda wrote were developed in conversation with colleagues, administrators, and policymakers in response to the problems that they, typically urgently, needed to address. She, for instance, developed a book series project in collaboration with a large Austrian publishing house, which was looking for ideas for new methods for teaching English as a second language:

> I came up with the idea together with the publisher. At the time, it was a revolutionary idea for teaching English as a second language because as you know before English was a separate subject in schools, kids had, for example, maths, history, and an English class. But what we wanted was to integrate English in some other subjects. So my books focused on teaching English in a maths class, history class, or even in Phys-Ed. ... They were thinking of changing something because kids were not motivated. ... We brainstormed ideas and we came up with this method. These books were on the market for seven or eight years.

In another project, Magda joined an international network which focused on the environment, an issue Magda was personally invested in. This partnership was a pleasant experience for Magda as a multilingual writer:

> I started to work with international groups to develop learning projects, learning materials and resources for different subjects. One of them was energy management, the other one sustainability, diversity, and there was also other stuff. All this included multilingual approaches. We had the German government working on that, people from Italy, Spain. So we used English and a mixture of other languages.

A less formal – but not less important – type of textual collaboration also happened in Magda's household on a daily basis. Magda was constantly in conversation with the members of her family about her ideas, about what she wrote, and about what she read:

> A very important part of my reading is that I discuss it with my husband, or when my mother is here with her as well. I also read with my daughter and she reads to me. It's just a communal activity that we do.

The informal involvement of Magda's family in her literate life also turned into a professional relationship with her husband illustrating her textbooks. These examples show that it is difficult to comprehend Magda's technical writing trajectory without awareness about the collaborations (casual, official, visible, or hidden) that fostered text generations that eventually would be framed as the products of a single individual.

'Although academic publishing seems to be more receptive of multiply authored titles, particularly in the sciences and social-sciences, co-authors of critical and theoretical works in the humanities have been subjected to negative treatment in university promotion and tenure processes' (York, 2002: 14). Clarice worked in the humanities and was thus exposed to the same climate about collaboration in academic writing; however – similar to Magda – she actively sought cooperation to expand her writing experiences. By the end of the process of data collection and analysis for my project, she had published four co-authored articles (in English and Portuguese with Canadian, European and Brazilian colleagues). Perhaps less discernibly, she was also involved in constant discursive dialogue with the members of a number of research circles (in Canada, and internationally). The best example to illustrate Clarice's consciousness about writing as a collective act comes from my notes and memos about a panel conversation that she organized about academic publication for junior graduate students at her department. I attended the workshop and found it interesting that Clarice and the other panellists deviated from the usual focus of such events on technical skills and instead focused on the power relations involved in academic publication. Clarice's talk, in particular, focused on academic network development by inviting graduate researchers to pool resources and ideas for dissemination – an indication of her own mentality about the collaborative nature of academic writing.

The Washington Post recently reported that Yoko Ono had been recognized as the co-writer of John Lennon's 1971 song 'Imagine' after almost half a century (Schmidt, 2017). Our dominant economic dynamics, hiring procedures, and academic structures tend to hide complex forms of collaboration that contribute to the creation of each text. Similarly, our pedagogies ignore the communal nature of act of writing, or at the best of times, encourage physical collaboration as long as it leads to a final product that could be evaluated based on clearly demarcated division of labour. Writing teachers should create space for students to generate writing topics collaboratively, practice effective ways of providing peer feedback, and develop strategies for supporting each other's work without judgmental punishment-and-award strategies in the process of assessment. Educators should think of ways that can help learners look at themselves as members of writing communities rather than students to be graded in compulsory general education writing classes – communities that have clear visions formed and shared by all their members.

Psychological research into human cognition in terms of its dynamics in teaching and learning processes has helped us understand how the brain functions when learning. Nevertheless, it has also had practical ramifications, impacting everyday pedagogies. Most importantly, it has solidified an orthodox belief in the role of individual intelligence in the process of writing. This mentality has typically prevented educators from reflecting on collaborative dimensions of writing and developing activities that can connect students with one another and also with other people outside the classroom.

Writing circles and communities

Writing circles and communities have always been the main environment where authentic writing occurs. Too often we forget that great writing (literary, scientific, or professional writing) existed long before the establishment of modern educational settings, in which most of our current drills-based pedagogies are rooted. Before Western industrialization, what facilitated writers with the support they needed were intellectual communities which writers were part of and the writing circles which grew out of those communities. Studying the lives of Magda, Choman and Clarice, I saw that the same communities and circles were still functioning efficiently although invisibly in out-of-school contexts. The examples I shared about collaborative writing in the previous section could be re-read as examples of such communities. Here, however, I focus on Choman's experiences to illustrate the significance of meta-institutional writing communities.

Choman's creative writing career would be far better understood through learning about the writing communities Choman belonged in than cataloguing and chronologizing her publications. It took me a while, in the process of data collection, to learn that Choman's literary foundations – as a Canadian writer of English fiction – actually formed in underground literary circles in Tehran long before her immigration to Canada. The unofficial nature of that experience – which cannot be reflected in a curriculum vitae – and the fact that the written products produced in those circles were never published, concealed this period in Choman's life in our conversations until we consciously attempted to uncover the impact of unofficial out-of-school collaborations – in any language – on Choman's recognized works. When we took this approach, Choman opened up to say:

> When I was doing my graduate studies in English literature [in Tehran], I realized that, unlike in Kurdistan, there were some underground fiction writing workshops in Tehran. I tried almost all of them, and decided

to join the Gol circle. I attended the sessions for at least three years, no matter where in Tehran they were held. I spent hours and hours with the other members of the workshop, developing stories together and exchanging thoughts.

Once in Canada, Choman actively took part in writing groups, writers' associations, and literary circles until she found her place in the community of Toronto's non-white writers. Professional partnerships in that community led to the publication of her first novel in Canada by a publisher that specialized in printing books by writers from Canadian minority groups. The intellectual community that had embraced Choman exposed her to North American discourses about race, gender, and ethnicity, which would deeply impact her future journalistic writing about the Kurds. Even after Choman moved to the United States, the concerns of her Canadian writer friends still informed her activities. A few days before I wrote these lines, I found Choman in an online community of non-Caucasian Canadian writers criticizing cultural appropriation in an ongoing heated debate in Canada about the hegemony of white writers in Canadian literary magazines and the media in general, which has resulted in the exclusion of coloured voices and their stories.

An analysis of the elements shaping Choman's writing life, more than K-12 and college writing classes, would point to the profound impact of writing circles that Choman had been a member of. If a writer's productive writing life – despite the hegemony of centralized official schooling – has its roots in out-of-school and in organic writing circles, we need to answer serious questions about our current writing syllabi and pedagogies: How much do our writing classes resemble writing circles? What are some of the dynamics of organic writing communities that mainstream writing classes can borrow from? Also, next to an attempt to simulate writing circles, how can educators connect their students with authentic writing communities; or if the students are already members of any circles, recognize and use their writing in classroom activities and in the official assessment regime? Both in simulation of and authentic connection with writing circles, 'the facilitator creates the perfect environment before receding like the Deists' god' (Blythe & Sweet, 2008: 314), an environment where members can collaborate and exchange thoughts and ideas with one another and also with thinkers outside their own communities while the teacher keeps his or her distance from students' activities with least amount of micromanagement or direct interference.

Less visible intellectual associations

An emphasis on fostering well-defined partnerships and circles should not overshadow the significance of looser forms of intellectual community that can nurture literacy and inspire writing activities. Similar to literacy discourses – discussed in the previous chapter – empowering writing communities should be regarded as flexible and fluid, ranging from circles with clearly defined structures to loose, abstract, occasional, and even accidental partnerships. Choman, Magda and Clarice had vivid memories of such collaborations – in some cases after decades – and weighted their impact high. In this section, I share three specific examples of such less visible collaborations to stress the importance of what I call *less visible intellectual associations*: (a) the role of unofficial mentors, (2) ethnolinguistic communities, and (c) imagined communities.

In my conversations with Clarice, Magda and Choman about the most impactful experiences in terms of learning writing, references to the role of mentorship (in and out of school) outnumbered mentions of the impact of particular institutional experiences, such as a particular writing class or assignment. Influential writing mentors could be teachers, experts, intellectual role models, colleagues, friends, family members, or even strangers who accidentally or briefly enter learners' writing journeys. Such mentors provide support and encouragement. They read learners' work beyond the power relations latent in the official classroom situation and offer organic feedback unlike those received from often industrial institutional evaluation regimes, which rely on mass prompts and rubrics and also tightly quantified grades. Emerging writers feel safe to share their writing with such mentors and believe in their judgment.

The relationships that Choman, Magda and Clarice had with their mentors were imprinted on their memories mainly because of the mentors' recognition of their literate potentials. Choman, Magda and Clarice's guides helped them make sense of their writing, understand their ground in relation with other writers, navigate the publishing industry, and envisage possible literate futures. In the previous section, I wrote about the underground literary circles in Tehran, which embraced Choman and created a literary foundation for her (in Farsi) that she would use as a base for her future English fiction. In one of these underground writing communities, Choman met and established a close intellectual relationship with one of the coordinators of the club called Sia (pseudonym). Sia generously mentored Choman at the beginning of her career as a novice writer. Sia, also, interestingly, inspired and encouraged her to continue writing in Canada after her immigration:

> Sia, who ran the workshops, didn't like my first story. He didn't like the second story. But he loved the third one. When I was moving to Canada, he advised me not to quit writing. He said he saw a future for me as a writer. And his words mattered to me.

This type of intellectual partnership can take different shapes at different times and at different places and thus cannot be formulated in a syllabus to be recommended in a fixed manner of implementation. An emphasis on the impact of such partnerships though can highlight the benefits of increasing students' exposure to academic, artistic, and professional communities where such bonds can organically develop. In many of our large school and university classes, it is unrealistic to imagine that a writing teacher could be every student's writing confidant for a long and continual period of time; nevertheless, it is not farfetched to create pedagogies that assist students in forming mentorship bonds with individuals outside the classroom. Such pedagogies could include involving senior students, artists, writers, and community members in students' writing activities.

Less visible mentors can offer much more than intellectual, academic, or literary support. Literacy learning does not occur in a vacuum; it takes space, access, power, and funds. Some of these could be provided by individuals who are willing to share resources at their disposal with learners who need them but are unaware of their whereabouts or are unable to have access to those resources. Clarice spoke with me about one of her teachers in Brazil without whose help Clarice – as a published writer of English academic papers today – might not have learned English at all:

> My parents got a divorce when I was 12. And at that age, I remember, we were going through a lot of financial problems especially because my father wasn't contributing financially. ... I was very interested in learning English. The only way to learn English was to go to a language school. So I went to my dad and was like 'Okay, I know that you haven't been paying child support, etc, but can you please pay my tuition?' I was 12 at that time. Actually my mom said, 'I cannot afford it; go ask your dad'. I went there and he said 'Sure, I'll do that'. So he started paying and paid for two or three months of the tuition and then said, 'Okay, money is running out. I cannot afford it anymore'. Because my dad couldn't pay for my tuition, I had to drop out. And one of my classmates came to my house once and she asked why I wasn't going to English classes anymore. I said my dad couldn't pay anymore. She told my teacher about my situation, and my teacher wrote a note to me and asked my friend to give it to me. I opened the note and it said 'don't do anything before you talk to me'. And I had no idea what that meant. I told my mom, 'Mom, here is what my teacher has sent me. What do you think I should do?' She said why don't we go there and ask what is going on'. When I got there, my teacher wasn't there but the director of the school was. My mom said 'Okay, stay there in the waiting room and I'll be right back'. She had a conversation with the director and the director basically said that I was very motivated to learn the language and I was really good; I was super-passionate and they decided to give me a lifetime scholarship. So I studied for three years for free.

As much as official educational structures are an essential part of today's learners' education, they are not the only source of education – as exemplified by Choman's experience with the Gol circle. Moreover, educators should be made aware that by activating their agency, they can open up new avenues for students to better navigate existing structures, which – as illustrated in Clarice's case – are often too complicated and cumbersome to intelligently address students' issues. Experiences with dominant writing pedagogies show that ignoring these two facts will generate drills-based teaching methods and insensitive evaluation techniques that might satisfy the statistics-oriented checklists of dominant educational structures but would hardly produce successful writers (Innes, 2016; Jones & Clark, 2014; Parkinson, 2014).

Being part of certain ethnolinguistic communities in Toronto was another unstructured intellectual connection that, Magda, Choman and Clarice felt, significantly informed their cultural lives. Magda, for instance, had a close association with the Hungarian community in Toronto. She was active in developing educational programmes for Hungarian children and their families. She created educational videos for Hungarian-Canadians in the guest room of her rental apartment in her free time. The videos were broadcast by a Hungarian broadcasting company in Toronto. Similarly, Clarice had her finger on the pulse of cultural and social Brazilian events in Toronto. I cite two particular examples from my notes documenting my observations of Clarice's social media activities. As a response to the impeachment of Dilma Rousseff – 36th President of Brazil from 2011 until her removal from office on 31 August 2016 – Clarice attended Brazilian gatherings and protests in Toronto and posted pictures on Facebook of herself demonstrating. The second example is her engagement with the Brazilian film festival in Toronto, about which she shared news, photos, and videos on her online platforms. Choman, similarly, saw such community involvement as an effective form of identity negotiation and power-relational communication. Choman found belonging to Kurdish circles and associations an effective way for carving her identity between two dominant cultures – Canadian culture and Persian culture – being a minority in both, a Kurd in Iran and an Iranian in Canada:

> When I came to Toronto, I joined a Kurdish dance group mainly as a political act. I thought if I wanted to mingle with the Iranian community in Toronto, I should represent Kurdish culture through Kurdish dance, music, and costumes. I thought if they tolerated our dance and music, we would be able to develop dialogue about other things as well.

Choman, Clarice, Magda and I had a few group conversations about the significance of the communities we belonged to and the impact of such associations on our literate lives, discourse practices, and philosophies. There was a consensus among us that the impact of invisible communities that we were a part of – or we wished to belong in or to engage with – should not be underestimated. An emphasis on the impact of invisible (or less visible) communities led us to share the *imagined communities* (Norton & Pavlenko, 2019) we felt we belonged to, believing our imagined memberships could tell something about our sociopolitical, ethical, and philosophical inclinations and about the literate practices that would hail from them.

> Imagined communities [first coined by (Anderson, 1983)] refer to groups of people, not immediately tangible and accessible, with whom we connect through the power of the imagination. Our communities include our families, neighborhood communities, our workplaces, and our educational institutions. However, these are not the only communities with which we are affiliated. ... Imagination – 'a process of expanding oneself by transcending our time and space and creating new images of the world and ourselves' [(Wenger, 1998: 176)] – is another important source of community. (Kanno & Norton, 2003: 241)

Imagined communities, thus, are communities that we imagine we belong to, although we may never actually meet their members, or all of their members. If, as I tried to underline in this chapter, collaboration in literate activities – as a source of empowerment – could be discursive as well as physical (actual co-authorship), imagined communities can profoundly impact a learner's discourse practices and accordingly their writing practices. Unearthing students' imagined communities or assisting them in constructing such associations can open interesting intellectual horizons and affinities for them. As an example, here I present the imagined communities that Magda, Clarice and Choman felt that they were part of. It is not difficult to see how these writers' imagined communities have indeed helped them in their multilingual writing practices. In one of our group interviews, I invited the participants to share, in writing, the communities in which they imagined they belonged:

Clarice:
- Academic writers in applied linguistics.
- TESL/TEFL/TEAL writers.
- Drama educators.
- Critical thinkers.
- People who appreciate cinema, theatre and the arts.
- People who like indie music (punk rock, indie rock).

Choman:
- Writers with an accent.
- People who admire literary fiction.
- People who admire literary fiction set in a foreign world.
- People who care about the Kurdish cause.

- People who genuinely want democracy and peaceful coexistence everywhere in the world even if that means zero profit.
- People who recognize and admit multiple levels of oppression are happening because of age, race, class, sexual orientation, or disability.

Magda:
- Hungarian writers who write in foreign languages.
- Teachers and educators who are constantly trying to find new ways and methods for making learning more effective.
- People who like to read in original languages because it feels more real.
- The international community of open-minded, always curious and very critical readers.
- Writers who are humbled by the literature written before them but are innovative at the same time.

As these notes show, Clarice, Choman and Magda's imagined communities highlighted their consciousness and sensitivity about writing in English as a learned language. At the same time, however, they saw themselves not as exceptional writers but another member of the community of non-native writers. This perception helped them see multilingual writing as a normal practice and, as a result, imagine creating quality texts in English as a feasible possibility. Moreover, Clarice, Choman and Magda listed communities (artistic, literary, cultural and political) with rich intellectual and creative conventions feeding their literate, literary, and academic lives. Also, they imagined their identities as deeply affiliated with communities inspired by critical agendas. Choman wrote about 'democracy' and 'oppression' and Magda and Clarice professed to belong to communities made up of 'critical thinkers' and 'critical readers'. Additionally, Clarice, Choman and Magda's imagined communities revealed their attachment to cross-cultural communication.

Dominant writing pedagogies do not often attempt to make learners' discursive allegiances visible inasmuch as they consider writing as an individual skill. It is, however, worthwhile to think of written texts as power-relational artefacts carved in ideological exchanges between different communities: the dominant and the minoritized; native speakers and the 'accented'; managers and report writers; and also experts/teachers/editors and 'novice writers'. Exploring educators' and learners' imagined communities can unearth learners' inclinations and thus their potentials. Moreover, at a more practical level, learning about students' intellectual associations can help teachers better understand their writing habits and their rhetorical choices. Also, conversation about such abstract communities can create possibilities for emerging writers for new imagined memberships especially in communities with critical commitments. Consciousness about imagined communities can help writers elevate their identities from apprentice writers to agents of change by trying to imagine new associations. Also, allowing students to construct new imagined partnerships can prevent a sense of alienation and isolation.

Summary

Although suggestions for highlighting power-relational aspects in everyday writing pedagogy are often frowned upon as impractical and controversial (see for instance, Fulkerson, 2005; Haswell, 2005), in disciplines such as philosophy there is little doubt about the role of writing (broadly defined as including text production, discourse generation, and narrative creation) in power battles. Employing such philosophical theories (for instance, Derrida, 1979, 2001), in this chapter I shared examples of Magda, Choman and Clarice's literate behaviours to highlight the significance of approaching writing as praxis and a vehicle for claiming agency. Moreover, inspired by Danto's (1964) *Institutional Theory of Art*, I highlighted the tribal and hierarchical nature of what I named the *writingworld* (teachers, editors, grant application reviewers, search committees, and so on) in order to create a theoretical context for reflections on publishing, distribution, and dissemination as part and parcel of the act of writing.

One important form of resistance against the subjectivity of the writingworld's older members' power-laden evaluations of emerging writers' works – especially those who write in new languages and new cultural contexts – is collaboration. Collaboration in writing can occur in at least three different forms: (a) co-authoring texts, (b) participation in organized writing circles with common discursive agendas, and (c) initiating other intellectual partnerships like unofficial mentorships and reflecting on one's membership in abstract (imagined) discursive communities.

Better understanding of the relation of writing and power can improve pedagogical practice. Educators need to explore teaching methods that approach writing as praxis. Writing is often used by dominant populations to define and control the oppressed, the marginalized, and the minoritized. Writing can empower learners in sociopolitical interactions and writing teachers should see their classes as spaces where they can help students find their voices in societal interactions. Moreover, by unveiling the collaborative aspects of writing, educators should help build critical communities of like-minded writers, especially when it comes to multilingual writers who can feel vulnerable when writing in adopted languages. Membership in such communities, also, can help emerging writers have access to the publishing apparatus – often controlled by privileged circles – by pooling their resources to challenge the balance of power through strategies such as *community publishing* (Mathieu et al., 2011).

6 Written Texts as Organic Outgrowth of Complex Linguistic and Cultural Repertoires

Although written texts are often presented as self-contained monolingual and mono-rhetorical intellectual artefacts, they are in fact select simplified presentations of individuals' complex plurilingual, multiliterate and cross-cultural interconnections. These fluid and ever-evolving networks of language and culture are often too amorphous to be readily visible in our highly compartmentalized, streamed and levelled educational centres and also workplaces. Hence, as rich as they might be, literate, linguistic and cultural legacies are often ignored and remain hidden well beneath finalized written products. In this chapter, I discuss how seemingly self-sufficient written texts – meant to be constructed according to teachers' rubrics or publishers' requirements – (a) are linguistically shaped by the writer's knowledge of all the languages he or she knows, (b) are semantically connected to the writer's non-written semiotic engagements, and (c) nourish on the multiple cultures of which the writer is, or has been, a member. Unpacking these relations, I also write about pedagogical possibilities that arise when one regards written texts as rooted in complex plurilingual, multiliterate and intercultural activities. First, however, I explain the theoretical context for the content laid out.

In an influential multiliteracies manifesto, the New London Group (1996) highlighted the significance of learners' multiple literacy practices, which include but are more than traditional forms of reading and writing. Similar to other scholars who have been advocating for broadening the concept 'literacy' to include students' native literacy events and their new literacies such as digital and multimodal textual practices (for instance, Coiro, 2008; Lankshear & Knobel, 2003), the New London Group saw the necessity of a multiliteracies turn as a result of two contemporary developments, more diversity in urban centres and multimedia technology:

> First, we want to extend the idea and scope of literacy pedagogy to account for the context of our culturally and linguistically diverse and

increasingly globalized societies, for the multifarious cultures that inter-relate and the plurality of texts that circulate. Second, we argue that literacy pedagogy now must account for the burgeoning variety of text forms associated with information and multimedia technologies. (New London Group, 1996: 61)

Such conceptualization of multiliteracies frames the Group's article as offering a solution for a specific problem peculiar to a particular context: an issue in contemporary Anglo-American world with its unique migration patterns and technological development. Regarding multiliteracies through a different theoretical prism, I here present the findings from my research, embedded in a philosophical foundation in order to stress the significance of multitextual practices not only as a contemporary issue specific to Western urban centres, but as part and parcel of literacy learning and effective text generation in general.

A Philosophical Approach to Multitextuality

Dominant product and process writing pedagogies frame teaching writing as teaching particular product models or a formulated process. This tendency indicates that such pedagogies are profoundly *essentialist* in that they assume there are universal templates (kinds of writing or a certain process) that, once learned, can standardize students' future writings. I am using the concept 'essentialism' in a philosophical sense as understood and discussed in mainstream Western philosophy:

> Kinds ... are prior to their members; they determine, so to speak, the identity of their members. As Aristotelians have characterized them, kinds mark out their members as *what* they are. ... Thus, we can iden-tify what a given person is by saying that it is a human being, what a given animal is by saying that it is a dog, and what a given plant is by saying that it is a geranium or, perhaps an oak tree. Now, the insight underlying the Aristotelian conception of a kind is that to identify *what* a particular concrete is to identify its core 'being' or essence. So the kinds to which concrete particulars belong mark them out as things having the essences they do; hence, those kinds are essential or necessary to the concrete particulars that are their members. (Loux, 2002: 126)

Stemming from a similar theoretical ground, essayist pedagogy (Farr, 1993; Trimbur, 1990) is popularly adopted in writing education on the assumption that teachers should teach the basics, the base, or the essence of writing to be employed in real writing situations later in students' academic or professional lives – a tacit admission that most classroom writing drills are context-less and thus neither meaningful nor engaging. The popularity of teaching the well-critiqued five-paragraph essay (Brannon *et al.*, 2008; Campbell & Latimer, 2012; Foley, 1989; Nunnally, 1991; Wesley, 2000) is indicative of a philosophical belief that the 'hamburger' persuasive model is the essence of academic writing:

> Every piece of great expository writing I have read, from the best of my students' research essays to the essays of Oliver Sacks and Virginia Woolf, adheres to that *essential structure* [emphasis added]. It's no coincidence that the scientific method demands a similar process: hypothesize, test, conclude. High school students should not be allowed to graduate, let alone get a high score on a standardized test, unless they can demonstrate those skills in an essay. (Smith, 2006: 16)

The history of ideas about the scientific method (in Western philosophy only) from Bacon (2000) to Hume (2000), Popper (1972) and Kuhn (1970) hosts dramatically more complex conversations about the nature of scientific inquiry than the simplistic formula 'hypothesize, test, conclude'. Examples of impactful prose in Western intellectual tradition also defy claims of the supremacy of the argumentative essay, which is in fact in a very young written genre (practiced in Europe from the 16th century with Montaigne and in the English language from 18th century with British empiricists) undergoing constant change from field to field, society to society, and language to language. Counter-examples include Greek philosophical poetry, Socratic dialogues, the complex prose of German idealists such as Hegel, and the intentionally decentralized writing of poststructuralist thinkers. This list of counterexamples can be stretched further by listing non-Western rhetorical traditions that would not fit the proposed model in order to reveal the Eurocentric mentality of the advocates of dominant rubric-based expository and argumentative essays (Canagarajah, 2002). Despite such genre diversity, current practice still reflects the belief that we have successfully identified the essence of academic writing: the five-paragraph essay (and its variations), which has turned into the main model for teaching writing at K-12 schools, for college composition (expository writing and argumentation), and for the writing modules of standardized tests such as The International English Language Testing System (IELTS), Test of English as a Foreign Language (TOEFL), and The Graduate Record Examinations (GRE) for youth and adult English learners.

Most forms of essentialism are reductionist in that they explain 'the behaviour of concrete (that is, many-sided) objects by reducing them wholly to (or reading them off from) just one of their abstract (that is, one-sided) constituents' (Sayer, 2000: 89). This reductionism has consequences. In previous chapters, I wrote about how genre reductionism has created essayist supremacy discrediting oracy and oral cultures (Farr, 1993; Trimbur, 1990). I also discussed the hierarchy of written genres in educational centres – with essay writing at the top – which marginalizes non-prose, non-Western, and feminine genres. Such a bias in favour of a fabricated essence for writing hardly offers any philosophical, moral, or pedagogical potential for embracing students' linguistic repertoires, their non-written semiotic performances, and their native knowledges.

An alternative philosophical stance to essentialism is *family resemblance* (Wittgenstein, 1953). 'Wittgenstein introduced this concept in order to attack the traditional doctrine that all the entities which fall under a given term must have some set of properties or features in common' (Wennerberg, 1967: 107). Similarities, Wittgenstein held, are loose and slippery resemblances similar to those shared by members of a family. Family members do not exactly look alike; however, they often have enough resemblance to be recognized as belonging to the same family:

> I can think of no better expression to characterize these similarities than 'family resemblances'; for the various resemblances between members of a family: build, features, colour of eyes, gait, temperament, etc. etc. overlap and criss-cross in the same way. (Wittgenstein, 1953: sect. 67)

From this perspective, an emphasis on a single shared essence is replaced with exploration for recurring features among multiple members that determine a family, features that change and evolve based on different membership groupings.

Now, how can a theoretical recalibration from 'essence' to 'resemblance' inform teaching writing? If we accept that there is no essay format that can represent all non-fiction writing in English, we can question the necessity of teaching different simplified forms of the expository and persuasive essay as our main pedagogical focus. Instead, teachers could engage in facilitating activities that can help students make sense of genre families by interacting with a variety of textual possibilities as opposed to copying a single model. These interactions would include identifying rhetorical behaviours acceptable in various academic circles and research communities and developing genre agility by engaging with different written genres and also rhetorical alterations and sub-genres within a single field. Moreover, an attention to genre diversity in classes hosting English language learners requires creating space for students' native textual practices both for identity affirmation and for opening the space required to build rhetorical bridges between the writing traditions in home and learned languages.

Next to such interlingual considerations, adopting the concept 'family resemblance' can also create pedagogical room for students' non-written literacies. If good writers are not seen as masters of a certain genre but connoisseurs of rhetorical resemblances emerging from textual families, conceptual and symbolic overlaps between what students write and non-written semiotic systems gain significance – resemblances including tone, content, structural organization, cultural relevance and personal interest. In this sense, learners' official traditional-looking assignments – essays for instance – can only be meaningfully created if we already make room for written and non-written texts that should surround the assignment to let it evolve through affinities to neighbouring texts and also through their differences. In other words, through a family-resemblance lens, students will make sense of the traditional essay as one textual construct among many, whereas an essentialist approach would wrongly represent the five-paragraph essay as the DNA of all academic writing. Within the former framework, we invite learners to write the Anglo-American essay as an outcome of constant engagement with multiple genres, languages, and semiotic systems; and based on the latter by following a rubric that outlines the ultimate components of the essay.

Here I further clarify the said distinction by a description of Swiss linguist Ferdinand de Saussure's (2011) theory of signification. In Western metaphysical traditions, linguistic 'meaning' has been mainly understood through the mimetic theory of language. If language is mimetic, every word is a symbol referring to an object in the outside world. Therefore, the meaning of a word is its 'referent' – the thing the word refers to. Saussure (2011), however, introduced a new theory of meaning, or a model of 'signification'. He said that when, for instance, we hear or read the word 'tree', it conjures up a 'concept' in our mind, which is practically the meaning of the word 'tree'. In other words, unlike the traditional view, which asserted that the meaning of the symbol 'tree' was a physical tree in the world, Saussure explained that despite the assumptions of mimetic theorists of language, there is no innate or natural correspondence between the signifier and the signified and the link is purely arbitrary.

Discrediting the definition of meaning as 'reference' – a symbol referring to a referent – Saussure believed that meaning was 'relational' and based on a question of 'difference'. Accordingly, we do not understand what the word 'tree' means because it refers to an object in the world or because there is a natural link between this sign and an image in our mind. Instead, we recognize the word 'tree' thanks to the difference between this sign and other signs. We recognize 'tree' in that 'tree' is different from 'free', 'three', 'glee', 'plea' and 'flee', all sharing a strong phonetic resemblance through the vowel /iː/. We practically use the phonetic rules governing these linguistic signs to decode the sign 'tree'. For this particular example, these rules can include the phonetic differences between the consonants /t/, /f/, /θ/, /g/, /p/ and /f/. Thus, phonetic differences (and similarities) generate the unique character of the sign 'tree'.

To connect Saussure's view to the focus of the chapter and the intro-ductory remarks up to this point, Saussure challenged the essentialist signification theory that deemed meaning as the natural connection between words and objects. Saussure's theory of meaning hence made way for Derrida's *différance*, meaning both 'to differ' and 'to defer': '[D]*ifférance* makes signification possible. Only to the extent that we are able to differ, as in spatial distinction or relation to another, and to defer, as in temporalizing or delay, are we able to produce anything' (Biesecker, 1989: 117). Similar to Wittgenstein's family resemblance, Derrida's *différance* can highlight the importance of diverse genre interactions for learners to identify textual similarities and differences that can help them construct the 'right' genre based on their audience and their purpose. Saussure, as a structuralist, and Derrida, a poststructuralist, belonged to opposing philosophical camps. Whereas the Structuralists maintain belief in an ultimate structure that regulates signification, Derridean theory highlights the absence of any solid reference. Despite this tension, Derrida's work is predominantly seen as complementing Saussure's project and not its negation (Bennington, 2004).

This theoretical backdrop can hopefully clarify the significance of the semiotic and cultural networks in whose context we make sense of the act of writing as a form of human communication. A text's process of signification will not occur if writers and readers do not engage with the semiotic webs that surround the text. Thus, literacy engagement is always multiliterate, and multiliteracies should not be framed, as was done by the New London Group, as a state-of-the-art solution to an urgent local problem: effective writers, and readers, constantly engage with various semiotic interactions. Such a theoretical shift is necessary so that a pedagogy of multiliteracies is not regarded as experimental teaching but as basic and everyday practice. This change of mentality will make it more comfortable for all writing teachers to ask: How should we change our writing pedagogies, knowing that texts gain significance through similarities and differences between sets of (a) written genres, (b) languages, (c) non-written semiotic systems, and (d) cultural rhetorical and communication patterns? Previously, I discussed the participants' genre agility (the first item listed). In this chapter, I focus on the other three semiotic family relations by focusing on my participants' translingual, multiliterate, and intercultural experiences in order to show organic writing practices significantly flourish through such interconnections.

Multilingual Writing, Plurilingual Lives and Translingual Practices

There is no shortage of research documenting the benefits of multilingualism from a cognitive perspective (Bialystok *et al.*, 2012; Diamond, 2010; Higby *et al.*, 2013). Moreover, home, heritage and minoritized languages have also been discussed as valuable sources of knowledge and literacy in available socioculturally inclined literature (García *et al.*, 2006; Hornberger, 2002; Polinsky, 2011; Schecter &

Cummins, 2003; Skutnabb-Kangas, 2000, 2006; Skutnabb-Kangas & Heugh, 2012; Soltero, 2004). According to the Saussurean-Derridean framework that I laid out above, texts do not exist in vacuum but constantly (though often invisibly) interact with the semiotic webs that surround them. In the case of multilinguals, these webs include texts in multiple languages; nevertheless, in settings favouring monolingual modes of education (hailing from policy, curriculum, and/or teaching practices) such interlingual connections are not always taken advantage of or even recognized if not suppressed. The data from my research project underline the importance of successful writers' engagements with multiple languages and the impact of translingual connections on multilinguals' writing practices. In this section, I illustrate some of the participants' interlingual practices in three areas: the participants' multilingual texts, their plurilingual existences and their translingual practices.

Choman, Clarice and Magda wrote in multiple languages. Although the impact of their non-English writing on their careers varied from participant to participant, they all used their multilingual textual repertoire as a context to make sense of their English writing. These writers used their non-English writing as a point of reference to evaluate their writing in English, and they saw what they wrote in their mother tongues as a conceptual and stylistic foundation for their current English writing.

Choman's non-English writing was as extensive in size as it was formative in terms of influence on her fiction writing skills and literary personality – although her non-English writing was entirely hidden from the English CVs she used in North America because it would not be generally perceived as carrying additional value. Choman started diary writing when she was at primary school long before she learned English. Later she wrote fiction in Farsi when she attended a number of literary workshops in Tehran. Her stories would never satisfy the government's censors to receive the required publishing licence for public distribution and the only audience they had was the instructors and the members of the workshops. Also, Choman for a while taught English literature in a college in a small town in southern Iran, where she wrote teaching materials in Farsi about English literature. She also dabbled in writing poetry in Farsi most of her life. All these writing activities were unofficial, they were never published, and they were not written in response to an institution's requirements. Nevertheless, I learned that these non-English writings were strongly connected to Choman's English fiction. These were the backbone of Choman's writer identity and her career as a journalist after immigration. Choman's first book published in Canada was a collection of stories relating the lives of Iranian women in a variety of situations. The feminist themes shaping this book had already evolved in her Farsi stories and were thus ready to be used in her English fiction after her rather unexpected immigration to Canada. Moreover, Choman's identity as an intellectual confidant enough to participate in the Canadian literary scene was formed thanks to interactions in non-English writing communities that created the space for her growth as a thinker.

Similarly, Clarice told me about her grounding in academic writing provided by her Portuguese writing in Brazilian educational institutions which she had attended as a student. She, as I will discuss in more detail in the next section, believed that the conceptual and rhetorical ability that she had developed by writing in Portuguese enriched her English writing in ways that made her work in Canadian higher education look uniquely profound in comparison with many of her peers who were native speakers of English. For instance, Clarice believed her knowledge of critical theory – rooted in her Brazilian education – was appreciated in Canadian higher education institutions as an important achievement in academic writing while it was simply norm in Brazil even at high school level. As for her published academic work, she also wrote a few articles in Portuguese after establishing herself as a graduate researcher in Canada: in her words, 'I actually challenged myself because of the awareness I am having of myself as a plurilingual academic'.

The same kind of return to the mother tongue for status checking was also performed by Choman. After the publication of her collection of short stories in English in Canada, Choman was recognized in the Iranian diaspora in Toronto and was invited to speak in an event in a panel next to a few famous Iranian writers. The writers were supposed to read passages from their works. Choman decided that instead of reading from the English book for which she was invited, she should read from her unpublished Farsi stories. She edited one of her older works and she read it to the event's large audience. When she was finished reading, Choman was 'delighted to see the audience's reaction to my reading ... as if the strength of my Farsi prose had overshadowed the voices of the famous writers on the panel'.

Magda's experiences with writing in multiple languages were slightly different from those of Choman and Clarice. While Choman and Clarice had to periodically focus on either English or the other languages they knew, mainly Farsi and Portuguese. Magda, before immigration to Canada, had written learning resources in multiple languages. When in Hungary, as a turning point in her writing trajectory, Magda had joined an international (mainly European) project to develop educational materials for a variety of programmes including energy management, sustainability, and diversity. 'All this included multilingual approaches. We had the German government working on that, people from Italy, Spain. So we used English and a mixture of other languages'. Although when I met Magda she mainly created English educational materials, she drew heavily on her previous experiences and borrowed from methods that her colleagues and she had developed together, methods such as the rhetorical approach, organization of topics, use of visuals, and so on.

What do these experiences tell us about the significance of writing in multiple languages? From a Saussurean-Derridean point of view, linguistic signs signify as a result of association with other signs. Inspired by this notion, in order to understand and nurture learners' writing in additional languages – for our purposes English for youth and adult immigrants – it is important to create space for the texts that students write and/or have written in other languages, and also to encourage further generation of such texts. Texts do not exist in isolation but in intertextual association. As a result, ignoring students' writing in languages other than the dominant language – English for instance – is an erroneous pedagogical tendency in that it damages fertile intertextual contexts needed for linguistic growth in all languages.

Moreover, according to Wittgenstein's theory of *family resemblance*, textual quality is hardly the result of copying universal models; in contrast, textual characteristics are developed in subtle connections between textual webs. The more crowded the family is, the more conceptual, rhetorical, and stylistic traits there will be to choose from. Multilingual writing, thus, is an important practice for rhetorical agility. In accordance with this theoretical framework, my analysis of Choman, Clarice and Magda's core English writing and their writing in other languages bore significant (family) resemblances including similar subject matter, conceptual relevance, discursive harmony, and rhetorical similarity. In many ways, these writers transplanted a lot of what they were writing in other languages into their English writing. This, however, does not mean that they did not borrow from the rhetorical traditions of English writing. While they enjoyed exploring new compositional possibilities, their rich textual backgrounds supported their survival and growth in their new rhetorical and discursive contexts.

I was curious to know how Choman, Clarice and Magda felt about writing in and between multiple languages. I wanted to learn from their perceptions of their plurilingual practices and their understandings of interactions, interconnections and interdynamics between the languages they knew. To present the participants' perceptions of their interlingual practices, I here use the concept 'plurilingualism' since it highlights processes 'where languages are interconnected and not just juxtaposed' (Piccardo, 2014: 183). 'Plurilingualism … is focused on the fact that languages interrelate and interconnect particularly, but not exclusively, at the level of the individual' (Piccardo, 2013: 601). Whereas multilingual education mainly focuses on the use of multiple languages in social (for instance, in schooling, home and community) contexts, plurilingual pedagogies draw upon individual linguistic repertoires as usually untapped educational resources. Here, I exemplify some of these plurilingual dynamics to strengthen the argument put forth previously that the quality of writing improves not solely by drilling abstract models but by recognizing the textual webs that students are currently engaging with (mainly outside the classroom) or could potentially engage with – and again especially multilingual texts for plurilingual students.

Although she was never published in Iran, Choman wrote in Farsi abundantly and shared her work with friends and other writers. Her prose took form in a tradition that was sensitive about linguistic ornaments and prose aesthetics, an ability which would be seriously hindered in a learned language and in a new literary tradition – especially in English fiction, where dramatic plot can outweigh decorated language. Choman gave me an example of her inter-literary experiences:

> In story writing in Farsi when I only read the dialogues and the language that the characters used, I could tell you what their job was, for instance, or their social status. I could tell how educated the characters were and where they came from only from the way they spoke. The most powerful aspect of writing in Farsi – although it was my second language [my mother tongue was Kurdish] – was my prose rather than plot or characterization. But I still don't have this ability in English. When I write stories in English I feel I'm a sprinter put in a wheelchair by force because her legs are broken. After all these years I feel I can replace the wheelchair with walking sticks, but it is still difficult. The slope is steep and my armpits are sore. This is writing in English for me.

Travelling between these two traditions, although painful, had only enriched and expanded Choman's experiences, especially considering the fact that she was only officially published and publicly recognized as a novelist when she wrote in English. Clarice, on the other hand, reminded me that migrating back to one's mother tongue for serious writing experiences could also pose its own challenges. Unlike Choman, Clarice wrote academic articles in Portuguese – her mother tongue – only after publishing her work in English. She said:

> [I recently published an academic paper in Portuguese.] I actually challenged myself to do that. ... I started reversing. Everything that I learned in English about writing, I was applying to my Portuguese writing. But some things don't work that way as you know. So it was very interesting. But what comforted me was that I had connections in Brazil, so I asked two people to read it and give me feedback. They gave me feedback and they had noticed the English influence. It was good. I was proud of myself because I didn't know I could write academic papers in Portuguese. I even had to learn their punctuation and referencing system. It was very liberating.

In addition to such challenges, which often turn into learning opportunities, adopting new languages might offer language learners perspectives on their learned language that most native speakers lack. The case of grammatical consciousness among language learners and also non-native language teachers in comparison with native speakers is a well-known phenomenon echoed by Magda:

> When I was doing a writing course in Canada after immigration, in a lesson that focused on editing, one of my classmates – a Canadian girl [native speaker] – she turns to me and says, 'Oh it's so easy for you because you learned it [English grammar]'. I was like, 'Oh ...' I never thought about that. She said, 'We never learned grammar at school, so it's easy for you'. There are different aspects that should be considered. Yes, I know English grammar pretty well.

In order to understand the participants' interlingual practices while writing at a more technical level, in an email group interview we spoke about *translanguaging* (Canagarajah, 2006, 2013; García, 2011) in their writing practices. Translanguaging is 'the ability of multilingual speakers to shuttle between languages, treating the diverse languages that form their repertoire as an integrated system' (Canagarajah, 2011: 410). After describing the concept translanguaging as a catalyst for a conversation focusing on tangible instances of the participants' shuffling between languages when they write in English, I asked Choman, Magda and Clarice how often they thought they experienced translanguaging. Here is an excerpt from our exchange with instances of the participants' translingual experiences:

> Choman: Since my stories are often set in Kurdistan but written in English, I constantly switch back and forth. I write my first few drafts trying to set up a Kurdish setting and then revise it to make sure it all makes sense in English. So I have to read it from a Kurd's perspective, making sure the setting is authentic and then read it from an English-speaking reader's view to make sure it's tangible.

> Magda: It is more natural for me to think contentwise in the language I am writing in but when it comes to grammar, I still might think in Hungarian and then translate it to the given language.

> Clarice: When writing academic essays/papers in English or Portuguese, I tend to translanguage when I get stuck. Sometimes I fail to remember words in the language I am writing and I tend to resort to another language I know or a variety of the same language. For example, if I'm writing an academic article in English, I sometimes think of synonyms in English first and then go to Portuguese or even Spanish, which is not a very strong language in my repertoire. I've noticed that when I write in Portuguese, my tendency to code-switch

[between Portuguese and English] is even higher as it seems my academic Portuguese proficiency is not as high as English. I find this to be a very natural phenomenon and something that I take as an advantage rather than a deficit. In fact, I enjoy going from one language to another as it gives me more opportunities to be creative in my own writing and improve its quality.

Identifying interlingual processes is an interesting area of focus, yet it is beyond the purposes of this book. The above examples are tokens of plurilingual dynamics that illustrate multilingualism can enrich one's writing practices. This statement – which might sound like a truism – does not always translate into pedagogical strategies that are interested in learners' multiple languages. Nevertheless, the academic and professional advantages of plurilingualism are significant. Here is an example of Magda's experiences in the workplace:

> I don't speak French, but my manager asked me if I could read the letters we received from French publishers we were dealing with. I said, 'I don't speak French'. She said, 'Oh I know, but you will figure out'. Oh yea, because English is not my first language, so if I'm already doing it in English ... and if I know German and Hungarian ... And I did manage to figure out, which was surprising for me. I read the letter and I understood what it was about. But she [the manager, who spoke English only] didn't. She didn't have the confidence, although she had studied French at school.

Plurilingual practices, as I tried to illustrate in this section, can have multiple manifestations from lexical, grammatical, and phonetic to conceptual, rhetorical, and discursive. I will discuss some of those in more detail by framing them as 'non-written semiotic interactions' and 'intercultural rhetoric' after I briefly discuss some pedagogical implications of approaching interlingual dynamics as a resource rather than a problem in the following paragraph.

One clear pedagogical direction, in an attempt to tap into students' plurilingualism as a valuable educational resource, is creating space in writing classes for multilingual text generation. Students' multilingual engagements in the classroom can range from multilingual note taking and outlining in the pre-writing research process to writing finalized multilingual assignments. Our current industrialized writing education with its standardizing rubric-centred assessment approaches is not accustomed to the flexibility and creativity required for recognizing and appreciating students' multilingual text production. The industrial nature of the system has heavily narrowed genre possibilities to increase centralized control over curriculum and assessment. Any endeavour to normalize multilingual text creation in the classroom would also entail broadening genre possibilities that challenge current understandings of academic genres. Thus, any pedagogy friendly to students' plurilingual practices would also appreciate allowing some genre fluidity in the syllabus. Such an approach would also provide possibilities for inserting non-written semiotic elements like visuals in writing assignments. It is not difficult to imagine how such multilingual genre-fluid assignments can help unearth students' rich literate backgrounds and incorporate those into students' current writing practices.

Non-Written Semiotic Engagement

Magda, Clarice and Choman significantly engaged with non-written semiotic systems. To borrow from literacy research terminology, they were highly *multiliterate*; they engaged with (or had at some point in the past) a variety of non-written textual performances including art, music, and drama. Drawing on the Saussurean-Derridean framework, explained previously, we make sense of signs (and in the same virtue semiotic systems including written texts) by comparing and contrasting them with the signs that cloud around them. Based on this theoretical model, it is legitimate to imagine that the richer and more variant the semiotic webs that scaffold our writing are, the more sophisticated our writing performances become. These semiotic webs can grow across languages – as discussed in the previous section – or can connect with non-written semiotic systems, for instance musical or visual texts.

A multiliteracies approach to literacy teaching and learning has been a constant source of inspiration as a pedagogical possibility since its theorization by the New London Group in the wake of the New Literacy Studies (NLS) movement (for a historical overview, see Baynham & Prinsloo, 2009a). Multiliteracies is particularly attractive because of its character as authentic pedagogy – as opposed to didactic – with room for 'Situated Practice, Overt Instruction, Critical Framing and Transformed Practice' (Cope & Kalantzis, 2015: 1), which could foster inclusion for different students and varied literacy practices. The following passage provides a definition of multiliteracies as understood by the New London Group:

> We decided that the outcomes of our discussions could be encapsulated in one word – multiliteracies – a word we chose to describe two import-ant arguments we might have with the emerging cultural, institutional, and global order: the multiplicity of communications channels and media, and the increasing saliency of cultural and linguistic diversity. The notion of multiliteracies supplements traditional literacy pedagogy by addressing these two related aspects of textual multiplicity. What we might term 'mere literacy' remains centred on language only, and usually on a singular national form of language at that, which is conceived as a stable system based on rules such as mastering sound-letter correspon-dence. (Cope & Kalantzis, 2000: 5)

Despite recent proposals for complexifying the initial arguments of the New London Group (Baynham & Prinsloo, 2009b; Collier & Rowsell, 2014; Cope & Kalantzis, 2016; Kafle & Canagarajah, 2015), the pedagogies and philosophies of multiliteracies are still framed as a current need in response to two contemporary developments: new technology and 'emerging' multicultural societies, marked by increasing ethnic and linguistic diversity. By adopting a philosophical approach to this debate, I hope to highlight the stance that engagement with multiliteracies occurs in all meaningful teaching and learning experiences and not only in specific contexts. The current mono-literacy curriculum has mainly been a product of centralized Western educational systems after the Industrial Revolution. In contrast with the London Group's proposition that the 'emerging cultural, institutional, and global order' necessitates a pedagogy of multiliteracies, I hold that multiliteracies has always been an empowering pedagogical approach for literacy learning. Multiliteracies is not a contemporary Western invention. This argument could be fleshed out in a different project (in an attempt to decolonize literacy research) by examples of pre-colonial multiliterate practices among indigenous populations, non-European nations that remained immune to colonial pedagogies, and also pre-industrial Western pedagogies. However, in this book, by highlighting the philosophical foundation for the significance of multisemiotic and hence multiliterate engagement, I intend to reframe multiliteracies as part and parcel of any rich literacy experience as opposed to a 'new' pedagogical solution to a 'new' problem.

Most of the referenced multiliteracies publications attempted to recognize learners' multiliterate activities, to celebrate them, and to create space for them in identity negotiation and community building processes. Building on that valuable work, I would like to take one step further and emphasize that not only should we recognize second language writers' multiliterate backgrounds, teachers should proactively encourage new multi-semiotic activities to complexify learners' semiotic world and increase their semiotic agility. A multiplication of multiliterate events can increase new semiotic entanglement, which will lead to exposure to new topics, discourses, genres and forms of information organization. This change of mentality, although simple, can transform pedagogies that regard multiliteracies as educational charity to save minoritized students into a genuine exploration of new horizons for both teachers and students (privileged and marginalized) in a democratic way. Once achieved, this horizontal (as opposed to hierarchical) relationship will automatically make room for displaying unprivileged literacies. Through this lens, I present some of the data my participants shared with me, re-emphasizing that these multilingual writers experienced schooling and developed intellectually far from today's diversifying Western urban centres and earlier than the multiliteracies shift in Anglo-American academia, yet still they engaged with *radical semiotic interactions*.

The findings from my study show our pedagogical and institutional practices hide writers' multiliterate backgrounds that might have enriched their writing in different ways. Clarice's recent academic writing, for instance, was a link in a long chain of multiliterate practices. During my research, I learned that without unearthing and studying those practices Clarice's ability and will to write – as an epistemological tool and a power differential – would not be fully comprehended. Clarice studied drama, taught drama and wrote plays in multiple languages. She was the lead singer of a rock band in her early twenties. Clarice formed and led the band, which actively contributed to the indie music scene in São Paulo for three years. Clarice also dabbled in drawing and animation making, and she took advantage of her artistic skills in dissemination of her research through videos and elaborate visual presentations. Her YouTube videos summarizing her research papers have attracted thousands of viewers. She was a serious theatre and movie goer. She occasionally invited me to the theatre and we often talked about our favourite international films. She also helped start an art film club in her department at university with other graduate students.

Looking at Clarice's writing through the prism of her rich multiliterate experiences prevents the reduction of her semiotic production to 'academic writing' only. Clarice's English academic writing, instead, should be viewed as only one component of her larger semiotic life, or in other words, as a semiotic engagement tightly connected to her other literacies. An interest in drama, for instance, is still a major motif in her research trajectory. Clarice has conducted (and published) research about employing drama in the classroom to create space for students' heritage languages. This research interest shows also another broader theme in Clarice's multiliterate experiences, which links her different semiotic activities together: the struggle to give voice to marginalized populations be it by writing, art or music. A multiliteracies approach to education should track down such conceptual threads in students' literate maps and also expose them to new semiotic experiences for encountering new concepts and discourses.

Choman similarly engaged with a variety of non-written semiotic systems. Although a writer of literary fiction, when she was a child she interacted with a sizable amount of 'lowbrow' Iranian music (Choman used the word 'lowbrow' as a word with positive connotations). Choman told me she was her aunts' 'walking jukebox'. 'I knew hundreds of songs by heart and could sing any song you requested'. The same command of Kurdish and Farsi oracy had also enriched her career as a writer in English, both as a novelist and a journalist. The quality of Choman's oral texts – including speeches, readings and interviews – were on par with her written work. I observed Choman's oral performances in different venues. As well as a promotional function, Choman's speeches and interviews displayed the same wit and intellectual depth as her writing. In another example, most of Choman's writing in English has been concerned with – in her words – 'the Kurdish cause'. Her act of writing about the Kurds, I learned, could not be understood without identifying the cultural thread that tied her English writing to her other activities such as Kurdish dance and her involvement in Kurdish media as a video producer, for instance, although the readers of her novels might see very little of those activities and the way they informed her writing.

Do Kurdish dance and Brazilian rock help multilingual learners write better English essays? It is impossible to tell (at least within the scope of this project). Nevertheless, the findings presented here can show effective multilingual English writers have complex multiliterate engagements. More importantly, the findings illustrate that the participants' multiliterate lives have strong cultural, discursive, and conceptual links with their writings. Also, my study of the multiliterate activities of these writers has helped me see that the multi-layered semiotic foundation that these writers have at their disposal would support further text generation and even social functionality and growth.

Familiarity with a multiplicity of semiotic systems facilitates the process of signification and hence enriches the process of meaning making in writing processes. Accordingly, writing pedagogies benefit from connecting learners' writing with their other semiotic interactions. A pedagogy of rich semiotic engagement might be difficult to be implemented in our current industrialized educational structures, which separate composition courses from content-rich courses, first language writing from second language writing, and, in second language education, writing from other skills and areas such as reading, listening, speaking, grammar, and vocabulary. Our current compartmentalized structures, ironically, have been engineered to limit semiotic interactions to fewer sign families in each class so that they can be offered in separate classes in a Fordian-conveyor-belt design: written text for reading in one class, written text for writing in another class, visual engagement in another, music in the next class, and so on. Nevertheless, writing teachers should find or create opportunities to recognize learners' out-of-school non-written semiotic involvement and also pro-actively seek to expose their students to new intellectual, cultural, discursive, and conceptual paradigms through various semiotic interactions. Such an approach can be adopted by moving beyond traditional assignments that require students to write in response to written text. Writing teachers should ask how often their students write to react to film, drama, and music. How often do our students use orality as the main substance of their writing, for instance, writing based on interviews with community members? Also, why don't we utilize ethnographic methods in writing classes to invite students to write based on observational data? Teachers could also think of inviting their students to walk out of the classroom to write in cafes, subway stations, concert halls, theatres, museums and different neighbourhoods to capture their experiences in those places.

Pedagogies conscious of the significance of multiliteracies, incidentally, create channels for intercultural interactions through music, art, film, and virtual text. Intercultural competence, which I discuss next, can help multilingual writers deal with rhetorical challenges involved in writing in new languages.

Intercultural Competence

> Switching between cultures is complicated particularly when language is added to the mix. When you change from one language to another, your cultural discourses automatically change. The language shift creates some cultural limitations, but at the same time creates some freedom for expressing new concepts. I'm neither entirely this or that; I am standing somewhere on the hyphens of my Kurdish-Iranian-Canadian-American identity. I borrow from all the components of these multiple identities. On the one hand, I have the chance to feed on all these cultural sources when I need to. On the other hand, you may never be 100% of those when you need to. (Choman)

Connections between intercultural competence and language learning have been the focus of many publications (see for instance, Arasaratnam & Doerfel, 2005; Connor *et al.*, 2008; Flower, 2003; Lambert, 1999; Lo Bianco *et al.*, 1999; Samovar & Porter, 2001; Scollon & Scollon, 1981; Taft *et al.*, 2011). Some major themes in this body of research include the significance of intercultural communication amidst globalization, creating dialogue between cultures, challenges of engaging with culture in the classroom, undermining cultural invasion and hegemony through language teaching, pedagogies of peace, identity in additional languages, and the (cultural/linguistic) third space (Bhabha, 1990). Building upon these research trends, I argue that an emphasis on culture in linguistic performance not only creates intercultural harmony (which is the main impetus for most conversations about intercultural competence), it also improves linguistic competence. It is important to stress the impact on linguistic performance, so that intercultural competence is not viewed as a bonus that language learning offers but a *necessary* step in the process of learning languages. Such an emphasis would make clear that intercultural competence is an important area of pedagogical focus both in diverse and in homogeneous classes. The following passage shows the common stance that regards developing intercultural skills as a desirable addition to language education, but not as a necessary component:

> A focus on intercultural competence has been mainly meant to, redefine language education in more precise terms for the important role it has to play in preparing children and adults of a rapidly globalising world to

know how to swing the pendulum of cross-cultural encounters towards the experience of enrichment, discovery, wonder, principled compromise rather than domination, and peace rather than confrontation and war; this in the private as well as public spheres. (Lo Bianco *et al.*, 1999: 5)

Consistent with this view, most of the research in intercultural education research has been interested in 'how culture is to be infused into language instruction, what items to include, and to what effect' (Lambert, 1999: 65). The findings of my research, however, indicate that intercultural competence should not be treated as only an add-on pedagogy needed because we are currently living in a globalized world. Effective language learning, in fact, can hardly happen without cross-cultural experiences. Also, the infusion of culture into literacy education should happen both inside and outside school. If semiotic agility increases – as described previously – through sophisticated plurilingual and multiliterate engagements, intercultural experiences also facilitate language learning inasmuch as culture is the seedbed of knowledge, expression, and literacy. This argument is particularly important when we focus on writing in additional languages, in whose dynamics discursive and rhetorical patterns rooted in one culture are to be processed in another.

In an attempt to create a model for intercultural communication competence, Arasaratnam and Doerfel (2005) reported findings including qualities of 'competent intercultural communicators':

[C]ompetent intercultural communicators are person-centred (me), sensitive, and kind, have experience with different cultures, want to learn about cultural matters, and are good at these processes. The attributes that are described resemble empathy. ... [They also] are open to others, better in communicating ..., show interest in differences and are aware of these, and have a level of exposure ... to these differences that make them able to pick up on these. (Arasaratnam & Doerfel, 2005: 157)

Arasaratnam and Doerfel's emphasis on 'exposure to difference' echoes the Saussurean-Derridean model of signification best evolved in Derrida's *différance* (Derrida, 2001), in which (a) we make sense of signs thanks to difference rather than similarity and (b) the process of signification is neverending. If cultural practices are considered as semiotic units, cultural competence would mean a desire to be exposed to different cultures, to move between them, and to have rich collections of cultural practices to pick from. Clarice, Choman and Magda enjoyed such intercultural disposition both at a textual level and in actual movement and migration between societies and cultures.

As for textual intercultural experiences, all three participants cherished engagement with literature and art produced in different cultures – a tendency leading to and at the same time strengthened by their multilingualism. Clarice had a serious interest in Anglo-American pop culture, she had an expert knowledge of European drama, and an impressive command of international cinema. Choman constantly read world literature in different languages. Two particular bodies of literature that she frequently referenced to in our conversations were Persian poetry and the English novel. Magda also had a solid grounding in European literature (in different languages), which she perceived crucial not only in her literate life but in her worldview and beliefs. It should be noted that the participants' interest in textual diversity, rooted in cultural difference, had developed before serious involvement with English. Thus, as much as learning languages opened new horizons for them, their comfort with additional languages was a result of their cultural curiosity manifested in engagement with texts from varied cultures.

Clarice, Choman and Magda's interactions with texts from other cultures did not occur without significant critical reflections. Clarice said she was aware her interest – as a youth – in American pop music was somehow the result of a systematic linguistic and cultural invasion and the hegemony of American culture and the international dominance of the English language. Clarice regretted not having (easier) access to the Spanish music produced in Brazil's neighbourhood in Latin America. She was critical of the cultural industry which privileged the English-speaking world. Choman – as a Kurdish activist – was very sensitive about the dominance of the Farsi language in the multilingual context of Iran. On the other hand, although she appreciated English fiction, she was aware that as a non-white English writer, she might not receive the same recognition from the community who controlled the Canadian publishing industry. She was specifically active in circles of writers of colour who were fighting for more ground in the Canadian literary scene. Similarly, Magda (along with her husband) often spoke with me about the distorted image that Anglo-American literature and media had created of Eastern Europe including Hungary, where they were from. In the course of this project, I learned how delicately Clarice, Choman and Magda maintained warm intercultural connections while navigating uncomfortable power relations between cultures and languages.

Next to textual intercultural experiences, Clarice, Choman and Magda physically moved between cultures; and as importantly, they actively sought possibilities for cross-cultural lived experiences. Clarice – by design – moved from a small country town – where she was born – to São Paulo and later to Canada's Ontario. Magda also migrated from a city in Iran's Kurdistan Province to the capital, Tehran in search of new educational possibilities. Also, before immigration to Canada, and later to the United States, she travelled to some impoverished places in the margins of Iran to teach. Magda also had travelled and worked in a number of European countries before her immigration to Canada. These cross-cultural migrations and movements had helped these writers to hone their intercultural communitive abilities through exposure to and shifting between cultural practices in different contexts. The transformative impact of such intercultural experiences should not be underestimated. Magda once told me:

> I think it's very important for people to see different countries and live in different countries, because even my Hungarian friends ... even my family ... they have such views ... it's unimaginable for me right now.

Similar to the fluidity of their discourse practices and genre performances – discussed in previous chapters – Choman, Clarice and Magda displayed a common breed of ever-evolving cultural existence, guided both by their pride in their mother cultures and an appreciation of different cultural practices. All three writers mingled with new cultures critically, yet partook in practices that would let them evolve as writers in an added language and also as humans. They examined and picked elements that would help them creatively build their cultural identities so that their choices would lead to their individual growth and the betterment of communities which they were living in at each point in their lives.

Are our mainstream curricula informed by our knowledge of the benefits of intercultural competence? What can we learn from a critical review of our policies, syllabi, pedagogies, and the educational material we share with the students? How multicultural are our pedagogical and textual canons? '[E]ducators are still far from understanding how to develop intercultural competence' (Deardorff, 2009: x); hence, a conversation about the impact of textual and physical movement between cultures is indeed a worthwhile endeavour.

Intercultural rhetoric

> To tell people [immigrants] who are 30 years old and wrote in certain way – often successfully – for 15 years ... you simply cannot say, 'Just because you're here, you have to write differently'. But there should be a balance between changing your attitude and adapting and also keeping your previous approaches. (Magda)

In second language writing scholarship, the significance of inter-cultural competence has been comprehensively discussed in the field of intercultural rhetoric (Connor *et al.*, 2008), or as previously called 'contrastive rhetoric': 'Contrastive rhetoric is an area of research in second language acquisition that identifies problems in composition encoun-tered by second language writers and, by referring to the rhetorical strategies of the first language, attempts to explain them' (Connor, 1996: 5). Intercultural rhetoric research reminds us that rhetorical strategies are neither individual decisions nor universal practices; in contrast, rhetorical patterns are cultural and local and thus change from society to society and from time to time. Educators understandably tend to teach writing notions that they have inherited from their cultures; nevertheless, their students' notions of 'great writing' might be entirely different from those of their teachers based on the cultures or subcultures they come from. Writing in adopted languages, accordingly, is much more than a linguistic practice: it is cultural, political and power relational. It is cultural in that rhetorical patterns are developed and practiced differently in different cultures. It is also political inasmuch as rhetorical traditions dominate each other and seek hegemony, often hand in hand with political oppression of minoritized populations and cultures. It is, moreover, power relational because, in addition to the said political hegemony sought through cultural invasion, writers' rhetorical abilities are constantly evaluated by teachers, editors, and publishers whose judgments are subjectively formed by their cultural and field-related perspectives beyond which they might have little rhetorical experience.

Since its beginnings, the field of intercultural rhetoric – initially called *contrastive rhetoric* (Kaplan, 1966) – has had to deal with an ideological albatross, which despite significant attempts (Connor *et al.*, 2008), still overshadows most of its speculations: Intercultural rhetoric is often essentialist and engages with cultural reductionism (Kubota & Lehner, 2004). Intercultural rhetoric has often deemed Western and non-Western rhetorical practices as static traditions monolithically practiced by all the members of a culture all through its history. This essentialist approach has been tainted by a tendency – more vivid in Kaplan's 'contrastive rhetoric' and less visible in 'intercultural rhetoric' – to view Anglo-American rhetorical practices as fixed, logical, clear, and coherent and thus superior to non-Anglo-American writing models, often discussed as non-linear and hence vague and incoherent. Most of these issues were raised and addressed by Kubota and Lehner (2004) advocating for a more critical approach to intercultural rhetoric:

> Some scholars have criticized contrastive rhetoric for its reduction-ist, deterministic, prescriptive, and essentialist orientation (Leki, 1997; Spack, 1997; Zamel, 1997). Their criticisms call for more attention to plurality, complexity, and hybridity of rhetorical patterns within one language as well as similarities among languages or cultures. (Kubota & Lehner, 2004: 10)

I spoke with Magda, Clarice and Choman about the rhetorical challenges that they faced when writing between cultures and languages. The findings of my research indicate that, as an important additional area of focus to what the aforesaid researchers suggested, we need to have conversations about institutional, economic, historical, and political circumstances that create 'plurality, complexity, and hybridity of rhetorical patterns'. Choman, Clarice and Magda's thoughts about intercultural rhetoric encouraged me to think of rhetorical cultures as much more than writing traditions; many rhetorical patterns are developed as a result of historical, political and economic dynamics that rule text production activities and also the institutions that fund and regulate them. In this sense, if we are studying international students' experiences with Anglo-American academic writing, which is often the case in intercultural rhetoric research, we need to highlight the fact that the dominant from of academic writing in English speaking universities and colleges is in fact a form of report writing that allows best to seek funding and share findings with funders in capitalist societies. Thus, essayist literacy, which has turned into a major form of report writing, has less to do with knowledge creation and more with cash flow.

Likewise, dissemination formats, popular in Anglo-American academia, have mainly solidified because they allow neoliberal higher education, journal, and conference industries to effectively package and sell written and oral texts to a domestic and international audience. Through this lens, instead of an emphasis on Western vs. Eastern writing cultures in the field of intercultural rhetoric, it would be more accurate to talk about writing in a capitalist/colonial structure vs., for instance, non-funded writing in community-centred intellectual circles with texts (written and oral) shared for free for local consumption.

Although probed explicitly, the participants in my research did not engage much in detailed descriptions of rhetorical strategies that they found difficult to adopt while writing in English apart from brief statements such as 'Portuguese is more flowery and creative', as Clarice believed, or the dominance of poetic language in Kurdish-Persian culture for instance in Choman's words that in 'Canada poetry has no connection to people's everyday life [and thus dominant Canadian prose won't embrace rhetorical complexity]'. Although these statements did not guide the main flow of our conversation about intercultural rhetoric, it should be noted that such observations, offering technical descriptions of differing rhetorical traditions, were not made to illustrate a problem but to highlight a source of added value and as Choman said, 'the luxury of looking at cultural interactions from a distance and choosing what you want'. Clarice, as an example of this privilege, recalled this experience:

> When I first started writing – you know for real – in a North American context, I was pretty much trying to assimilate my writing to that particular venue [Anglo-American academic rhetoric]. [After a while], I started using all my [South American] criticality into my writing and all of a sudden people started to like it. And I was like, 'Oh, OK, awesome'. Then I continued. … It is also a matter of being confident enough to know who you are and to know that there is value in it.

Next to such brief references to rhetorical differences as an advantage, the participants led most of our conversations about written rhetoric in Canada towards experiences with navigating written communication in a market-oriented economy with an international reach and the complex interactions it involves. Magda, for instance, said:

> I had to deal with a lot of changes regarding business writing because of the formality that exists [in Canadian transactions] ... you really have to choose your words carefully, and your style, and tailor it to different audiences. But not just business writing but business life is much more informal in Hungary, or used to be, so this was a change for me that I had to adapt to.

And Choman in the same vein:

> The shift from an oral to a written communication culture was an interesting experience [immigration from Iran to Canada]. If you are after funding to make a film, as a few of my friends and I intend to do, you should prepare an application package including letters, proposals, histories, but if you want to deal with a Kurdish TV station, there is no written application; it's all oral interaction.

These examples from Magda – as a Hungarian – and Choman – as an Iranian Kurd – are significant since they challenge contrastive rhetoric's stereotypical assumptions about writing traditions. Magda is a Westerner who finds Canadian transactional writing as strange as Choman does. Also, Choman's emphasis on an oral tradition should not be mistaken with high versus low context culture theories that often go hand in hand with conversations about intercultural rhetoric and assume naive and unrealistic demarcations between Eastern and Western cultures. Iranian written traditions, centuries older than European communication norms and millennia older than the Anglo-American writing traditions – host a large variety of genres including major forms of academic writing dominant in the English-speaking academia today. Choman's and also Magda's comments should, hence, be read as an invitation to see intercultural rhetoric as a form of intercultural consciousness that includes an understanding of the dynamics of text production in each culture, dynamics that are often dictated by economy, politics, and institutional structures as well as purely rhetorical legacies embedded in culture. In summary, intercultural rhetoric for the participants was the recognition that cultures – or 'systems' as Clarice calls them in the following quotation – produce their own criteria for textual quality. Mobile multilingual writers are in constant textual negotiation with the cultures they move into in a complex exchange of rhetorical techniques regulated by political and economic dynamics:

[When we movie into a system], we are a part of the system; and we are active in the system. And too be active in the system, you have to play the game. So if you don't play the game, you are not going to be part of the system. But being part of the system is also a way for you to impact the system.

I did not embark on a full-fledged systematic textual analysis of the participants' writings to find instances of their native rhetorical tendencies, which would be an attempt beyond the intentions of this project. Moreover, since the participants were 'officially' published in English, it would be legitimate to assume that their rhetorical practices were embraced by their English-speaking audiences, which left enough space for me to have a phenomenological approach to record the participants' perceptions of intercultural rhetoric. Nevertheless, flipping through the participants' writings, it was not difficult to see where the writers had infused their heritage rhetorics into their English writing. Intercultural traces varied but made perfect sense in the textual contexts they appeared or were absent. For instance, Clarice's English academic articles' structure, voice, and diction resembled those of native writers fully, yet Choman's literary prose – specifically in her fiction about Iranian women – bore close resemblance to contemporary Iranian literary styles that could be very broadly characterized as poetically realistic, with still-life descriptions of reality along with a certain amount of abstraction and enough space between the lines for readers' interpretations in a poetic style. Whereas the more tightly prescribed Anglo-American academic writing often had Clarice resemble the dominant research writing, the infusion of Iranian poetic realism into Choman's stories with Kurdish characters successfully recreated the local texture in the tone of the writer. Also, in Magda's PowerPoints and emails – although error-free – there were grammatical and lexical moments that might be reconstructed differently by a native writer. Nevertheless, the clarity and communicative powers of her educational materials made consuming her English texts such a pleasure for her consultees and colleagues.

An in-depth analysis of inter-rhetorical instances in the participants' writing samples is not the main focus of this study and would take a different research project. The above examples are merely some observations to stress that cross-cultural writing patterns could be traced in the participants' writings, yet the participants seemed to pragmatically highlight, ignore, or hide them if necessary, an ability developed by an attention to cultural – including economic, institutional, pragmatic, epistemological and power relational – 'systems' in which texts are generated, as Clarice emphasized. This broader view of culture is consistent with more critical conceptualizations of intercultural rhetoric in contrast with earlier less refined theories that considered 'writing merely as a reflection of cultural thought patterns rather than a social practice involving human agency' (Kubota & Lehner, 2004: 9). As these few examples hopefully show, the writers who participated in this project did not necessarily try to leave their mother rhetorics entirely to achieve rhetorical nativeness; instead, they consciously and creatively arranged the rhetorical fabric of their texts in negotiation with systems which would absorb their writings.

Developing a pedagogy cognizant of intercultural rhetoric cannot be avoided when we are teaching writing in additional languages. Teachers consciously or unconsciously engage with cultural issues when teaching writing; as a result, an awareness of the complexities of cross-cultural experiences could only enrich teaching practices. Although there have been a variety of suggestions for pedagogies promoting intercultural competence (Kubota & Lehner, 2004; Thatcher *et al.*, 2017), such approaches are still far from the norm (for instance in Canada, Steinman, 2003: 88). Top-down centralized curricula, in English speaking countries, freeze, formulate and package writing genres and their rhetorical components and superimpose them on classroom practice. At the same time, different forms of standardized testing select oversimplified rhetorical patterns that are testable at an industrial level. Additionally, the corporate textbook industry makes enormous amounts of profit by creating rhetorical models that they can market as exemplary rhetorical formations. Such industrial writing education leaves little space for teachers to facilitate students' rhetorical negotiations unless they are willing to mobilize their agency to work against the said dynamics; in which case, they can consider the following strategies.

Key to addressing intercultural rhetorical connections in the writing class is creating space for rhetorical negotiation. Part and parcel of such negotiation is overt conversations about rhetorical migration from culture to culture and from language to language. Students need to develop consciousness about their rhetorical journeys and the malleability of genres when put in new educational and cultural contexts. Students need to become aware of the fact that an invitation to experience new rhetorical patterns is not a denial of their writing skills but an expansion of their writing trajectory and intellectual world. Creating space for students' rhetorical negotiation would entail providing opportunities for students to make their mother rhetorical practices visible, sometimes on par with dominant rhetorical models. In other words, writing between rhetorical traditions in second language writing classes should not be seen as a problem but as a norm than can enrich students' intellectual and literate lives. Such an approach would require a restructuring of our current assessment systems. Rubrics, for instance, are mainly used as a tool for mass assessment in our industrialized educational structures. A pedagogy of intercultural rhetoric moves beyond rubrics and relies on one-on-one connections that recognize the humans behind writing products and their unique cultural backgrounds. In such an assessment mentality, what is evaluated is not the rubricated components of a finalized written product but the quality of students' engagement with rhetorical negotiation. The same evaluation, should also happen for teachers' rhetorical negotiation and their eagerness to engage with rhetorical patterns that are new to them. It is important to stress that rhetorical negotiation is two sided and involves both the students and the school.

In this final section of the chapter, inspired by my participants' experiences, I tried to show that educators and researchers need to see that intercultural competence is not only an additional bonus to our writing classes but a necessity to increase semiotic and genre agility on par with and strengthened by multiliteracies and plurilingualism. Also, my participants' perspectives helped me demonstrate that the 'cultural' in 'intercultural rhetoric' is a broad, complex, and fluid notion. Rhetorical patterns cannot be simply formulated and taught to writers who write in a new language because rhetoric is partly a product of socioeconomic circumstances, and thus requires overt consciousness to navigate. A more productive way of teaching intercultural rhetoric might be teaching rhetorical negotiation with systems that are interested in consuming, publishing, and/or distributing one's writing, or in other words: teaching reflection on social, economic, and political dynamics that create writing cultures.

Summary

In this chapter, I shared analyses of Magda, Choman and Clarice's rich and complex plurilingual, multiliterate, and cross-cultural experiences. The theoretical backbone of the bulk of Anglo-American scholarly conversations about the significance of multilingualism, multiliteracies, and intercultural communication has been the argument interested in the post-World War II 'global village' mentality and the multicultural multi-ethnic fabric of today's most major urban areas in the West. Revisiting this theoretical foundation, best represented in the multiliteracies movement, I tried to highlight the importance of semiotic agility as an important intellectual asset whether or not it relates to globalization processes. It is important to show that plurilingual, multi-semiotic, and intercultural practices should not be framed as a solution for a unique problem, because, as a matter of fact, these practices are part and parcel of literacy learning in any context. What made them absent from Western schools before the current period was not because they were not needed; instead, they were wrongly excluded because of colonial and industrial philosophies of education. Thus, multiliteracies should not be discussed as a fancy invention but a belated correction.

I critiqued the view that favours teaching the Anglo-American argumentative essay as the essence of prose writing and offered a new model based on Wittgenstein's family resemblance theory, which opens the door for more genre possibilities in composition and writing classrooms. I used instances of my participants' plurilingual, multiliterate and intercultural experiences to illustrate how the multiplicity of the semiotic systems that they engaged with had helped them achieve high levels of semiotic agility enabling them to write in different languages and in different cultural contexts.

This theoretical consideration has profound pedagogical consequences. This view challenges copying universal models of writing and brings educators' attention to the importance of learners' multilingual, multi-semiotic, and cross-cultural lives in order to (a) tap into them as valuable resources and (b) enrich them by exposing learners to new communication forms and traditions.

7 Social and Institutional Lived Experiences

In previous chapters, I described Choman, Clarice and Magda's ontologies of literacy (what literacy is), their understandings of how writing and power are connected, and their multidimensional literate, linguistic, cultural backgrounds. In this chapter, I focus on some of their lived experiences as multilingual immigrants. Here, I try to add to the book's phenomenological and theoretical conversations by providing specific examples of the participants' social interactions that impacted their intellectual and writing trajectories. In my interviews with Clarice, Choman and Magda, a number of their social experiences loomed large in our conversations because of the participants' repetitions of the themes as well as the direction guided by the sociocultural lens which had informed some of the interview questions. I wished to learn in what ways the participants' experiences with literacy were rooted in sociocultural, discursive, and power-relational contexts. I also wondered how the participants' socioculturally informed literate lives had impacted their writing practices, particularly when they wrote in English as an additional language. The present chapter includes some concrete examples of social and institutional experiences that answer those questions. In what follows, I write about the participants' experiences in relation to discourses that label students as successful or academically lacking. I ask if my participants were 'exceptional' students at school. I also explore how the participants' socioeconomic class impacted their access to and experiences with education. Moreover, I write about the participants' experiences in educational settings; for instance, their interactions with dominant curricula and their reactions to discourses such as the native/non-native dichotomy. Finally, I briefly focus on immigration as an intellectual event and a valuable source of literacy learning, as experienced by the participants.

'Good' Student, 'Bad' Student

The labels 'good student', 'bad student', 'top student', 'weak student', 'A student', 'C student', and so forth, which are casually used in educational settings, the mass media, and on social media, have also been used by educational researchers in academic publications, particularly in educational research informed by psychological paradigms (see for instance, Janssen *et al.*, 2006; Kerkman & Siegler, 1993; Siegler, 1988). This research trend is theoretically fed by the premise that students can be categorized as better or worse based on their cognitive calibre; for instance, Siegler (1988) stated that 'children could be classified into 3 groups: good students, not-so-good students, and perfectionists' (Siegler, 1988: 833). Such a mentality has problematic practical consequences; this view can signify that research and pedagogy should be mobilized to identify 'good' and 'bad' students and also to reinforce the traits of 'good' students. The findings of my research problematize this view by refusing to corroborate the oversimplified notion that because 'good students' possess certain cognitive capabilities, they will succeed academically and thus – for the purposes of this book – will become good writers. Although it is conceivable that many students who meet different institutional academic standards become good writers (maybe in different languages), the participants in this study never belonged in the 'good student' category. Thus, my project contributes to an alternative body of research that questions the relevance of the good student vs. bad student dichotomy (Karwowski, 2010; Taylor, 2008; Weissberg, 2011). This research trend often tends to map onto race and class by showing marginalized and minoritized students are disproportionally labelled 'bad' students (Vasudevan & Campano, 2009).

I learned from my conversations with Clarice, Magda and Choman that, unlike psychological research that defines 'good students' as capable of higher-order thinking, they deemed 'good students' as being labelled so mainly because they conform to institutional requirements with creating minimum disturbance. In this sense, none of the participants described themselves as 'brilliant' students. Clarice for instance – now an established graduate researcher in a high-ranking university – viewed her undergraduate studies in Brazil not much more than a minimum response to the requirements of the institution for a delay-less graduation:

> I was a terrible student. [She laughs.] Yeah, I was a very average student. At that time, I was just … I just wanted to get my course done and get the hell out of there because I wanted to get a job and make money.

It is important to read Clarice's words in the light of other data to also reflect on her academic behaviour outside the particular context described above. My observations of her academic life as a graduate student in Canada contrasted with the interview data significantly. Clarice constantly upheld the utmost academic rigour and decorum. She was curious, involved and inspirational. She respected peers and colleagues and valued their work. She was organized, punctual, cooperative and reliable. Considering graduate studies standards in Canada, she was deservedly considered a 'good student' in her department! This contrast raises the question, what institutional, educational, and sociocultural contexts might create positive academic performances beyond innate cognitive ability? Listening to the other participants about the same issue in a group interview (with all three writers present) helped me better understand Clarice's proud pronouncement: 'very average'. As also highlighted in Choman's response in the following lines, Clarice's use of the adjective 'terrible' seems to have less to do with academic success and more with meaningful academic engagement. In her response to Clarice, Choman explained that she performed well as far as formal evaluation was concerned, but it took more than good grades to make her feel fulfilled academically:

> My English was also fine at school, which helped me land an admission for English Literature at university. I also learned French pretty easily and enjoyed doing it. My language grades at school were always high but I never thought I would study English at university. When I was accepted at university, I thought 'Okay, I'll do it'. I didn't really become enthusiastic about English until I started to interact with English literature when I started to read English fiction and English poetry in the second year of university. Now English, which by that point was only an academic chore, turned into love of the language.

In the previous chapters, I gave gravity to the argument that the writers involved in this project took ownership of their literacy narratives; they consciously shaped, reinterpreted, and reconstructed their literate histories to enrich their current academic engagements and maximize their intellectual involvement in different contexts. In the same manner, Choman, Magda and Clarice drew upon their linguistic and cultural repertoires to effectively engage with different literacy situations. In my conversations with the participants about their academic performance at school (whether or not they were 'good' students), I detected the same form of agency at work when they were remembering how they were perceived at school. In their reconstructions of their past schooling, they represented themselves as curious and intellectually involved but at the same time non-conformist. The images they pictured from themselves as students did not match the typical 'good student' criteria; they, instead, saw themselves as intelligent (and sometimes difficult) students who impacted the process of teaching and learning with their intellectual engagement whether it was encouraged or deemed problematic. Magda, for instance, talked about her debates with her teachers at kindergarten:

> I have to tell you that one day in kindergarten, I got a sticker from my teacher because I was not arguing that day. And when I went home, I didn't

know what to say … why I got the stupid sticker? I couldn't possibly say, 'The teacher has said, 'You're great, you haven't been arguing today'".

Magda's focus on the symbolic meaning of the 'sticker' – prize for 'good' students, or an incentive for 'good' behaviour – challenges typically broad and vague definitions of 'good student' and 'bad student' attributed to learners both at school and in the family. By 'bad students', for instance, 'we mean all predilections inimical to learning, everything from passive sloth to violent criminally' (Weissberg, 2011: 23). Choman, also, recalled memories of her school years, when she enjoyed upsetting the academic hierarchy in the classroom with the teacher designated as the possessor of knowledge. In our conversation, Choman remembered her childlike rebellion to show off her command of Farsi as her second language to her teachers:

> Even when I was in grade one or two, I corrected my teachers [who were Kurdish] if they didn't pronounce Farsi words correctly. Or I sometimes told them their sentence structure was not correct.

My findings indicate that although Magda, Choman and Clarice could be comfortably ranked as successful writers, and perhaps more importantly as successful immigrants, they hardly fitted the stereotypical criteria for 'good students'. I found no particular trace in my data reflecting that they were not academically enthusiastic; however, they were careful not to picture a conformist image of themselves at school through the remembrances they shared. The interview data based on which I am offering this discussion is also consistent with my observations of how these writers carried themselves in institutions where they studied and worked; they, from time to time, swam against the tide to preserve their academic and/or professional dignity even in the face of serious consequences. Clarice, for instance, was once entangled in complicated micropolitics at her department about a required grade for an examination that would let her qualify to start her doctoral research. She was graded lower than expected but was given the chance to retake the examination after one year, an option many – including me – advised her to try. She instead requested an appeal to prove the high quality of her writing, knowing that a second rejection would abort her doctoral studies. The new readers luckily approved Clarice's work, or she would not have been able to complete her PhD. Choman, in another example, decided to quit a teaching position in a college in Toronto because she was critical of the policies of the institution – measures that had isolated her as an international adjunct instructor. She did not find the ambiance dignified and left the college – a noteworthy move considering the unpleasant situation of the teaching job market in Toronto, particularly for a 'middle-eastern woman', in her words.

Naive binaries such as 'good student/bad student' are problematic; it is, thus, imperative to think about discourse formation processes in educational settings that create such labels, identify their reductionism, and resist them through policy and pedagogical practice. As shown in the case of Choman, Clarice and Magda, such concepts can hardly help teachers understand their students and support them and are practically irrelevant to the process of teaching writing. On the negative side, however, they cause students to imagine themselves as lacking ability. Such an approach, hence, will never help learners construct strong writing identities.

Financial Resources and Education

There is no shortage of evidence showing that children born into affluent families have more access to literacy artefacts, engage with literacy earlier in their lives, and perform more satisfactorily in educational settings (Blanden & Gregg, 2004; Desforges & Abouchaar, 2003; DiMaggio et al., 2004; Hochschild, 2003; Lareau, 1987). This phenomenon, however, has less to do with 'literacy', per se, than the synchronicity between home and school discourses and practices (Gee, 1999). Providing publicly funded financial resources for education has also often been a heated issue in politics in different contexts including North America (see for instance, Fabricant & Fine, 2015; Gunter et al., 2017; Noguera, 2003; Posey-Maddox, 2014). The common theme in such policy debates has mainly been a question of public funding for education for all. In my explorations of Choman, Clarice and Magda's literate histories, issues related to their financial ability were not infrequent. All the three participants came from households which sometimes struggled with money shortages to different degrees; nevertheless, not only were they educationally successful in their native contexts, but they also used their academic background to their favour as immigrants in their host country, Canada. I was curious to learn what cultural and societal networks had facilitated Choman, Clarice and Magda's academic growth despite financial problems, and also family issues such as parental separation. Three themes emerged from the data that could address this issue. First, although not abundant, the financial resources of the participants' families were thoughtfully managed for calculated contributions to Clarice, Magda and Choman's education. Second, the participants were surrounded by networks of family members who, although not very rich, valued education and thus regarded its costs as high financial priority. Third, governmental policies regarding the promotion of literacy that affected the participants' lives were crucial, most importantly the participants' access to publicly funded education.

Clarice often remembered her literacy learning processes occurring in her childhood with references to her family's financial situation. Clarice was brought up by a single mother with a background of little formal schooling, in charge of a family with three children and meagre financial resources. In this context, even some most basic forms of literacy engagement such as purchasing books or extra-curricular language learning would turn into economic burdens challenging the family's budgeting practices:

> My parents got a divorce when I was twelve. And at the age I remember how we were going through a lot of financial problems, especially because my father wasn't contributing financially. There were three children in the family me and my sisters. ... I don't come from a family where my parents would read me a story before I went to bed! They didn't have time for that. They were working. Or did they buy me books? No, I would mostly read my sisters' books because they were ahead of me at school.

The financial challenges could have hindered Clarice's literacy learning, yet the attitude of Clarice's mother towards the value of education, as Clarice recalled, turned the obstacles into an advantage:

> My mom basically gave us the idea that 'if you want to get out of this, it's going to be through education, so start reading'. She was extremely present in our lives in terms of ... 'Oh, I have this homework to do. What does this word mean?' And she was like 'Oh, I don't know go and look it up in a dictionary'. I became addicted to reading dictionaries probably because of her. When I was twelve my mom had just finished grade three. She valued education because she didn't have it and she saw that the three of us could have it. ... I think the fact that we were not privileged financially made me really want to do something more significant.

Choman, similarly, grew up in a home with financial and relationship problems. Choman's parents were teachers. Whereas teachers in North America are usually considered middle-class with sufficient economic stability, public school teachers in Iran are under enormous financial pressure and often deemed as lower class. Teachers from minority populations, such as the Kurds, are typically under double pressure being away from the resources available in large cities like the capital, Tehran, and also being viewed as potential dissidents because of racial, linguistic, and religious differences. Choman often highlighted the struggles she had to undergo in a low-income Kurdish home with serious family disaccords. She, nevertheless, emphasized that family's educated background and their personal library inspired her love for learning and writing:

> My parents didn't get along and expression of affection didn't have a place in the family. Writing was my only channel of expression. I talked to my notebooks. ... My father had higher education. When he went to university, very few people in Kurdistan even had a school diploma, at least half of the population of Kurdistan. At that time though, my father had a master's degree, my mom had a bachelor's. And many of my aunts

were teachers. They all had studied in Tehran. There were no universities at the time in Kurdistan. We had a huge library in our house. I had an educated family, but we were very poor because my dad had been fired. He was actually in prison because of political reasons. The only bread-winner in the family was my mom. My mom was a teacher. And being a teacher in Iran means being poor. Yes, money was a real problem. Sometimes I didn't have shoes to go to school. What is really important is when you grow up you should see books in your parents' hands. When you're a kid, they are your heroes. When you see them reading books, reading becomes second nature to you. Then when you're bored as a kid, you always have this option: reading.

Magda, similarly, grew up with divorced parents. Magda did not talk about severe financial hardships but still highlighted the significance of having enough (not necessarily abundant) access to literacy artefacts and resources. She described the economic status of the family as middle class with enough money to purchase books:

We always had a lot of books and reading was just part of our everyday life. I didn't have to struggle to have access to literacy artefacts partly because books were really cheap [in Hungary at the time]. Textbooks were also extremely cheap, so we almost paid nothing at school for buying textbooks. Now, however, they are very expensive [in Hungary], and I think it is a very important factor for literacy.

In addition to sufficient financial resources and positive familial and communal attitudes towards education, Magda's statement shows a third crucial factor in the development of Magda, Clarice and Choman's literate and writing lives: publicly funded educational infrastructures even in imperfect sociopolitical and economic circumstances, in the participants' case: Communist Hungary, post-revolutionary Iran, and among the disadvantaged populations of Brazil, where a serious economic gap is continually a problem (Messias, 2003). Magda went to school during the communist era in Hungary. Her comments in the above quotation should be put in the context of the economic dynamics of the time. Although a critic of the USSR dominated political epoch in Hungary, Magda was also worried about the challenges that the emerging neoliberal models in Hungary were creating, problems such as unaffordable book prices.

My research project was not intended to focus on policy in terms of public funding for literacy education, yet the theme loomed large in the literate histories told by the participants. There was a common pattern in the data indicating that public funding had significantly impacted Clarice, Choman and Magda's everyday experiences with literacy and language learning. Clarice, similar to Magda, was aware of the role of the publicly funded education that she had received: 'We were in a public school, not a very good school but we were still doing it'. When she went to the public primary school, Clarice became interested in learning English, for which she had to attend a private extracurricular programme. Clarice's father paid the tuition for a short while, but he ran out of money soon. Clarice would never learn English – an experience which became the foundation of her academic existence today – if it had not been because of an institutional scholarship that her teacher guided her family to apply for: 'I was super-passionate about English and they decided to give me a lifetime scholarship. So I studied for three years for free'.

Choman also thought that the development of her literary imagination more than anything was thanks to the books she read at home and also in the public library of a state-run cultural centre in their neighbourhood:

> When I was a kid, my mom used to take me to a youth cultural centre. She went to work, and I stayed there from morning to evening. And I couldn't have enough of reading. Even when she came to pick me up, I didn't want to leave the place.

Policy strengthening the foundation and reach of publicly funded education can impact students' literacy engagement, and, consequently, writing practices, especially those of students with limited financial means. Effective learners understand this and take advantage of educational possibilities offered to them by society. These opportunities might arise in favourable historical circumstances such as times of economic prosperity when supporting the public good does not feel costly, or they might be accessed with more difficulty in situations when financial resources are scarce. Regardless, thoughtful policies that aim to provide education for all can help individuals like the participants in this study grow intellectually, sometimes with no other alternative available to them. The case of the writers involved in my research, in particular, shows how even less systematic and scattered opportunities even in not very prosperous historical conditions can change students' lives, opportunities such as a small internal grant or an isolated cultural centre with a small library, or simply having access to cheaper books.

Power Relations in Educational/Cultural Settings

> Relations of power in the wider society (macro-interactions), ranging from coercive to collaborative in varying degrees, influence both the ways in which educators define their roles and the types of structures that are established in the educational system. (Cummins, 2009b: 263)

In an attempt to capture significant aspects of the participants' literate histories, in our conversations, references were made to power-driven interactions with their teachers. I opened this section with Cummins' words on how wider societal power relations (macro-interactions such as racism, sexism, political hegemony, language dominance and colonial pedagogical traditions) can be reinforced or resisted in the classroom in everyday micro-relations between educators, students, and their communities. 'Micro-relations ... are never neutral' (Cummins, 2009b: 263); they are loaded with power relations that will be remembered by students for years. Clarice, Magda and Choman's remembrances of such interactions were significant in that they revealed the imprint of micro power relations on students' lives.

A theme emerging from the participants' words connoting the impact of micro-relations in educational settings (and also in writing communities) was their consciousness of the power-laden layers of everyday interactions in the classroom. Magda for instance talked about her classmate whose interactions with their teacher revealed power-relational challenges involved in immigrant adult education:

> I think I am quite conscious of how ideologies in society impact us. I need to get more powerful. ... I really need to know who I am and what I can contribute. And then I can be more powerful. ... I had a classmate [in a writing course in a college in Toronto]. He was teaching all kinds of stuff, business and other stuff. His English. ... He was from Pakistan I think and his English was perfect, really good. And he always challenged the teacher, 'No that's actually wrong'. And he explained his point. And he was always right. I love him ... that you can do that. But you have to be confidant. You have to be right to do that.

The class that Magda spoke about is an example of numerous courses and programmes that skilled immigrants are obliged to take for Canadian qualifications since their foreign credentials – although accepted by the Canadian government for immigration – are not typically recognized in the job market, and thus immigrants, experiencing a de-skilling process, are actively excluded 'from upper segments of the labour market' (Bauder, 2003: 699). The lack of an effective system to quickly absorb the immigrant talent into professional fields in Canada is a reflection of societal macro-interactions that are mobilized based on the belief that newcomers are academically and professionally inadequate. These ideological perspectives are also at work in the classroom, putting both teachers and students (especially youth and adult students with successful backgrounds) in difficult positions. Magda's story about her Pakistani friend illustrates the complexities of classroom interactions intensified by racial, ethnic, linguistic and power differences.

In the above quotation, Magda advocated for awareness about such power relations in everyday ideologically laden micro-interactions in the classroom as a factor that could challenge the balance of power in the learner's favour. Clarice, similarly, spoke about the confidence needed in processing the teacher feedback that students receive on their writing in a learned language:

> It didn't impact me negatively if people pointed to my mistakes in my writing. You know, ideas are more important than any kind of grammar mistake. What I'm worried about is my content. If my content is rubbish, then I get upset. If somebody challenges my content I feel really upset. ... And I think this is liberating too: When you are a good writer, you don't have to be a good writer *all the time*. And you shouldn't because that's pedantic. ... It's liberating to feel we don't have to be grammatically super-correct all the time. It's not important. ... Power relations are there. They are always going to be there. You should learn how you navigate the system in a way that you are going to be successful but at the same time you are not going to get hurt.

Clarice highlighted the significance of one's stamina and diplomatic manoeuvring in one's journey as a writer, especially when one is writing in an additional language. Instead of focusing on negative feedback, successful learners 'navigate' micro-interactions with potential teacher allies to foster relations that provide them with the technical and social support needed to create quality writing that is both meaningful for the writer and is transformational in some sense. References to such teacher-student alliances, intended to challenge relations of power reproduced in schools based on larger societal patterns of discrimination, frequently appeared in our conversations about the participants' experiences with schooling.

For instance, Choman explained her methods of navigating forces of ideological coercion and potential collaborative resistance by remembering herself as her high school's 'ugly duckling' who 'swam against the social tide' in post-revolution Iran. After the revolution, the ministry of education trained and placed special teachers – referred to as *parvareshi* teachers (nurturers) – in all schools to spread the doctrines of the revolution among the youth. Choman as a curious and creative young girl who 'challenged the norm' was seen by *parvareshi* teachers as an 'ailment to be treated' (Choman's words). Ideological coercion, thus, became a daily experience for Choman. On the other hand, however, the other teachers tried to alleviate the situation by highlighting Choman's academic progress in order to protect Choman's image as a respectable student in her own eyes and to resist, at the school level, the damage that could have hindered her education. Time shows that the forces of collaborative resistance won; Choman's picture of herself today is much more similar to the identity portrait that she co-constructed with her supportive teachers: an asset to society rather than a problem.

In a different context, Magda, in an editing course in Canada confronted her doubts as a non-native editor of native English writers with supportive insights of a Canadian teacher who commented on Magda's ability to judge native speakers' language use in writing although English was not Magda's mother tongue:

> At that time my English was not particularly brilliant, but I was editing [native] English writers and … they made mistakes! I was editing something that was supposed to be totally okay. I doubted my edits, but my teacher admired my work over and over again. … That was eye-opening for me: 'Okay, it's not only me. If native university students make mistakes in writing, it's fine if I do too'.

Magda's story is also another reminder of how significant everyday unstructured micro-interactions in classrooms are. It shows how a few comments made by a supportive teacher can challenge grand discriminatory narratives such as the native/non-native dichotomy, which I will return to in more detail later in this chapter.

Clarice, similarly, benefited from relationships with teachers who used their agencies to create change despite structural restrictions that they had to comply with. As I also previously wrote about, Clarice would not have been able to learn English if it had not been because of the supportive action of one of her primary school teachers. Despite her successful performance in an extra-curricular English class, Clarice – a primary school student at the time – had to quit lessons because her family could no longer afford the lessons. Aware of Clarice's interest in the class, her teacher used her contacts and knowledge of the inner workings of the system to acquire a scholarship for Clarice, which let her study English for free for three years.

Macro discursive patterns and hegemonic societal ideologies are reproduced in the classroom on a daily basis. It is naive to imagine classrooms are ideologically neutral. Even in most innocent everyday micro-interactions, educators should make a choice between reinforcing unjust societal relations or resisting them. Educators can make a difference and should be aware of the potential impact of collaborative resistance. Such collaborations could include a range of measures from recognizing students' identities and 'unofficial' (sometimes banned) knowledge, to co-constructing activities and assignments with their students to challenge dominant curricula. What teachers say and do in everyday interactions matter and can make or break the future of their students.

Dominant and Canonical Curricula

The data that I collected for my project indicated a tendency among the participants to move beyond mainstream and canonical curricula. Here 'mainstream curriculum' is intended to mean centralized curriculum designed by governmental officials, education administrators, and/or academics imposed on classrooms over large geographical regions (often across a province or nationwide). 'Canonical curriculum' in this chapter is considered curriculum offering the dominant literary canon as the main source for students' textual events in language, literacy, and literature classes.

Centrally controlled curriculum is a legacy of the Prussian model of education popularly adopted in Europe for nation-building purposes and construction of 18th and 19th European nation states (Cubberley, 2005). Although the Prussian model has been modified over time in different Western countries and evolved into more refined variations, its tenacious interest in centralizing curriculum and assessment is still present. The shortcomings of centralized mainstream curriculum have not remained unnoticed: '[M]ainstream or dominant curriculum theory treats knowledge as something to be managed and consumed' (Giroux, 1987: 175). Also, a more recent voice critiquing the assumptions of the centralized curriculum model by highlighting its industrial mass-production mentality:

> Within this modernist frame of reference, dominant curriculum change models all carry assumptions of linearity, purpose, control, identifiable objectives or outcomes, and well-articulated plans for implementation be they at the teacher, subject, school or systemic level. (Macdonald, 2004: 75)

Such a top-down approach to curriculum development, more than student success and satisfaction, aims to create or maintain a certain social order by streaming students into roles deemed appropriate for them. 'The dominant curriculum constructs the subject in such a manner that it can be readily inserted into the existing social order' (Zavarzadeh & Morton, 1986: 2). In such a model, students are deemed as cogs in the machine. Any curriculum with such an approach is bound to generate alienation and frustration.

One of the functions of dominant curriculum is the reinforcement of political and cultural hegemony by spotlighting the literary canon in students' literacy activities. When I was analyzing my interview and observation data from interactions with Clarice, Magda and Choman, I realized that those writers had all struggled with dominant curriculum. A close analysis of my participants' reading histories showed their uncomfortable relationships with the textual canons imposed by mainstream curricula. Clarice for instance said:

> I remember rejecting a lot of books, especially at school. The books that were part of the curriculum, 'Okay, you have to read this collection'. ... Most of them I just hated because there were horrible books. And then again I would read the good stuff. I remember the first book I read in

English was *1984* by George Orwell, and I loved it. I was probably 13 or 14 years old. I just loved it and I thought 'that's the kind of thing that I want to read'.

Further in this conversation, Clarice and I tried to understand why she felt the books were 'horrible'. There was no simple explanation; Clarice did not like the books because of a combination of different factors. The development of the curriculum in Brazil did not involve any student or community participation. Lack of student voice in curriculum development had severe consequences especially for underprivileged families in less affluent areas, as was the case with Clarice. Clarice felt she was studying someone else's curriculum. Moreover, the pedagogical approach and evaluation strategies hardly stirred interest in students to approach the canonical curriculum content enthusiastically. Clarice did not think the literature was *innately* 'horrible'; instead the manner of framing and presentation of the content did not strike a cord with students like Clarice.

As for Choman, the canon of Persian literature was perhaps the first topic we discussed when we first met. I first met Choman through a mutual friend in a coffee shop in Toronto. She was introduced to me as a Kurdish-Iranian-Canadian writer. She, in return, was aware of my Iranian background. Immediately after greetings, we engaged in a conversation about our favourite Iranian writers. Seemingly innocently, we listed the writers we liked; nevertheless, the exchange was, at a different level, a mutual inquiry about how close to the official Persian canon we stood. Looking back, I feel this conversation determined the future of our friendship based on the writers we liked and their places in the history of Persian literature in regard with official power. 'I read a lot of Shamlou and Forough', she said. 'Me too. I loved them', I replied. One should not underestimate how loaded those few words were. After the Iranian revolution in 1979, the centralized national curriculum became overtly intolerant of any writer who did not echo the official ideology of the revolution. Ahmad Shamlou (1925–2000) and Forough Farrokhzad (1934–1967) were among a long list of writers blacklisted and banned by the government. Choman's interest in uncanonized Persian literature, meant she must have been involved in a number of out-of-school activities including reading 'forbidden' writers, frequenting bookstores where you could purchase illegal books, and mingling with underground intellectual circles where you could discuss the books and discover new dissident writers. Our conversation about those writers told much about our literate backgrounds as well as our political and ideological inclinations. Fortunately, there was enough overlap between us that sustained our friendship and facilitated our collaboration in my research project.

Magda's relation with the canon was also significant. Relating her experiences with transition from dominant Hungarian curriculum to Canadian curriculum, Magda indicated that neither curriculum was perfect. She thought the Canadians could enrich their content, which was too watered down literarily, and the Hungarians should be less strict and develop more child and youth-friendly content; yet she did not specifically complain about the canon promoted by the two curricula. The way Magda challenged canonical, mainstream, and official literature should be described in a slightly different manner from Clarice and Choman. Magda – along with her family members – had a long history of engaging with intellectual and literary European schools of thought, which were more rooted in cultural practices than schooling. I had many conversations with Magda, her husband, her daughter, and her mother about the books they read. The textual legacy of the family (in multiple languages) was of a size that made mainstream curriculum and its suggested canon only a very small part of what the family understood as literature. The family clearly had a personal canon which overpowered the canons reinforced by educational systems both in Hungary and Canada. Magda's family, for instance, interacted with many more titles, read in multiple languages, and read books from a diversity of cultures. Textual content in official curricula is often monolingual and monocultural; it tends to lack diverse presentations of gender, race and ethnicity. Furthermore, our current centralized curricula are designed far from classrooms by policymakers, administrators and business owners (in the textbook industry) who seek to impose their own agendas through canonizing curricular content (Applebee, 1992, 1997; Wixson *et al.*, 2003). These dynamics do not reflect serious consideration for maximizing the quality of students' textual interactions. As a result students' individual out-of-school canons should be treated as a valuable alternative or at least an important complementary component.

The experiences of the three writers who participated in my project show that the scope of the literature that they engaged with does not match the official canon promoted in mainstream schools. Moreover, I found no data in my pool to suggest a strong belief in the significance of canonical curricula. In contrast, sentiments demonstrating resisting dominant curriculum were noticeable both in the participants' words – as shared previously – and their cultural consumptions observed in the process of this study. In all three cases, the participants' literary (and artistic) repertoires were much richer than the content offered in the official curricula.

Magda, Clarice and Choman's experiences with dominant and canonical curricula corroborate the pedagogical recommendations that – often through the paradigms of culturally responsive pedagogy – invite teachers to reflect on the cultural, political, and ideological foundational of curriculum in hand in order to broaden and connect it with students' cultural, textual, and linguistic legacies. In other words, teachers need to take a stance in relation with the curriculum which they are working with. They need to ask if they should teach a centrally controlled canon passively or instead highlight possibilities that the curriculum offers for creating textual diversity. Such a decision often requires a mentality that drives teachers to regard learners as having come to the classroom with rich literate backgrounds. It also requires a willingness to learn from students. Teachers, hence, need to think of ways to engage with students, their families, and their communities in the process of interpreting the curriculum with a genuine desire to recognize learners' organic textual practices. Centralized curricula often reinforce dominant ideological hegemonies. Teachers need to mobilize their agency to approach the received curriculum critically and to interpret it creatively for allowing the formation of culturally responsive pedagogical practices. The fact that curriculum is abstract and the teacher's interpretation is the concrete manifestation of a curriculum document, provides teachers with a reasonable amount of power. It is up to teachers to decide if want to use that power.

Native vs. Non-Native English Users

Choman, Magda and Clarice shared thoughts that indicated their writing journeys would be better comprehended through the conceptual lens of the native vs. non-native speaker debate. There is a growing trend in second language education discussing that judgments of linguistic capability, nativeness in particular, are not made entirely based on linguistic performance, but racial considerations impact listeners' evaluations of speakers' linguistic backgrounds. White English speakers tend to hear accent and syntactical imperfection while they communicate with non-white non-native speakers of English and also non-white native speakers of the language (Amin, 1997; Braine, 2010; Curtis & Romney, 2006; Faez, 2011). The same racial bias towards non-white and/or non-native speakers is also at work in other areas of linguistic performance such as writing. Non-white writers of English are often under double scrutiny.

Magda, Clarice and Choman studied, wrote and edited in a variety of capacities in Canada, experiencing moments of anxiety and doubt caused by dominant nativeness notions that are reinforced by power relations and micro aggressions that challenge adult immigrants in academic and professional settings. The participants' experiences showed that despite being accepted professionally and socially as competent users of English, they still had to wrestle with nativist ideologies in ways that differed from participant to participant and context to context. Choman, Magda and Clarice's responses to judgments about their non-nativeness and *nativist microaggressions* (Ramjattan, 2017) were too various to be presented in a single theme. This might have been caused by racial and linguistic differences among the three participants. Nevertheless, in order to exemplify the significance of multilingual writers' inner dialogues about their perceived nativeness or non-nativeness, I provide some statements by the participants that can represent three major defence strategies in the face of power-ridden judgments of the degree of their nativeness: (a) acceptance of their non-nativeness; (b) problematizing the concept of nativeness; and (c) highlighting linguistic strengths which matched or even overpowered those of native speakers.

None of the participants denied their consciousness about their 'technical' non-nativeness. They shared their vulnerabilities in this regard and spoke about the uncomfortable struggle of writing in a learned language in literary, academic, and professional conditions that required highly complex linguistic performances. Choman, for instance, said:

> I have always felt very vulnerable as a 'non-native' English writer. I feel uncomfortable when I write a passage which is grammatically sound but my editors change my sentence structures. ... When I write stories in English, I feel I'm a sprinter put by force in a wheelchair because her legs are broken. After all these years I feel I can replace the wheelchair with walking sticks, but it is still difficult. The slope is steep and my armpits are sore. This is writing in English for me.

This response by Choman – which I am using again in relation with the nativeness debate – does not mean she was not aware that even native speakers found editors' corrections of grammatically sound structures unpleasant. Choman was also conscious that the discomfort she felt when writing fiction in English might have been only partly connected to her non-native English and it could have also been caused by other factors such as culturally constructed rhetorical patterns or different fiction writing traditions, which could similarly challenge native speakers of English when they start to write fiction professionally. In this dialogue, I was interested to record the emotional reactions of the participants, resultant of the consciousness of the perceived gap between native and non-native linguistic performances. Choman's case is an informative representation of such feelings of vulnerability since as an 'accented Canadian writer' (Choman's words) she was frequently judged by literary communities, who are typically more sensitive about the aesthetics of writing than academic or technical writers, represented by Magda and Clarice in my study. Despite the psychological pressure involved in creative writing in a learned language, what encouraged Choman to write in English and, perhaps more importantly, to enjoy writing in that language was the complexities of the concept 'nativeness', particularly because of the status of English in today's world. The status of English today, with its spread and varied forms, opens enough space for non-native writers to claim ownership over the language. With English functioning as a *lingua franca*, it is quite reasonable to ask, who is a native English writer after all? A question also asked by Magda to problematize the nativeness discourse:

> [Academic papers are sometimes rejected with the excuse that the writers are not native English users.] When they tell you, 'have a native speaker edit your paper, then resend it' ... that is wrong at so many levels. Who is a native speaker? Who should read it? This girl behind the counter [in the coffee shop]? This lady behind me? Or a guy walking on the street? Who? They are all native speakers. Can they understand my article? No. If they said, 'Professor X, an expert in something, should read this', that might make more sense. Do they think native speakers speak better English? That is so wrong. I know some native speakers like my colleague who cannot write properly.

It is not easy to define a native speaker based on technical criteria that purely measure linguistic performance in that 'native speakership ... is more than privilege of birth or even of education. It is acceptance by the group that created the distinction between native and nonnative speakers' (Kramsch, 1997: 363), or the privileged social group that claims the ownership of correct English. Magda knew that claims to objectivity in editing process in regard with nativeness are not accurate and that at times judging someone's writing as non-native sounding might be yet another lever in societal power relations.

The participants' conscious complexification of the idea of nativeness helped them see through the superficiality, inaccurateness, and also the racial charge of many institutional, structural, and standardized forms of assessment. Despite claims to objective methods of assessment, most of such evaluations rely on rubric-centred readings of a small-sized textual product; for instance, an application letter or an article. No matter how imperfect, a single textual performance, such as an essay, cannot be used as a base for judgment of non-nativeness. An essay might be badly written or have grammatical issues and could be rejected for those, yet template emails with comments critical of 'non-native' prose sent to authors who are perceived to be second language writers are indicative of larger systemic problems. Such practice compares with casual judgments of nativeness in everyday social interactions where 'native' speakers feel entitled to pass opinions on other people's linguistic competence based on a small talk. Magda, Clarice and Choman, knew that nativeness could not be measured by a single linguistic performance. Nativeness involves a large number of lexical, syntactic, phonological, pragmatic, and rhetorical manifestations, in some of which – depending on the context of communication – non-native language users can outdo natives. Choman talked about syntactic/grammatical competence as an example of one of the layers of nativeness where non-natives' conscious approach to grammar gives them an edge over native speakers:

I decided that I would like to take an editing course to see what goes on the other side and, when I want to publish something, what Canadian editors expect to see. All the students in the course were native speakers but me. And to my surprise, I did much better than everyone else when it came to grammar and structure because I had studied them systematically as a language learner. This really boosted my confidence.

Grammatical nativelike (or rather above-native) competence is not the only linguistic performance challenging nativist views. Conversational skills were, ironically, among the most visible linguistic strengths which Choman, Magda and Clarice had in comparison with native speakers of English. I wrote 'ironically' because judgments of nativeness, if not led by invisible racial motives, are often naively made based on phonological features in casual conversations. When I observed the participants speak with other people in English, however, instead of asking how accurately they sounded, I was curious to see how often they effectively communicated in a 'native' context (in a conversation with native speakers). I, for instance, wanted to see if they ever led the conversation and how much attention they received from their audience. Through a pragmatics lens, the question of 'how a native speaker sounds' can be replaced with 'what a native speaker does with language in different communicative contexts'. From this angle, it was not difficult to observe that the participants not only matched native speakers in oral exchange but at times outperformed them because they carried their native communicative strategies and semiotic agility into their interactions in English.

I observed Clarice in a number of her doctoral courses. Clarice was among the smaller group of students who proactively participated in conversations and generously shared opinions. She broke the classroom silence much more frequently than most native speakers present. She posed questions, changed the course of the conversation, and inspired others to talk. In my conversations with Clarice about her communicative performance, Clarice suggested that she might have inherited her interest in engaging with conversation from Brazilian culture. Clarice saw oracy as an important tool for knowledge generation and community building. Choman, in another example, had given interviews in Kurdish, Persian and English. I studied online reactions to her interviews on social media and learned her audio English interviews did not receive less attention than her interviews in Farsi or Kurdish. It did not feel that delivering messages in English had, by any calculation, alienated her English speaking audience. Choman came from a culture with rich oral communication traditions. This cultural oracy helped Choman explore non-written informal channels of communication in structurally complex institutions which she was part of in order to network and reach out to likeminded people.

Additionally, in different conversational contexts, she took advantage of her storytelling abilities, which made her voice a centre of gravity in gatherings with native speakers in them. Magda came from a highly educated Hungarian family. Magda and her husband, an artist and musician, often talked to me about the challenges of breaking into the Canadian job market. We especially talked about the challenges involved in translating non-Canadian professional experience for Canadian employers. Despite the odds, Magda emerged as a successful professional in Toronto after a few years of looking for a job, and in a career that required regular high-risk linguistic performance. The intellectual foundations formed by Magda's upbringing in an educated house gave Magda's presentations and the coaching materials she wrote a depth that would make questions about accent and sounding like natives irrelevant. As these examples show, it is not only in grammar where English learners can show their strengths. If nativeness involves smooth initiation and completion of a conversation, millions of users of English as an additional language meet this criterion in different contexts on a daily basis.

To recap this section, Magda, Choman and Clarice were cognizant of the native/non-native dichotomy and where they 'technically' stood as non-native English speakers. They were also aware of the racial judgments that tended to exaggerate non-natives' underperformance. Consciousness of the complexity of the non-native debate helped Magda, Choman and Clarice to take control of their linguistic existence with more confidence about their communicative abilities in English. This approach to defining language competence among adult immigrants has also been observed by other researchers:

> Unpacking competence as a relational construct – through the lens of adult migrants' lived experiences of language – points to how embodied experiences such as internalization of the view of the Other (i.e. manifested through the use of reported speech) and emotional perspectives (such as highlighting the importance of self-confidence) are an important part of constructions and perceptions of competence, thereby extending more traditional views of competence used in language education. (Rydell, 2018: 108)

The pedagogical indications of my participants' views of nativeness are twofold. First, educators need to be conscious of the invisible presence of societal power relations in seemingly objective judgments of students' nativelikeness. This consciousness is necessary for challenging larger societal discriminatory patterns that find their way into the classroom. Second, writing teachers can re-adjust the paradigms based on which they assess second language writers. Most of the rubrics that we inherit from our school departments, teacher education, or other English teachers have been designed to mass evaluate students' activities. As a result, most of these rubrics, in the name of objectivity, focus on painlessly observable entities such as length, syntax, and structural components (thesis, topic sentence, examples, and so on). As my research shows, effective writers do engage with such formalistic elements, yet they do much more than that. They show curiosity, they research, they question, they translate, they embed themselves in intellectual and artistic communities, they draw upon their ethnic cultures, and so on. If educators rethink their evaluation paradigms to include the aforesaid engagements, they could create new definitions of 'native' English writing which would nurture emergent multilinguals more comfortably and judge their performance more justly. Simplistic assessment is not always objective although our rubrics would make it look so. You are not objective if you do not do justice to the complexity of writing and the multidimensionality of your students' engagement with writing.

Assimilation and Cultural Conformity

The linguistic nativism discourse also exists in sociopolitical forms as expectations from immigrants to assimilate into mainstream culture; thus, assimilation and social conformity have always been among key issues discussed in terms of immigration (see for instance, Abramitzky et al., 2016; Alba & Nee, 2009; Grote et al., 2014; Sayegh & Lasry, 1993). Despite aggressively imposing their own values on colonized populations (with many violent episodes), English speaking cultural and political forces in the Anglo-American West have often been concerned about the protection of their 'core values' against outside 'barbaric' cultural practices. Assimilationist voices have been very strong in colonized territories such as the United States, Australia and Canada (the context of this inquiry) despite the fact that the dominant Anglo-Saxon culture is ironically non-native to those lands and has been merely a guest culture for a relatively brief period of time. Questions about assimilation have mobilized political forces, impacted the decisions of policymakers, and created grassroots movements, some in support of multiculturalism and some in pursuit of its demolition. In education, considerations about assimilation and multiculturalism have provoked conversations about bilingualism, multilingual education models, and the role of students' home and heritage languages. These conversations have also given momentum to policy and research trends that focus on student and teacher demography based on racial, ethnic, and linguistic groups.

In postcolonial theory, assimilation has been discussed as the practice of *mimicry* (Ashcroft et al., 2003; Lawson, 2004). Colonized populations, and immigrants in the same manner, often experience periods of mimicry as a result of a desire to assimilate into the dominant culture. In order to feel at home, minorities copy dominant cultural practices including language use, dress code and lifestyle. Mimicry, however, often fails to create respect or recognition. Minorities, postcolonial theorists argue, soon realize that they will never be treated as equals to the dominant population no matter how they speak, look, or behave. As a result, mimicry will only lead to disillusionment and indignation, often followed by identity movements that help highlight the subtle othering strategies of dominant populations.

One translation of postcolonial debates regarding mimicry into identity debates in education is theorizations about a race-neutral education, which is rooted in 'traditional claims of legal neutrality, objectivity, color-blindness, and meritocracy as camouflages for the self-interest of dominant groups' (Ladson-Billings & Tate, 1995: 52). Similar to mimicry, the naivety of thought in suggestions for colour blindness in education has also been critiqued and regarded with scepticism (Cochran-Smith, 1995; DeCuir & Dixson, 2004; Dixson & Rousseau, 2005; López, 2003).

Borrowing from the above matrix of conceptual frameworks, Clarice, Magda, Choman and I discussed their experiences with assimilation after immigration. I was interested to learn how they perceived their experiences with demands for conformity particularly when those impacted their literate activities. Clarice, Magda and Choman felt very strong about their cultural heritage and native identities while they actively contributed to mainstream Canadian society and were appreciated in return. Each of these writers, however, added different layers to our conversation. Here I share reports of two group interviews in which we discussed assimilation and how it impacted writing practices.

Our conversation about assimilation in the first group interview started with a focus on writing and rhetorical practices but soon moved beyond those to include social expectations, gender, and race. As for rhetorical assimilation, Clarice, for instance, said:

> The thing is a lot people who come to Toronto, or Canada, they feel that they have to assimilate in order to have access to whatever they are going to do. If they want to write, and if they want to be part of a certain journal, they feel they have to assimilate to that particular style and stick with that and that's the only way to have access to it. It might be that they will have access to it, but ... I don't know ... it's conformist ... I don't necessarily like it.

Choman had also experienced pressure for rhetorical assimilation in the literary world, yet she considered the presence of a rhetorical hegemony as a sign of larger societal forces which expected cultural conformity from immigrants. Despite the popular notion that 'Canada is a multicultural mosaic', Choman had felt the weight of Canada's assimilationist culture and found it to be tightly connected with writing.

Choman's multifaceted view of writing in new cultural contexts might have been rooted in her perception of writing as a social act. Choman's writing life showed her tendency to treat the act of writing as resistance against dominant social and ideological norms. Choman said she 'wrote as a form of rebellion and resistance', an idea which was in fact the core of Choman's writing identity: being punished at home for writing in a home culture where girls were mainly responsible for the housework; writing fiction at school when one was supposed to focus on academics; writing stories in underground circles with no publication prospect because of dealing with banned content; writing about women's rights; writing about the Kurdish cause; and writing to break into the North American corporate literature industry as a lower middle-class immigrant of colour. This background helped Choman to see rhetorical conformity as connected with cultural and political dynamics.

Magda, among the three writers, was the quietest in sharing experiences struggling with othering and discrimination, both in conversations between me and Magda and in this group interview. One reason for Magda having a smaller share of this exchange might be a question of genre. I had approached Magda as a technical writer, and thus her perception of her role in the research project might have led her to leave more space for Choman as the novelist and Clarice as the humanist academic to share experiences with assimilationist forces. After all, creative writing and qualitative research often make authors' discourses, legacies, and histories more visible and hence are prone to pressure from dominant paradigms. Magda's relative silence in this regard might have also had another reason: perceived racial similarities with the dominant Canadian elite. Could it be that Magda's perceived whiteness might have mitigated othering and assimilation dynamics that otherwise would be aggressively employed? I never followed up with Magda with a conversation about whiteness; nevertheless, I conducted another group interview in which I asked how 'being a woman' formed the writers' social experiences that impacted their literate and writing lives. In the course of the conversation, issues were raised regarding race, ethnicity, gender and Islamophobia. In what follows, I share an extended excerpt of our conversation in its original organic flow. As you will see, the exchange corroborates the views of feminists of colour that minoritized women are often under multiple layers of discrimination because they are not white and often not rich; religion also could be added to the mix when, for instance, women like Choman are perceived to be Muslim, only because they come from the Middle East:

Choman: Growing up in a small town in Iran, I didn't have many other ways to entertain myself and fill my free time but to read unlike my brothers, who could play soccer with friends, hang out with friends in the streets. I'd also write to protest to the gender inequalities in the only way I knew, filling up my diary with angry sentences. ... So I'd read and write to create an alternate world in which things were better. That was not a conscious decision, just something I'd do because I had no other options.

Clarice: My parents got divorced when I was 12 and the house was populated with women: my mother, my two sisters and I. Because we were financially deprived, my mother would go to work all day and go to school at night so she could finish her studies in primary school. She came from a family that was not school educated, which was very common in Brazil at the time. I also feel that my mother encouraged the three girls to study and try to do our best all the time. I knew from a very early age that I would have to use knowledge as a powerful tool, not necessarily for economic but intellectual ascension. ... Strength is something my mother always instilled in us. Although we were comfortable talking about our emotions at home, we were always encouraged to show that we were strong. ... Besides, I grew up in a male dominated society, which to this day is still somewhat sexist, sometimes even misogynist, so I always wanted to show this strength.

Magda: My story is kind of the opposite of Clarice's. My parents also got divorced when I was 14 but I had two brothers. Then I met my husband pretty soon and my son was born when I was 19, so I spent a lot of time with boys and men around me. But when I think about my readings as a child, I usually read the books that were written for girls. I was never interested in those adventure books written for boys. Also, most of the writers we studied at school were men and usually (I don't know who chose them) they had tragic lives or lived in poverty. So as a girl, writing was not appealing for me. In our culture however there was no distinction between boys and girls, everybody had to read the same books, every year there were mandatory readings. Business writing is also interesting, there were some attempts to teach women how to write as a man ... can you imagine? For example they told women not to use the word 'sorry' so many times ... that's crazy.

Clarice: ... [As for my experiences in Canada,] I don't see myself as a 'woman of colour' and I'm not sure people see colour in my writing. They may notice that I have a different linguistic and cultural background than people who were born and raised in Canada, though. I never hide the fact that I am Brazilian. In fact, I use my cultural and linguistic heritage as social capital because for some reason, Brazil tends to be seen as trendy and progressive.

Choman: I see myself as a marginalized voice, like many other women of colour who get published but not warmly received by the mainstream media. I got great reviews in various websites, but not a single mention in the mainstream media. So far I have been able to function at the margins without censorship but there are lots of ceilings and not all of them are glass! It seems that my best is never enough! [As a published writer, I got a job as a writing teacher to teach academic writing to college freshmen]. The students would say here is someone with an accent standing in front of me; how good is their English? Is she really able to teach me writing if she makes grammatical mistakes when she speaks?

Clarice: [In response to Choman] I did encounter problems of this kind mainly back in Brazil and surprisingly not here in Canada because I'm not a native speaker of English. I'm of course mainly talking about my experiences as a TA [Teaching Assistant].

Choman: It's a very good point. I believe the situation might be slightly different as a TA or RA [Research Assistant]. I, for instance, worked in a writing development centre as a graduate student and I rarely thought about 'nativeness', I experienced this specifically when I was teaching writing to vocational college students who didn't know why the institution was ripping them off and requiring them to do courses that they thought they didn't need such as academic writing. And the students would ask 'who are you to teach me English writing?' And it wasn't only the students. It was the whole structure: the way the chair treated part-time teachers; the dean didn't even know who I was; and full time teachers didn't have a good relationship with us either, and we were not part of the union. And don't forget, Clarice, you're from Brazil and I am from the Middle East. They might trust a Brazilian teacher but I'm not sure it would be the same case with me.

This conversation reveals some of the complexities involved in the dynamics of multilingual writers' identity negotiation, particularly when they encounter assimilationist and, at the same time, othering practices. I started the two group interviews with questions about conformity and assimilation in relation with writing in adopted languages in new sociocultural contexts. The responses, understandably, started with considerations about intercultural rhetoric and the alienation of heritage rhetorical practices, but the conversation gradually swayed to a number of different directions that could provide an insight into multiple dimensions of the writers' identity negotiation in their new context. In the course of our exchange, for instance, the participants' identities as women were highlighted, propelling us to think about othering and assimilation in parallel with the function of Anglo-American patriarchy in connection with women of colour. Magda, Clarice and Choman, also, spoke about how in professional workplaces in Canada one's lower position in the institutional hierarchy could reinforce racial and gender discrimination, leading to increased alienation. Choman's position as a Middle Eastern – and thus perceived Muslim – woman immigrant added a new layer to the conversation. It was interesting to see that the dialogue between the participants showed complex connections between rhetorical assimilation and a myriad of identity layers such as gender, race, and religion.

The presentation of the highlights of my conversations with Choman, Clarice and Magda about assimilation in this section is not meant to specify identity layers that are impacted by the imposition of rhetorical conformity. Such an objective requires more in-depth analysis and data collection. Instead, I am using my research data to, broadly, highlight the existence of less visible dimensions involved in the seemingly objective process of teaching rhetoric. When teachers invite learners of English to write in dominant Anglo-American genres and rhetorical patterns, they can inadvertently strengthen larger societal assimilationist ideologies. That is why rhetorical migration can be experienced as invasion of writers' native identities. Our current factory model writing education treats genre and rhetoric as formalistic moulds that can be used by all students to produce homogeneous texts. The system takes very little responsibility for severing students' identities from rhetorical practices. The data that I showcased here can hopefully remind us that rhetorical migration is a delicate process and cannot be harmless if not encouraged critically and with ample space for identity negotiation. Such an approach in practical terms could include: discussing histories of Anglo-American genres in writing classes, discovering parallel genres in students' cultures, assessing rhetorical exploration and critique as well as rhetorical reproduction, and also awarding students for genre experimentations and creating rhetorical fusions. Such rhetorical tolerance can not only create agility but also it can create space for identity negotiation and thus undermine the process of alienation. It is ironic that assimilation could in fact function as a strong form of othering by constantly sending this message to migrants that they are different. The same contradiction can also slow down effective adopting of rhetorical patterns if rhetorical migration is not conducted holistically, with all the identity layers involved.

Immigration as an Intellectual Catalyst

> I don't know how I dared to come to Canada. I didn't know one single person in Canada. No one I had ever met in my life had seen Canada or knew about it. It was indeed 'the road not taken'. All I relied on was an iffy scholarship. How would I make money in Canada? I was really scared. It was the biggest risk I took in my life: Immigrating to Canada with no money. (Choman)

Familiarity with other cultures and 'knowledge of other languages [have] always been the hallmark of educated people' (Cummins, 2015). Michel de Montaigne, Geoffrey Chaucer, Samuel Beckett, Ezra Pound and Goethe are only a few icons revered in the history of

Western thought because of their multilingualism and intercultural knowledge. In the same manner, traveling to other lands has been admired as a source of honour in the West. This cultural significance, for example, created the 17th-century Grand Tour tradition observed by the European (especially British) nobility, whose trace can still be seen today in the traveling gap year. This tradition, however, has a dark side. Multilingualism and exploring new geographical places have been typically admired when experienced by the European rich and powerful and regarded as a problem when sought after by people from other cultures, for instance, refugees and immigrants to the West. In Western colonial history, when speakers of European languages landed on other people's territories, they were celebrated as explorers and history makers, although, ironically, they inflicted terror and genocide upon indigenous populations. For other populations who reached the same lands, there has been less of a celebratory tone.

In the US context, for instance, policies have failed to uphold universal linguistic rights, and instruction in students' mother tongues has been rarely proactively supported by the government (Wiley, 2007). At the social level 'accented' immigrants have been harassed and asked to 'go home', although some have been legal American citizens. On the other hand, however, more affluent Americans tend to provide multilingual education for their children. In English Canada, teaching French often turns into a mere formality required by law, and average students and parents complain about ineffective French education in Canada and poor results. Nevertheless, the limited French immersion system with a defendable track record of creating bilinguals is mostly serving the children of white Canadian upper classes. Conversations about plurilingualism in Europe seem to focus on a celebration of dominant European languages and fall silent when it comes to voicing concerns about the languages brought to Europe by refugees and immigrants. There is also often uproar if demands are made for more funding for the maintenance of immigrants' heritage languages, but seemingly there is continual consensus on supporting institutions such as The British Council and its French equivalent *The Organisation Internationale de la Francophonie*, which have been effective instruments in linguistic imperialism and cultural colonialism. Seemingly, multilingualism and multiculturalism are good for some but not others.

The societal power relations and discourses that regard immigrants' intellectual legacies irrelevant can alienate minoritized and racialized learners both socially and academically. They can have schools approach learners as backward, lacking and problematic. In contrast with this misconception, immigrants and their children are, in fact, intellectually privileged travellers with rich experiences, typically beyond the reach of average citizens of host countries. Campano and Ghiso (2011) urged:

> We should regard immigrant students—and all students—as cosmopol-
> itan intellectuals. … In our work with immigrant, migrant, and refugee
> populations we have learned that students' literacy practices and knowl-
> edge are not merely relevant for their respective communities, but also
> have value for the world we share. We understand this capacity to make
> claims of universal significance as part of what it means to be a cosmo-
> politan intellectual. (Campano & Ghiso, 2011: 164)

This change of lens should not be seen as an act of charity for
immigrants but a recognition of true facts distorted by social discourses
that dehumanize and demean immigrants as criminals, savages, and
inferiors on a daily basis. In other words, regarding immigrants as
cosmopolitan intellectuals is not a theoretical suggestion for creating
pedagogies to empower students but a discursive action to radically
reform dominant teaching practices in the Anglo-American world. What
needs empowerment is our education systems, not immigrant children.
Such learners have rich backgrounds, which have deepened and become
more complex thanks to immigration and cross-cultural existences.

The writers that I worked with in my research are examples of
such cosmopolitan intellectuals and their lives show that they took
advantage of immigration as an *intellectual event*. Clarice defined this
intellectual event as 'international awareness' or experiencing the local,
wherever you reside, with a universal consciousness, which requires lived
experiences in a variety of cultural contexts. 'Writers develop in relation
to the changing social needs, opportunities, [and] resources' (Bazerman
et al., 2017: 355). Clarice's life is an illustration of how a desire to
learn more about the world can shape one's educational foundation
by connecting one with different learning possibilities and also with
different educational institutions. Clarice spoke with me about her
journey from a small town in Brazil to the capital and then to Toronto,
Canada:

> [I studied hard] to get out of this city, where I was born, because it was
> a small city. I was a country girl, so I wanted to go to a big city, which
> wasn't very far, just 50 kilometres away. And when I was in the big city
> I thought, 'this is still not working. It has to get bigger than this'. [Then
> I moved to Toronto.] It's not because I'm ambitious. I think because I'm
> aware of … I have an international awareness. I mean I don't see things
> at a local level only. If I'm watching TV or if I'm watching a movie, I see
> local movies, local TV, but I'd like to see what is going on in very remote
> areas … not only 'Oh, I wanna see what's going on in Paris or England; I
> wanna see what's going on in Uruguay or in Africa'.

Magda, who had frequently worked with international groups to
develop learning projects, also highlighted the impact of the experiences
that Clarice framed as 'international awareness':

I think it's very important for people to see different countries and live in different countries. Because even my Hungarian friends ... even my family they have such views that it's unimaginable for me right now.

The intellectually privileged status of immigrants, migrants and refugees as global intellectuals is the result of a two-fold advantage. First, they employ immigration as a vehicle for literacy – a catalyst for new literate engagements through living new languages, discourses and sociocultural practices. Second, migrating learners bring with them the knowledge of their native lands and cultures. The latter has important pedagogical potentials. Our current industrial education systems rely heavily on ready-made curricula and off-the-peg programs that deliver mass lessons to populations sorted by standardized tests or admission processes. Such an educational structure would regard the admission of English learners as a challenge, if not a shock because they are deemed to require customized treatment. In a more organic teaching and learning context, where humans mattered more than the system, immigrant and refugee students would be regarded as sources of knowledge that could enrich academic, artistic, and literary communities. In writing education, for instance, teachers, instead of imposing genres prescribed by a centralized curriculum, could ask what forms of writing would best help students share their stories. Also, writing teachers, at least from time to time, should put themselves in a listening position to learn about their students' rhetorical backgrounds. Opening space in class for democratic sharing of rhetoric would be a great educational opportunity for domestic and mainstream students to learn from other cultures. In a deindustrialized second language writing education, the syllabus is not imposed on English Language Learners; in contrast, emergent multilingual writers' rhetorical repertoire should be treated as an unwritten part of the syllabus, as a learning opportunity for the teacher and mainstream students.

Summary

In this chapter, I focused on major themes underlined by the participants in my research about the impact of their social lives on their writing. These themes were pooled together under the umbrella 'social experiences' after three chapters which discussed the participants' literacy discourses, the relation between writing and power, and the participants' multi-semiotic engagement. In a sense, this chapter was the outcome of a thematic design for moving from abstract concepts to more tangible social experiences or, in other words, from the participants' belief sets to everyday social interactions.

Despite what could be reasonably assumed, none of the writers participating in this project were 'good', 'stellar' or 'brilliant' students at primary and secondary school, although later in life they succeeded both academically and professionally, even in the face of the hardships involved in immigration and the challenges of living in a new culture and language. An important question to ask is how assessment practices failed to show the potentials of these individuals at school, which is supposed to be the main function of evaluation. It is, thus, essential to think what new assessment strategies, both pedagogically and policy-wise, can be incorporated in our practices to avoid creating unrealistic categorizations of students.

Another important theme was the impact of publicly funded schools on the academic trajectory of the participants. The sample size of my research was too small for generalizable conclusions; nevertheless, my participants' literate and intellectual achievements might not have been reached without support systems funded by the public. What may be particularly noteworthy for policymakers is the fact that the programmes that at times saved the academic lives of the participants were not necessarily grand plans requiring astronomical budgets; instead, the public support – instances of which were presented – was provided by local administrative bodies and activated by the initiatives of individual managers or teachers within the community.

The participants thought that the power relations between them and their teachers directly influenced their writing practices. The findings of this project are consistent with the views of researchers that regard the role of educators as reinforcing or challenging larger discriminatory societal practices inside the classroom (Cummins, 2009b). Next to a concern about the academic content to be delivered, teachers should consciously think about how their interactions with the students could challenge dominant societal ideologies, discourses and stereotypes, which constantly paint minoritized and racialized students as less able because of perceived cultural and linguistic inferiority. One significant example of such everyday micro-interactions is resisting the dominant curriculum superimposed by administerial hierarchies formed and chaired by racially, culturally, and linguistically dominant populations. As for literacy education in particular, educators should engage in critical readings of canonical curriculum to create room for more textual diversity in the curriculum. 'The dominant curriculum, with its unproblematic, standardized definitions of knowledge and its standardized tests, has no room for such activities [creating room for racialized and minoritized populations]—it is too busy being accountable' (Kincheloe, 1993: 258).

As an important example of micro societal interactions that impact relationships in the classroom, the participants in my research shared their struggles with forces pushing for assimilation. For instance, they talked about a constant demand for proof for linguistic nativeness. Educators should ask how their pedagogies create a safe space in the classroom where students' identities, native literacy practices, and accents are not constantly hammered to resemble the dominant models. Policymakers, also, should consider the same questions when developing curriculum. They should ask if their curricula see minoritized students as a problem for the system or an opportunity. Immigrants, migrants and refugees should be seen as global intellectuals with dearly earned lived experiences and as possessors of rich knowledge traditions.

8 Mechanics and Practicalities

Suggestions to reform dominant writing pedagogies that give essayist literacy centre stage are sometimes met with suspicion based on the argument that alternative methods are impractical in dealing with the realities of everyday teaching (see for instance, Fulkerson, 2005; Haswell, 2005). Product and process strategies are established, predictable and 'assessable'. These strategies also comfortably fit the dominant factory-model writing classroom, where all students should write in the same genre, about the same theme, according to the same rubric, and at the same pace. This book calls for developing pedagogies with more attention to sociocultural, political, discursive and power dimensional aspects of writing. So far in this manuscript, I have stressed the importance of pedagogies that take students' narratives and discourses of literacy as seriously as the written texts that they generate. I have discussed the connection between power and writing. Also, I have advocated for creating space for students' plurilingualism, native cultures, multiliteracies, and social lives in the process of teaching writing especially in second language writing. In this final chapter, I focus on a number of themes regarding mechanics of writing and stylistics. This focus, I hope, will attract the attention of educators who view stylistics as the main priority in teaching writing.

In my conversations with Magda, Clarice and Choman, their thoughts about their philosophies of writing and their literate histories outweighed expressions about mechanics of writing. They did not deem the teaching and learning of the formal aspects of writing irrelevant; instead, there was a consensus among them that, based on their experiences, hard writing skills such as grammar and punctuation would be developed much more effectively when writing occurred in authentic writing contexts. Despite this general trend in the data, from time to time I invited the participants to speak about the practicalities of writing in a learned language such as syntactic or lexical command, and also about experiences with ESL classes. This chapter highlights these conversations by focusing on learning the mechanics of writing, migration from pen-and-paper to digital writing practices, and standardized tests for English learners.

Learning Writing Mechanics

As discussed in detail in the introduction of the book, the philosophical foundation of this study is the notion that language use is a form of life and that we learn languages when we socioculturally *do/live* them and make sense of the power relations surrounding linguistic performances including writing in additional languages. The pedagogical proposals based on the findings of my research are a contribution to a long conversation about language education in the English-speaking West with two opposite sides: one camp emphasizing the importance of the mechanics of reading and writing and the other reminding that the so-called 'basic skills' won't be mastered if not learned in authentic contexts created in accordance with students' backgrounds and identities. In theoretical scholarship, this debate can be best illustrated in the stance taken by critical literacy (Christensen, 1999; Freire, 1970; Freire & Macedo, 1987; Janks, 2013) versus skills-based approaches, ontologically inclining towards functional literacy theories (Behrens, 1994; Perry *et al.*, 2017) with their emphasis on literacy engagement for everyday life skills. An example of the same clash in educational policy and practice is the debate between the advocates of phonics and whole language approaches (see for instance, Baumann *et al.*, 1998; Dahl & Scharer, 2000; Krashen, 2002; Weaver, 1988). In second language education, also, the same conversation has manifested itself between grammar oriented and drills-based audiolingual methods, and, on the other hand, different variations of Communicative Language Teaching (CTL) (Littlewood, 1981) and its offspring such as the *Dogme* movement (Meddings, 2009).

A focus on how Magda, Clarice and Choman engaged with stylistics in the process of learning writing – with particular attention to writing in English – took centre stage only towards the end of the process of data collection. The participants' philosophical and cultural understandings of their linguistic performances dominated the interviews partly as a result of the nature of the research questions and partly because of the interest of the participants and the direction that they guided the conversations towards. Considering the debate sketched schematically in the previous paragraph and our stance on language learning as a holistic experience with sociocultural dimensions, we thought we should also reflect on dynamics that helped the participants acquire the stylistic features of writing – especially in English – such as grammar, syntax, punctuation, diction, and so forth. I asked Clarice, Magda and Choman how they learned the 'boring stuff': spelling, vocabulary, grammar and punctuation. I asked them if we were underestimating the importance of stylistics by emphasizing the societal and power-relational aspects of writing. Their response – in short – was the mechanics of writing were neither boring nor power free. They said they enjoyed learning the formal aspects of different kinds of linguistic performance, yet they emphasized this sense of pleasure was tied to the passion that they felt about becoming familiar with a body of literature written in a different language and communicating with a different culture.

An important realization for me in my exchanges with Choman, Magda and Clarice was the fact that the theoretical distinctions emphatically represented in functional and holistic teaching methods did not resonate with them. Nor did they sympathize with discourses such as 'the challenge of teaching grammar and punctuation' or 'learning the basics', which indicate students' need to drill basic formalistic techniques that can be extracted from the 'real' writing process to be experienced later in students' lives. Clarice offered an explanation of the complexity of the process of learning stylistics, challenging dominant one-dimensional notions:

> Let me start by saying that the mechanics of a language are not boring at all. It's the way it is taught that may be boring, but grammar, stylistics, punctuation, vocabulary, spelling, diction, etc. are all necessary parts of a language, both for oral and written representations. Language is social. Without the social aspect there is no point in having language. It is important to learn how to use language in different forms according to a given audience.

For Clarice, thus, stylistic strategies have developed as a result of the social nature of language and not despite it; basic stylistics, hence, are not everlasting universal rules. In other words, mechanics of writing are not *at the service of* communication; they *are* the communication. Grammar, punctuation, and other formalistic features are communicative vehicles and should be treated as such: they should be taught and learned embedded in authentic communication contexts. It is impossible to move away from the power-relational aspects of language to focus on the form only because stylistic choices also are often cultural and/or political decisions. Clarice continued:

> The power relational aspect of the language also includes the mechanics of the language. I will mindfully choose the lexical terms and/or grammar styles necessary so I can have access to a certain type of publication or audience, may this audience require strictly academic or informal language. For example, when communicating with family and friends back home, I make sure to use the lingo they use in Brazilian Portuguese so I don't appear as 'the posh super educated Brazilian who lives in Canada and who doesn't care about Brazil anymore'. Another example is the use of style. In a recent North American journal, I noticed that the use of 'whereas' instead of 'while' was pretty much the norm, so I went over my manuscript and made those stylistic changes

just so I had more chances of having my manuscript accepted. The problem is when major changes are necessary in order to have access to an audience. In this case, I have to make sure I'm not 'selling my soul to the devil', that is, changing my language to the point that the meaning of my message doesn't represent what I originally wanted.

Although grammar is often seen as closely related to style, for Clarice grammar and diction are sociocultural and power relational; moreover, stylistic choices have ethical ramifications and to a degree that could be likened to 'selling one's soul to the devil'. This understanding of the complexities involved in learning and applying stylistics was also echoed by Choman and Magda – the notion that formal elements cannot be separated from larger personal passions and agendas that motivate people to engage with new languages. Choman said:

> I don't understand the question 'how you learned the mechanics of writing'. I just learned them. They are not that difficult to learn actually. What I think is important, however, is that my passion for English literature was the reason I learned the English language. If it weren't for Sylvia Plath poems or Emily Bronte, Orwell, Hemingway or other great English writers, I probably wouldn't have a reason to master this difficult language.

Magda similarly had no particular complaints about a grammar approach to language learning especially because it was the dominant pedagogical model when she learned Russian as the compulsory additional language at school in Communist Hungary. Nevertheless, like Clarice, her conciseness about larger intellectual goals made her believe an obsessive focus on stylistics was irrelevant:

> Grammar, and stuff, has always been part of my learning but the main reason to learn languages for me was to be able to read authors in original and not the translations. Hungarian translations are most of the time excellent but of course the number of available books is limited in translation. I think that reading in original languages is so much more than reading. It gives you a much better sense of the literary culture, feelings and people's understanding of the world without any misrepresentations.

Previously, I described the participants' ontologies of literacy and writing using a number of concepts including 'literacy narratives'. Using this concept, I emphasized the necessity for learners to proactively construct their own literate pasts while marshalling literacy discourses in arrangements that can present their intellectual abilities in a positive light to nurture their future literacy activities. In my conversations with Clarice, Choman and Magda about writing mechanics and stylistics, what loomed over our exchanges was again the writers' larger literacy narratives and their intellectual identities, which directed the conversation away from providing formulaic strategies for other writers to copy as a model of success. In other words, Magda, Choman and Clarice's intellectual and professional identities showed a level of maturity that a question about punctuation and grammar played a very small role in their literate journeys. A lack of interest in learning grammar and stylistics in our students, more than anything else, might be an indication of literacy narratives that need discursive nourishment to grow to a size that can embrace more meaningful interpretations of literacy engagement. Such an approach, of course, is challenging since our current educational structures deliberately seperate learning stylistics from authentic writing practices to offer new courses. In an organic English Learning program, Vocabulary, Grammar, Reading and Writing would not be offered as different classes. Severing these skills apart would make the process of creating a writing identity, based on a nourishing literacy narrative, extremely difficult. As a result, English learners would find the curriculum content irrelevant.

From Paper to Digital Literacy Practices

There is a growing body of research which focuses on digital literacy and online writing practices (see for instance, Barton & Cummings, 2009; Dymetman & Copperman, 1998; Fortunati & Vincent, 2014; Grabill & Hicks, 2005; Merchant, 2007; Withrow, 2004). The development of digital and online writing venues has created a thirst for information about the pros and cons of moving from paper to the computer screen. In my preliminary conference presentations about my research with Magda, Choman and Clarice (while the work was still in progress), the audience asked questions about the digital writing practices of my participants. Most of the questions indicated an interest in learning about 'best writing practices' rooted in a process mentality that believes in an ultimate writing process, effective for all. Such questions, on the other hand, were reminiscent of newspaper and magazine interviews with famous writers, which depict the writing practices of bestselling authors as models to lead to worthy literary creation. Such journalism reveals an obsessive degree of curiosity about the writing practices and literary tendencies of celebrity writers as if societal discourses, the publishing industry, and the commercialized/politicized media oligarchy had no role in generating texts which the culture industry (Horkheimer & Adorno, 2002) exposes the public to. In response to this demand, I asked Choman, Clarice and Magda about their digital reading and writing habits and, considering their age as writers in their mid-life, their migration from paper to digital text.

Similar to my inquiry about grammar and stylistics, the participants were not particularly intrigued by my question about digital reading/writing inasmuch as they deemed adapting to new forms of text production as a natural dynamic in their writing journeys. They thought their use of new technology should be seen as adopting, yet again, another medium for textual presentation of their thoughts. In previous chapters, I stressed the significance of the participants' semiotic agility or ability to shuffle between different semiotic systems, especially between written and non-written texts such as oral texts, music, theatre, cinema, and so forth. At different places in this book, I also discussed the significance of the writes' genre agility or the ability to employ different written genres for expression. My conversations with the participants and my observations of their digital practices guided me to make sense of their digital practices as another application of their semiotic and genre agility. My participants did speak about some particular digital habits; for instance, Magda read a great deal online, Clarice did not use a pen to write any longer, and Choman had a heavy presence on social media; nevertheless, these practices should be analyzed and comprehended in relation with the contexts where these tendencies were developed. Here are a few examples.

For Clarice, digital mediums of literacy were only new formats for textual engagement. Rather than migration, using digital devices for Clarice was an expansion of her literacy practices – a welcome, or at least natural, expansion since, as I previously discussed in detail, literacy practices occur in physical space and thus in a variety of different mediums: 'I think my understanding of literacy has gone through changes over the years just because we have a larger number of mediums'. My observations of Choman's heavy use of social media in relation with her literate history also indicate the same mentality and tendency. As a multiliterate singer, dancer, photographer, novelist, journalist and activist, online writing for Choman was only another channel to contribute to her favourite causes such as Kurdistan, minority women's issues, and minority literature.

Magda described her digital literacy practices as a literate situation among many which helped her intellectual growth, whether she was engaging with paper or digital texts. Here for instance, she, after briefly touching on her multilingualism, connected her computer and mobile screen reading to the way she invited her family members to be part of her reading experience:

> I read a lot of books. I read a lot on the internet; sometimes I just print it; I like reading print-outs. I read in three languages: English, German, and Hungarian, whichever I can. A very important part of my reading is that I discuss it with my husband, or when my mother is here with her as well. It's very interesting because all these topics that I am reading now such as self-awareness, coaching, leadership, and all this is really new to her so I enjoy talking to her about this.

In another part of the same conversation, Magda answered the typical question 'whether traditional books or e-books provided a more fruitful or pleasant reading experience' by re-framing it as: 'how different media provide variety in text generation methods and thus lead to multiplication of expressive possibilities':

> I also see now in Hungary – and I think the whole Europe – a growing need for contemporary literature for there are a lot of writers ... a lot of poets who are just emerging now. There are so many new books and a lot of these writers are writing online.

For Magda, thus, a comparison between paper and digital literacy was more complex than drawing lists of pros and cons for each tradition. She thought such comparisons should include considerations about the different text-generation and distribution possibilities that each format offered, and also the manner in which each event – like online reading – occurred. In other words, the main question in this regard should not be, 'Which medium is a better medium, paper or computer?' We, instead, should ask, 'Why and when do people adopt one format or the other?' Magda's reminder that thousands of emerging independent writers only perform online stresses the fact that the choice of medium is not only a preference, but it is determined by positionalities, visions, identities and circumstances.

There is little evidence to show that new media make or break writers; they, instead, create, alter, or kill genres (Askehave & Ellerup Nielsen, 2005; Furuta & Marshall, 1996; Holdstein, 1996). The printing machine made the novel the dominant genre and overshadowed the significance of oral performance and agora culture. The advent of photography transformed classical painting into abstract representation, and the invention of cinema made theatre less mainstream. In normal circumstances, however, writers – in terms of popular education – with reasonable multiliterate, multilingual, multi-genre and multimodal competence can typically catch up with the multiplication of mediums. However, it is also true that lack of access to new mediums results in technological discrimination (Carvin, 2000; Weidmann *et al.*, 2016). Also, the dominance of newly emerged literacy mediums can reduce the frequency of traditional textual practices. The above propositions justify a re-statement of the theme that literacy is fluid and effective writers (and readers) adapt to a multiplicity of literacy practices and artefacts in different literate contexts.

Experiences with English Language Testing

Standardized testing has been an important area of scholarly conversation in the educational research community in North America (for instance, Allison *et al.*, 1998; Haney, 1981; Kohn, 2000; McNeil, 2002; Sacks, 1999). One important focus has been the aftermath of the No Child Left Behind policy in the United States and its effects on assessment strategies (Cochran-Smith & Lytle, 2006; Evans & Hornberger, 2005; Hornberger & Link, 2012; Hursh, 2007; Simon, 2014). This body of research typically discusses US students as a whole with less attention to language difference; however, there is also a niche trend that specifically focuses on standardized testing and multilingual students (Abedi, 2007). In addition to national and regional tests for mainstream K-12 students in the United States (and with much less intensity in Canada), there is a world-wide multi-billion-dollar business that offers English language testing for youth and adult international, immigrant, and refugee students. These testing companies claim that they verify the English competence of international students interested to study in English speaking educational systems (Ahern, 2009; Templer, 2004). Mainstream educators in Anglo-American educational settings often know very little about the dynamics of these examinations, most of which are administered internationally outside the borders of the host countries. This, however, does not mean there have been no voices in academia warning against the ills of standardized tests such as TOEFL and IELTS (Uysal, 2010). Next to a concern about the enormity of monetary profit overshadowing quality in such tests (Ahern, 2009; Templer, 2004), there have been reports about the unpleasant effects of these tests on examinees such as negative washback caused by the process of test preparation (Alderson & Hamp-Lyons, 1996; Cheng *et al.*, 2004; Green, 2007). Also, scholars focusing on linguistic human rights have criticized organizations such as The British Council and *The Organisation Internationale de la Francophonie*, which administer such exams, for acting as the cultural wing of neocolonialism by promoting linguistic imperialism (Phillipson, 1992, 2008, 2009; Zafar Khan, 2009).

Major writing genres evaluated in these examinations are short argumentative essays and in some cases add-on letter writing tasks, which are typically given less weight in assessment. The essay writing tasks in the writing modules ask examinees to write essays that are variations of the five-paragraph/hamburger essay model with slight differences from examination to examination. The TOEFL writing section, for instance, provides the examinees with a theme and asks them to write an essay of 4-5 paragraphs or 300–350 words in 30 minutes. Generally speaking, the quality expected for these essays, the writing circumstances (registration process, ambience of the exam rooms, and technology), and the assessment dynamics are well below desirable standards even in comparison with not very ideal essayist practices dominant in mainstream schools and universities in English speaking countries. This decline of quality seems to be the result of a combination of factors, but mainly of the large industrial scale of the exams, the highly commercialized nature of the service provided, and the business conducted far away from mother countries with reduced accountability. Despite these problematic characteristics, these tests have turned into the main gatekeepers of the international quota for higher education in English speaking countries, even imposing control over faculty members' admission decisions. It might be a shocking fact, but almost all colleges and universities in English speaking academia rely on the assessment performed by these examinations, although some institutions have also developed strategies such as offering their own English courses to international students.

If you are an immigrant to a country like Canada or an international student, the experience of dealing with standardized language tests overshadows your life for years, to name the major hurdles: language evaluation for filing an immigration application, for a university admission, for professional requirements, and for the citizenship test. Against this backdrop, it was no surprise that when I invited Magda, Clarice and Choman to speak about their experiences with assessment, our conversation soon moved towards standardized testing for English learners. I approached Magda, Clarice and Choman because they wrote successfully in English as an additional language. One would assume that such successful multilingual writers should represent the ideal kind of student or immigrant for Canadian universities and the government in terms of English language proficiency, yet it was not exactly the case.

Choman was a published writer who had received awards for her writing in English. She was also currently working as a full-time journalist regularly publishing articles in English. Moreover, she worked as a fiction editor, often polishing texts written by native speakers. Did the popular standardized tests, from which prestigious North American universities accept advice for picking international students, identify Choman's commendable linguistic potential? Choman shared her experiences with TOEFL:

> It's counter-intuitive and it makes me smile now, but I did really bad on the writing section of TOEFL! And I wrote the test so I could study a Master's degree in Creative Writing and I ended up studying the pro-gramme because my overall TOEFL mark was high, especially in reading comprehension but my writing skills got the worst mark. Go figure!

As indicated by Choman, the problems with such standardized testing are twofold. First, the testing strategies are not effective and the results hardly reflect the actual linguistic competence of the test takers. Moreover, the institutions receiving those results also treat them as mere figures to match check lists with little qualitative interpretation. Choman luckily was given a seat, yet she was never interviewed following the lower writing grade or asked for writing samples in English. This carelessness, fortunately, did not work against Choman, but it is credible to imagine that qualitative approaches to university admission could pave the way for the entrance of better candidates in general.

Clarice also talked about the structural formalities that render certifications of this kind meaningless. She also emphasized the problem of the irrelevance of the writing content in her experiences with IELTS and TOEFL:

> In IELTS I had to write a response to the editor of a magazine and the level of academic writing was somewhat minimal, which was a drag for me as I usually do it very well. Writing response letters to the editor is something I have never done in real life so I found the task very outdated and difficult because of the lack of relevance it had for me. Nevertheless, I got the full mark.

> I took TOEFL so I could do an MA in Applied Linguistics in Canada. I don't remember about the writing in my first attempt but I had to take this test a second time because I wanted to work as a teaching assistant and the score required was higher than the score I'd got (which was enough to attend the programme but not to work). The irony is that I used to be a TOEFL instructor back home, that is, I used to teach people how to get a high score. ... It was a nerve-racking experience. I hated both experiences and to this day, I will sweat to sit and write in a high-stakes test. I really hope I never have to do this again. I sense a bit of trauma here, even though I've been successful.

Similar to many other examinees who I met in my career as an ESL/EFL teacher, the participants had somehow managed to pass the exams, yet with terrible memories of wasting of time and money and also enormous psychological pressure. Most of these exams are typically taken when the examinees are going through dramatic transitions in their lives and the process of testing only adds to their anxiety and vulnerability; this pressure, however, becomes much more painful when the examinees realize that the assessment strategies are so poorly designed and performed that the exam results simply do not accurately capture their linguistic competence – in Magda's words, 'My biggest issue with the tests is that I don't think that most of the time the results reflect actual knowledge and skills'.

Summary

Emphasis on the significance of sociocultural contexts of learning is at times met with sceptical questions about the necessity of teaching 'the basics' in writing for instance: diction, grammar, punctuation, citation strategies, and so on. This book was intended to focus on writers' sociocultural lives occurring beyond their final textual products. Nevertheless, considering educators' interest in the mechanics of writing,

I felt it was important to report my research participants' experiences with learning formalistic aspects of writing, especially writing in an additional language with the lexical and syntactic challenges that it involves. This topic, of course, grows onto other territories such as navigating institutional writing traditions, emerging online writing practices, and assessment practices.

My research participants' reactions to my questions regarding learning the mechanics of writing can be summarized as follows. First, an emphasis on the sociocultural dimensions of writing does not equal a negation of the importance of teaching mechanics and stylistics. It is rather a suggestion that formalistic features such as word choice, grammar, and citation can be best learned in authentic writing events that are tied to learners' sociocultural and political existences. Second, learning stylistics is neither boring nor apolitical. Magda, Clarice and Choman did not mind learning grammar and punctuation and thought of stylistics as an important part of the process of learning a language. Moreover, they thought choosing tone, rhetoric, punctuation, and so on is deeply power relational and involves understanding the politics between writers and their audience. Third, if learners have enough semiotic and genre agility, adopting new writing practices does not have to be seen as a problem but an organic extension of a writers' skills. These new writing practices could include experiences such as migrating from paper to digital writing and less pleasant writing engagements such as standardized tests' writing modules. Effective learners are technically and discursively prepared to interact with new literacy events that emerge in the course of their intellectual journeys, be it new genres in new languages or new mediums born as a result of technological development.

9 Implications, Recommendations and Potential Further Directions

This final chapter brings together the main points presented so far to discuss some of the implications of the book's arguments for pedagogy, research and policy. In the previous chapters, the analyses shared included brief references to practice and curriculum possibilities based on the findings of my research. This chapter fleshes out those recommendations and pulls them together in one place.

A key concept to help readers comprehend the practical implications of the conversations offered in the previous chapters can be best framed as *deindustrialization of writing pedagogy*. Our factory-model educational structures were originally constructed to transfer skills, including writing, to large numbers of students in uniform pedagogical approaches. This factory model was developed in Europe in response to the Industrial Revolution and was rapidly adopted in most urban centres in the world. Despite superficial and cosmetic changes to the system, mainly in the form of a transition from industrial to neoliberal models, most of our educational settings still have the same administerial foundation: the factory workflow. In literacy education, for instance, there is still a belief that language is a cognitive skill that individual students can learn in the traditional physical classroom over a certain number of periods. Like factory workers, students need to show up at school at a certain time, leaving behind their out-of-school literacies and the communities that contribute to the formation of those literacies. They need to attend classes scheduled based on the needs of the system rather than the student. They are also required to produce homogeneous assignments and take standardized tests. Teachers, also, in such a system, are treated as technicians tasked to have the floors run smoothly rather than being regarded as mentors deeply invested in the growth of individual students. The teacher-technicians have their tools: homogeneous learning objectives, rubrics, grades for quality checking, and centralized curriculum.

The writing skill, in such a model, is only another cog to be installed on the machine at some point on the conveyer belt. Writing classes have been severed from content-based subjects such as history, philosophy, and also STEM classes. Even General Ed writing courses are ranked and pigeonholed: Introductory, Advanced, Test Prep, Academic, and so on. In second language education, specifically, writing classes have been separated from reading, speaking, and listening skills. Also they are taught in isolation from grammar and vocabulary classes. From another angle, all these writing courses are at the bottom of a hierarchical business model, which treats these courses as introductory material for later essential courses. In this pecking order, writing classes, viewed as 'service' courses, are often underfunded and their instructors are hired as adjunct or sessional instructors or lecturers with temporary contracts. In this context, prescriptions for teaching 'quality' writing are handed down to teachers in aging syllabi, typically with vague ancestry, to be shared with students through select genres, corporate textbooks, and standardizing rubrics. Such an industrialized writing education cuts off all the organic social, cultural, political, and identity related dimensions of writing. This book highlights those dimensions to show what we are missing.

The research project which the book is based on was launched resting on three theoretical stances which would challenge the industrial view of writing pedagogy. First, most dominant writing pedagogies are innately essentialist, meaning they have been developed mainly to teach the assumed 'essence' or 'basics' of 'academic' writing: often oversimplified forms of the Anglo-American argumentative essay. In previous chapters, I challenged this notion, adopting a nominalist approach to understanding genre. This approach is free of the illusion that all writing genres share the same essence; it, instead, attempts to expose learners to complexified genre representations rather than simplify genre possibilities. In accordance with this mentality, teachers, instead of focusing on genres, should teach genre agility, which is typically gained as a result of engagement with a diversity of genres. In classes taught accordingly, students do not follow genre templates and rubrics; they actively create their own genres, some of which, of course, would bear resemblance to dominant genres such as the argumentative essay.

Second, genres are often seen as static (as opposed to evolving) entities because language in modern and contemporary Anglo-American (analytic) philosophical traditions has often been treated as logical syntax and reduced to grammatical, syntactic, and linguistic formulae (Carnap, 1937). The same mentality has also compelled writing teachers to believe that there is a basic grammar for writing, a view resulting in the consensus that the five-paragraph argumentative essay is the mother of all writing. Although an analytic approach to language has helped us study the formalistic features of language more seriously, its pedagogical implications have been prone to criticism because of their tendency to reduce language to stylistic, formal, and rhetorical features. Writing is an act with a complex nature and multiple dimensions, one being its formal existence. The other dimensions of writing include cultural, political, epistemological, and other para-, meta- and intertextual layers. Industrialization of writing pedagogy, despite the good intentions of many educators, cuts off many of those layers simply because non-formalistic layers of writing are often too fluid to be captured, packaged, and formulated for student mass consumption. Such practice inevitably will resort to regulating stylistics, which can be universally administrated and whose results could be demonstrably documented and assessed. Moving beyond logical syntax by emphasizing all dimensions of writing can undermine the dominance of industrialized pedagogy and assessment.

Third, dominant writing pedagogy has failed to create space for intellectual and cultural collaborations. Writing is a social phenomenon and texts are generated as a result of complex partnerships and interactions. Modern educational structures – which were established after the Industrial Revolution and through the classic colonial period – disregarded organic and indigenous literacy practices and showed contempt for out-of-school and non-Western forms of literacy engagement. A separation from native and out-of-school reading and writing practices has disabled students' organic intellectual communities. Compulsory attendance in the 'modern' classroom – as the only venue where 'verifiable' education happens – has impacted writing pedagogy significantly. The belief that writing can only happen within the classroom space has made the collaborative sides of writing disappear simply because organic connections between students, their communities, and their out-of-school cultural mentors are typically undermined when students walk into our schools. In this book, I tried to highlight the collaborative dimensions of the act of writing. There is a growing pedagogical trend in North American schools towards inviting students to write together. I tried to show that although in-school co-authorship is valuable, there is a difference between the physical act of co-writing and intellectual collaboration. The findings from my research show that writers flourish and perform best when they belong to organic (often out-of-school) writing circles. Such intellectual partnerships can be formal, regular, and traceable (for instance, continual membership in a poetry club), but could also be casual or less visible collaborations (like the impact of a relative-mentor or irregular encounters with local artists, writers, and thinkers).

Pedagogical Implications

As exemplified by Clarice, Magda and Choman's histories, literacy practices do not occur in a vacuum. People engage with literacy in a discursive context: their intellectual legacies, their perceptions of literacy, their values, and the reasons for which they read and write. While trying to make sense of syllabi and rubrics, learners draw upon their literacy discourses in the writing events which they partake in. Writing curricula should make learners' discourse practices visible and encourage students to actively incorporate their discourses into curricular visions and content.

When crossing borders or cultural spaces, learners do not leave their discursive histories behind. When placed in new learning situations, successful learners actively reconstruct their *literacy narratives* with features that can help them maximize productive engagement with the learning material. Magda, Clarice and Choman actively created and recreated their literate histories to empower them as active participants in the new social and educational environments which they entered. Resynthesizing one's literate legacies and sociocultural discourses in new educational settings is particularly challenging in the process of learning additional languages and using those languages in unfamiliar cultural territories, as often experienced by immigrants in their host countries. It is, thus, crucial that educators facilitate this discursive negotiation.

In the above paragraph, I wrote successful learners 'actively reconstruct their literacy narratives' to emphasize that literate identities are not solid static entities that teachers can objectively identify and define at will. Literate identities are complex forms of consciousness regarding norms for semiotic consumption and text generation, which are constantly reformed as a result of our interactions with different discourse communities. Hence, any description of learners' literacy narratives is a *creative* act. Effective learners take charge of the process of their writing identity formation and creatively merge their native discourse practices with new cultural possibilities, imagining the most empowering outcomes in their current circumstances. Educators are an essential part of this identity negotiation and will, consciously or unconsciously, impact students' literacy narrative construction. They need to be aware of this process and nurture it towards positive identity representations. For instance, teachers can create space for students to make their literate histories visible and have overt conversations about students' perceptions of literacy. In this process, they should set up assessment strategies that reward constructive cultural and rhetorical exploration and creative identity formation. Creating a robust writing identity for learners who are to write in additional languages is a challenging and delicate task and requires teachers' support and utmost attention.

Also, writing teachers should be cognizant of their own literate legacies and the way those inform their understandings of effective pedagogy. Similar to students, teachers' backgrounds are unique and local. The positionality of teachers as the heads of the class, particularly in countries hosting newcomers, can lead them to assume that their understanding of 'great writing' is the norm and those of their students' 'non-standard'. Teachers should critically unearth their literate legacies and share their perceptions of writing with students (Britzman, 1989) to help them have a clearer view of their teachers' expectations. Such an approach will help the class regard new writing lessons as other possible forms of writing as opposed to the only form of correct written presentation. In a sense, in an effective second language writing class, teachers need to learn from students' rhetorical legacies as much as students learn about new genres and rhetorical patterns.

In addition to students' literate histories and teachers' intellectual legacies, educators should unveil hidden discourses dominating educational institutions and curriculum. Institutions, departments, programmes, journals, and academic circles have certain expectations in terms of writing style. However, these expectations, and their genealogies, are rarely explicitly articulated and remain invisible, especially to emergent multilingual writers. Educators need to realize that there is not a single norm for good writing. Writing is always evaluated according to dominant communication discourses, which change from institution to institution, and from discipline to discipline. Effective writing pedagogy, thus, does not aim to impose the dominant view of writing but to deconstruct and *re*construct it through a discursive dialogue between teacher and student perspectives. Effective writing pedagogy is the art of hybrid discourse practices.

An attempt to make literacy discourses visible could be facilitated by assignments such as expressive writing and/or autoethnographic inquiry. Autoethnographies help students treat their positionalities as part of the subject of inquiry, and thus help teachers have access to students' portrayals of their discourse practices. Duoethnographies, in addition, put learners in conversation with one another and create space for comparing literate backgrounds while the teacher facilitates that conversation. Multimodal writing, also, can help reveal aspects of students' intellectual and artistic lives which are difficult to see in written representation. Digital writing and arts-based inquiry will open new semiotic possibilities, especially for language learners, where students can communicate their perceptions and philosophies through visual art, sound and video.

Through a lens of discourse navigation and literacy narrative construction, even more traditional writing assignments can and should be treated as identity texts. It, for instance, should be noted that when students are writing, for instance, argumentative essays, not only do they assert and support their arguments, they also construct their understanding of the rhetoric required for the genre. Thus, rhetorical deviations from dominant essayist patterns should not be treated as a problem but an opportunity to comprehend students' rhetorical genealogies. Such an approach is particularly important when it comes to assignments written in additional languages in the wake of multilingual writers' rhetorical migrations across cultures. Accordingly, it is important to move beyond fixed rubrics and create rhetorical and genre space for students to include their native rhetorical patterns, and even their mother tongues, in writing assignments. In the narratives of their histories, the participants in my research presented their textual products as identity puzzle pieces that when put together, would portray their intellectual identities, even the writings which they did not necessarily like. Every writing assignment, hence, can contribute to learners' literacy narrative formation. Teachers' assessment should reflect this dynamic in addition to the traditional stylistic concerns.

An important component of a learner's literacy narrative is their *writing identity*: who they are as a writer, what writing communities they belonged to, why they write, how their writing has impacted the world and their lives, and how they imagine their history as a writer. A more practical question about writing identity for teachers in the process of everyday teaching is: what do I know about my student's *writing trajectory*. Our current industrialized writing programmes and syllabi are designed to deliver packaged lessons to large numbers of students with little concern about students' writing trajectories. It is important to remember that writing skills are developed in a trajectory and not in isolated assignments. Teachers need to learn about each student's writing trajectory and rhetorical repertoires in order to customize their assignments so that they organically connect with students' previous writing. In such an approach, writing assignments are not viewed as a means for teaching what the system deems as an important skill; instead, each writing contributes to students' writing identities by meaningfully connecting with their writing trajectories. In a pedagogy of writing identity formation, a writing assignment is not a self-sufficient writing experience, but a carefully constructed bridge between students' trajectories and their future writing lives.

It is much easier to see the shortcomings of rubrics as dominant writing assessment tools when one thinks of the significance of literacy narrative and writing identity construction. Rubrics function as factory floor checklists for evaluating the quality of finalized written products. Rubrics can hardly be used for facilitating students' rhetorical negotiation across languages and cultures. Instead of using rubrics, one-on-one conferences are a much better strategy for meaningful dialogue and exchange between students and teachers. Of equal importance, and sometimes with more impact, are micro-interactions with students: showing respect, interest, and curiosity in casual conversations and encounters. Every word and gesture communicated between teachers and learners can impact learners' writing identities. Informal exchanges are an important part of educators' feedback, particularly because they are not accompanied with grading dynamics and thus often appear to students as honest and non-judgmental. The process of feedback, thus, should be seen as a complex ongoing relationship, rather than a formal response to a writing assignment.

Besides the concept 'literacy narrative', another major theme describing my participants' understandings of literacy was *writing as a hermeneutic tool*. Clarice, Choman and Magda's perceptions of writing can remind educators of the multidimensionality of writing, often forgotten amidst the current hegemony of report writing and essayist literacy. More than a product or even a process, authentic writing is a complex form of communication with a number of metalingual features including emotive, conative, phatic, ideological and sociocultural contexts in which writers and readers interact (Jakobson, 1960). Effective writing teachers simulate writing situations for their students that aim to activate these metalingual layers of writing by inviting students to work on projects that are meant to involve authentic audiences and to address real sociocultural issues. Authentic projects direct students away from drills-based writing activities towards hermeneutic engagement in search of the best communication techniques. When viewed as a hermeneutic tool, writing is not considered a collection of prefabricated genres that students should copy. Instead, writing genres are constructed based on constant interpretive adjustments between the writer and the audience to maximize communication (Gadamer, 1975; Kent, 1993).

How does this notion translate into practice? Educators who are aware of the hermeneutic nature of writing assign projects (to be completed over time and in different steps) that resemble authentic writing genres such as researched-based writing, oral history, ethnography, investigative journalism, and so on. These projects are designed to target readerships beyond the classroom and are written in response to issues that concern students and their communities. These tasks also expose students to a variety of writing genres to choose from based on the project that they have in hand and the audience that they wish to speak to. Thus, they help writing classes step out of the traditional frame of argumentative composition. They also let students blend genres and meaningfully engage with creating multimodal and multilingual texts.

Regarding writing as ever-evolving hermeneutic interpretation, also, creates new pedagogical possibilities based on two other concepts: *writing as an epistemological tool* and *semiotic agility*. If teachers do not see written products as complete and closed semiotic packages but open projects that allow semiotic flexibility and experimentation, there would be less fixation on stylistics and also on rhetoric of assertion and persuasion.

If there were less emphasis on producing finalized and stylistically polished products, students could more often use writing to explore new concepts and issues in free-form and resolution-free writing. In this form of writing, what is assessed is intellectual engagement through language rather than formal aspects of a perfect written presentation with a single argument. Students in such an approach do not write to report; they write to learn, to examine, to explore, and to push their creativity further. Choman, Clarice and Magda frequently wrote to make sense of themselves, their environments, and sometimes their relationships. The dominance of report writing in our writing education has seriously prevented tapping into the epistemological potential of writing as a tool of inquiry. Most forms of Anglo-American essay writing, academic writing, and grant writing are forms of report writing for a superior in industrial and institutional hierarchies: for potential employers, professional supervisors, dissertation committees, funding councils, and of course classroom teachers. Dominant pedagogy, thus, teaches writing as a reporting and marketing tool rather than a medium for intellectual and emotional reflection.

Moreover, hermeneutic practices – which involve interpretive abilities in different communicative contexts (Rymes, 2014) – require semiotic agility developed through *radical semiotic interactions*. The ability to make sense of different textual ecosystems – in both reading and writing – cannot be effectively mastered by concentrating on individual genre prototypes such as the augmentative essay. In contrast, effective writers make sense of individual genres by making comparisons between the genre in question and other genres that they have been exposed to; and the more various the genres that they have read or written in are, the more accurate their understanding of new genres that they encounter will be. The main job of literacy and writing teachers, hence, is not to simplify genre possibilities – often by focusing on a small number of textual formats, moulded by templates and rubrics – but to complexify genre categories. In other words, instead of teaching genres, educators should teach *genre agility*.

I deliberately started the previous paragraph by using the concept 'semiotic agility' rather than 'genre agility' to emphasize that my research shows semiotic agility is sharpened by but includes much more than engagement with genres. Writing teachers should also be aware that students need to constantly engage with non-written texts: oral, visual, musical, and so on. Print-based genre consciousness is developed as a result of larger semiotic experiences. Effective writing teachers are curious about students' semiotic experiences, the movies that they watch, the art that they produce, the singers that they listen to, the fashion that they follow, and so on. Writing teachers should see these semiotic systems as connected to learners' writing. They should recognize and actively expand them. Students should be invited to write in art galleries, about quality films, about artistic traditions in other cultures, and in response to music concerts and dance performances. This is particularly important for minoritized language learners such as refugees and newcomers, who may have few connections with artistic and literary communities apart from their school, college, or university.

Multilingual writers, in addition, thrive on translingual practices, although most of these remain hidden in finalized monolingual written products. Through a lens of *radical semiotic engagement*, the presence of students' home languages, and the other languages they know, in their written products in the adopted language (and in the process of writing) should be encouraged. Students should be invited to write in response to texts written in their mother tongues. Writing teachers should employ translation as an effective form of writing and design assignments that allow translation between languages. These assignments could be translations of texts in students' home languages into the school's language of instruction, or translation as a quoting strategy, especially in projects that focus on students' cultural heritage. Moreover, learners should be invited to create multilingual texts. Students should be allowed to see all the languages that they know at the same place on a single page as a reflection of their linguistic repertoire. In the same manner, language learners should be able to manifest their code-switching and code-meshing practices in writing.

To sum up the discussion about writing as an epistemological tool and semiotic agility, writing classes should move beyond mono-genre, monolingual writing tasks and expose students to multi-rhetorical, multimodal, and multilingual possibilities. Such an approach, however, might prove challenging because of the shortcomings of the current industrialized educational planning, as a result of which writing education has been oversimplified by being torn away from other intellectual and semiotic activities. There is often little space, curricular foundation, and teacher training for promoting multi-semiotic practices in the writing class. On the other hand, multi-semiotic engagement is a lifestyle formed by communal and familial cultures. Thus, a culture of writing for learning and multi-semiotic engagement may not be easily created in the traditional writing classroom. Writing teachers, however, can use writing assignments as community building activities that connect students with intellectual and artistic circles that organically engage with multi-semiotic practices, hoping that those connections will continue to hold – after students leave writing courses – to enrich their semiotic lives. A shift from teaching writing to facilitating network building entails strategies such as inviting local artists to one's class to co-create with students. It also means that teachers should find ways to connect student assignments with cultural centres in their neighbourhoods. Teachers also should collaborate with students' communities to develop routines that hone students' multiliteracies.

Another theoretical framework with potential for pedagogical transformation is viewing *writing as a power differential*. The experiences of the writers who took part in my research show that texts are never power neutral: they are formed by and mirror macro societal power relations and micro interactions in educational settings. The reception of texts written in learned languages, like those written by English Language Learners, is impacted by macro societal power relations such as sexism and racism. For instance, 'accented' writers might face impairing challenges when trying to negotiate with the publishing or journal industries for disseminating their work. On the other hand, schoolteachers might have inaccurate assumptions about students' abilities and cultural backgrounds under the influence of dominant societal discourses. Those assumptions can manifest themselves in micro interactions such as feedback on student writing, creating a constructive mentorship, or assessment in general.

In order to illustrate the power dimensional aspects of writing, I proposed the concept *the writingworld* after Danto's (1964) theory of *the artworld*, which describes his Institutional Theory of Art. The notion writingworld indicates that written texts are not autonomous artefacts judged entirely based on their academic or aesthetic merits; they are developed, quality controlled, selected, and offered to the world for appreciation by the writingworld's members. The members of the writingworld consist of people who can amplify or restrict writers' voices and support or prevent the distribution of their writing. Those include teachers, curriculum developers, assessors, reviewers, editors, publishers, elite readerships, and also a writer's peers and communities. Teaching writing would change significantly if teachers were aware of the dynamics of the writingworld and tried to make those dynamics visible to their students. Such a shift would create a writing pedagogy that as well as focusing on composition and rhetoric would stress the sociocultural, ideological, and political dimensions of text generation and dissemination. In order to apply this change in writing classes, teachers would need to give more weight to (a) collaborative aspects of writing and (b) publishing and dissemination as a crucial component of the process of writing.

Providing space for *collaboration in writing* can embed student writing – which is typically seen and assessed as an individual cognitive act – in a writingworld where learners' texts are reviewed and appreciated by their peers. Collaboration could take place in the form of co-construction in activities such as brainstorming and peer reviewing. Learners also can be invited to craft multi-authored pieces. Successful collaborative writing typically happens when instead of assigning occasional peer review activities, teachers attempt to create writing circles with greater longevity than a few sessions. To sustain and support writing circles, teachers can invite non-student members, like professional writers, artists, scientists, and so on, to join their students. In addition to technical support, these guest members expand the territory of the appreciative side of the writingworld in which the students write. Providing this kind of support for students is important because most members of the writingworld outside students' writing circles – such as editors, reviewers, and publishers – are not necessarily responsive to novice writers' talent because they consider their role as gatekeeping. Inviting writers, artists and scientists to your class can challenge institutional, academic, and literary hierarchies by bringing together professional and emerging writers and thinkers. Moreover, such co-authorships can complexify the process of assessment in that students and professional writers will be assessed as equals with the same stakes in the quality of the work, even if with different responsibilities.

When thinking of collaborative writing, it is important to be clear about the difference between physical collaboration and *intellectual alliance*. Most research on collaboration in writing focuses on the former; my research generated much more evidence for the significance of the latter. Next to considerations for physical co-construction of texts, teachers should also think of creating discursive alliances between members of writing communities. Such alliances typically require inviting students to develop meaningful agendas for their writing projects; for instance, agendas aiming at contributing to social, cultural and political causes, or agendas for initiatives that address issues in communities that students come from. Attention to the significance of cultural and activist alliances will help teachers view writing classes as *writing communities*, where learners exchange discourses as well as writing skills. A writing teacher's job, first and foremost, is establishing a writing community. A student's writing community could include members from students' like-minded friends, their out-of-school mentors, their family members, and, as was explained, local writers, artists and scientists. The more connections a writing community fosters, the more possibilities for co-creation and mutual appreciation will be raised. Receiving such intellectual recognition is particularly important for learners who write in additional languages. They can employ safe collaborative spaces to address possible stylistic errors without the fear of being judged only based on the lexical and syntactic layers of their writing. This can only happen when people are more interested in what you say than how you say it, and, of course, are willing to support you to best frame your message.

It is important to underscore the empowering nature of intellectual collaboration in writing circles because the writingworld has dynamics that are not always as nurturing as those of supportive writing communities. Written products, both in school and in the publishing industry, are constantly quality checked, assessed and evaluated in accordance with criteria that are often influenced by the power relations between emerging writers, and, on the other side, teachers, editors, publishers and funders of research projects. These parties typically assume that their role as the writingworld's gatekeepers is to edit, reject, or reward texts based on the rhetorical traditions that they have inherited from their institutions, fields, and cultures. Although presented as neutral rhetorical criteria, these established forms of textual communication are carefully protected because they sustain the economic and/or ideological status quo. This gatekeeping entails complicated mechanisms and complex networks.

The most tangible example of gatekeeping dynamics and workflows is the process of *publishing and dissemination*. In this process, the dominant culture filters out (a) alternative rhetorical styles and (b) voices of 'the other' or writers who do not belong in dominant racial, economic, or linguistic populations. People who write in additional languages are typically the first targets of ongoing rejection strategies in the publishing process because they rapidly have the red flag raised: they come with a baggage of 'strange' rhetorical traditions and they write with 'accents' that disqualify them from being a member of the elite. A craft and *techne* oriented pedagogy fails to expose writing students to the publishing and dissemination process and multiple hermeneutic layers that it involves. Ironically, lack of attention to dissemination as part and parcel of the writing process even prevents students from engaging with stylistics in organic communication contexts. As a result of disconnection from the writingworld through publishing, school essay formats have turned into a unique genre on their own and are not usually re-created in other communicative venues. In our compartmentalized writing education, a focus on dissemination is a step that is often left out of the writing class for after graduation or completion of courses. Teachers need to treat publishing as an inseparable part of the process of writing and not something that comes after it. Teachers should view text sharing and dissemination of ideas as a necessary component of every writing project that students engage with.

Most traditional Anglo-American classroom assignments are written for an audience of one: the teacher. Communicating with such readership is by no means natural when one thinks of everyday organic writing practices that help writers, journalists, bloggers and scientists to communicate with the public or at least with their own intellectual, scientific or literary communities. The abnormal nature of writing for a one-member audience undermines the quality of writing. Finding ways to share student writing with the world can turn the current banking model of teaching writing into an experiential writing education, in which students interact with authentic audiences and experience the challenges involved in the dissemination of their views. Additionally, student publishing, especially of texts written by linguistic minorities, can provide learners with a voice typically silenced under academic, professional, economic, and also racial hierarchies.

Teachers can invite their students to interact with mainstream publishers. They can design assignments that require students to submit articles to journals and magazines. Students can write letters to newspapers' editors about current issues. They can engage with book and zine projects to create collections that are meant to be submitted to publishers. On the other hand, teachers and students can take advantage of current technological possibilities for different forms of self and community publishing. Students can create blogs, podcasts, and videos. The class can self-publish on e-stores such as Lulu or Kindle. Students can also write on social media platforms and engage with online writing practices such as textual mixing, remixing, sampling, re-posting, reacting and commenting. In the same way, students can contribute to open-access wiki projects by sharing the findings of their classroom research. Engaging with mainstream publishers will help multilingual writers navigate the complex structure of the writingworld. On the other hand, experiencing self and community publishing will teach emerging writers how to take control of the dissemination of their work and make their voices heard despite the writingworld's censorship practices.

A final recommendation for everyday pedagogy, based on my research findings, is *mobilizing teacher agency* to help students navigate structural complexities of educational settings in English speaking countries. Consciousness about the sociocultural and power-relational dimensions of writing can help teachers regard students' literacy practices in the context of their struggle to find their way through the education system into the job market and eventually in the social strata. Immigrants, refugees, and their children use language, read, and write in order to make sense of the complexities of the institutional and social make-up of educational affordances; for instance: national, provincial and local school and university structures; division of academic disciplines; employment and promotion practices; job interview and application cultures; student loan, grant, scholarship, and award applications; academic stratification, streaming and tracking policies; and accessing recourses such as non-mainstream educational settings ranging from student support offices and writing centres to alternative and bilingual schools. Although typically not required by official curricula, effective teachers use their agency to help minoritized students make sense of the complexities of the system. For these students, being placed in the right class or school or having access to publicly funded student support centres can have a larger impact on their textual life, and their exposure to future writing possibilities, than lessons about formatting a thesis statement or topic sentence, which are of course of great value.

From colonial to neoliberal education, Western schools have frequently failed marginalized populations, be it economic, ethnic, racial, linguistic or gender minorities. Broadly speaking, this malfunction is reflective of the fact that these educational structures are built and managed in the image of macro-sociopolitical power relations that often favour elite groups and marginalize other populations. Despite this problematic history, my research shows, teachers often can carve some space within the same structures to support minoritized students. Teachers can mobilize their agency in an alliance with the students to help them understand how the system functions and when it malfunctions. Teachers cannot control larger societal power relations; they, however, can choose to use their everyday interactions with their students to 'resist and challenge the operation of coercive relations of power' (Cummins, 2009b: 261) if they become aware that 'micro-relations ... are never neutral' (Cummins, 2009b: 263).

The experiences of the writers who participated in my research can exemplify how discriminatory societal power structures manifest themselves in educational settings. They spoke about immigrants' lack of access to resources and discourses; labelling students' academic achievement influenced by hidden racial and class-related presuppositions; silence about flawed standardized English tests sold to international students with high prices; mistaken notions of nativeness for linguistic minorities; forces of conformity and assimilation; and disregard for immigrants' advantages over local populations as a result of newcomers' multilingualism and hence connection with more knowledge sources. Despite such trends and practices, my participants spoke about individual teachers who protected and helped them grow by sharing their knowledge of the dynamins of the system and using its blind spots in favour of students. Teachers – and also teacher educators – should be aware of teacher agency and its impact on the process of teaching and learning.

Implications for Policy and Research

Many current educational policies and curricula have elements that indicate awareness about anti-discriminatory education and thus about linguistic and cultural difference. Any form of equity-oriented education planning creates space for considerations about *genre diversity* and alternative forms of text generation, and hence accommodation for multilinguals' *organic writing practices*. More specifically, however, policymakers need to find ways to *deindustrialize* writing programmes. In previous chapters, I discussed concepts such as fluidity of discourse practices, genre plurality, radical semiotic engagement, hermeneutic design, long-lasting intellectual alliances and authentic readerships. With a focus on regulated mass production of texts based on homogeneous rhetorical models, most of our writing programmes work against these essential components of organic textual engagement.

Centralization of writing curriculum and standardization of writing assessment have given prominence to pedagogical practices that sever writing from authentic contexts. In writing classes, students write about themes and subjects that are, typically, already determined by the syllabi and are formulated in detailed rubrics. These writing moulds often do not stem from students' organic intellectual engagements and thus raise little interest. A rubric oriented assessment regime, also, creates rigid genre restrictions. Furthermore, mass quantitative placement practices often lead students with diverse writing trajectories into the same classroom space. These placement practices ignore learners' intellectual, cultural, and academic backgrounds and rely entirely on questionable forms of linguistic assessment or seniority based on year of admission. Such an approach, especially in General Ed writing courses, makes creating intellectual bonds between students challenging. Homogenizing writing syllabi will only limit students' textual performances because this approach fails to tap into students' various writing legacies and their rich out-of-school literacies. The same is also true of students' future writing activities after completing writing courses. When students leave writing classes, they will usually engage with genres and rhetorical traditions different from those that they experienced in the writing class; thus, rendering the goals of standardizing writing classes in the name of 'practicality' questionable.

As a planning/policy response to this situation, writing curricula should become *open ended and suggestive* (as opposed to prescriptive) to lend themselves to localization in different teaching contexts and according to the backgrounds of individual students. Such writing curricula would allow teachers to invite students' out-of-school writing practices into the classroom. In the same manner, this approach would connect learners' home and neighbourhood cultural engagement with writing class materials and assignments. It, on the other hand, would create space for students to envisage their academic futures and the writing genres that they might engage with when thinking about what genres they should learn about at present. In a sense, a decentralized writing curriculum will be a plan co-constructed by teachers and students (and possibly students' communities) in local contexts and in organic connection with students' writing trajectories.

The current factory model educational structures treat writing classes as isolated credit earning courses with allotted slots separated from other courses, for instance as evident in compulsory freshman writing courses at college level. In contrast with this form of compartmentalization, writing programmes should create *inter- and transdisciplinary connections* to provide authentic contexts and meaningful contents for student writing. This approach could lead to important transformations. For instance, writing courses would connect with other courses for which students are already writing papers and could help students develop content for those courses. Also, experiential writing approaches such as community service writing and partnerships between writing classes and off-campus communities and organizations would be seen as mainstream practice rather than marginal experimentations. Writing classes, in this manner, would resemble writing centres and writing workshops to be frequented based on writing projects in hand rather than attended according to rigidly gridded compulsory timetables.

Still on the theme of deindustrialization, curriculum developers, also, should be aware of the *genealogy of rubric-centred pedagogy*. Rubrics are mass assessment and mass communication tools evolved in industrial educational structures. Curricula that heavily rely on rubric-driven assessment standardize students' writing assignments more than nurture their writing practices and their intellectual identities. Curricula and syllabi should treat rubrics as tools to facilitate writing; rubrics should not become the purpose of writing as grade earners and turn into redlines for potential punishment in the form of losing points. Rubric-driven standardization will only diminish writing quality, which flourishes best in authentic writing contexts where evaluation takes place organically in the course of close and continual interactions between the mentor(s) and the learner or the writer and their authentic readership.

Policymakers and curriculum developers, in addition, should attempt to *decolonize writing curricula*. The main focus of most current writing curricula is essayist and academic genres which are in fact different variations of a report writing tradition that highlights findings and opinions at the service of persuasion. These reports are often presented in transactional connections with supervisors, managers, committees, and councils as applications for promotion and funding, and in a similar fashion with teachers for being awarded in the form of marks and grades. The dominance of report and technical writing in educational settings is not accidental. Anglo-American colonialism – in its classic British tradition and American neo-colonialism – often reduces writing education to teaching report writing and transactional correspondence as the most convenient forms of communication with the ruling class at the top of institutional and political hierarchies. Reports and letters facilitate smooth communication between, on the one hand, mother countries and their colonies, and on the other, employees and business leaders, including researchers and their funding institutions. Schools have traditionally prioritized genres in accordance with the requirements of colonial and market-oriented neo-imperial agendas rather than focusing on students' needs, interests and aspirations and how writing can help them address those. Colonial institutions, additionally, favour monolingualism since it guarantees their access to all corners of the empire. Similarly, from the perspective of Western liberal economies, the dominance of a single language creates a more energetic flow of goods in the markets because all the parties involved in the manufacturing, distribution and consumption networks can utilize the same language.

As a result of this genealogy, linguistic minorities experience the erosion and disappearance of their native languages and genres when the dynamics of empire and market force them to write in the dominant language and its prioritized report writing genres. Students' native languages and genres should be recognized as essential reservoirs of their knowledges and should be protected by decolonized curricular practices. Decolonizing writing curriculum, first and foremost, involves creating new genre possibilities and opening space for *genre plurality*. Writing syllabi should move beyond argumentative and persuasive genres to include reflective, exploratory, creative, documentary, and open-ended writing formats. Also, polices and curricula should encourage writing teachers to incorporate non-Anglo-American rhetorical and writing practices. Such an approach would also lead to a recognition of multi- and inter-genre practices as legitimate writing activities. Students in such an environment will be allowed to create genre and rhetorical fusions. Students' writings could look like genre collages with components borrowed from different writing traditions. In other words, a decolonized writing syllabus is not meant to standardize genre practices but to enrich them by creating new genre possibilities. Moreover, especially in classes hosting multilinguals, students should be allowed and also encouraged to write multilingual texts. *Multilingual text generation* should not be perceived as an experimental approach. Writing texts in multiple languages has a long and rich history and is an organic writing practice that is nurtured in societies with tolerance for cultural pluralism.

Decolonization of writing curriculum also includes *moving beyond the positivist view of inquiry* and the scientific method. Most writing activities in our schools and colleges are organized based on a positivist epistemology that has a strong focus on reporting findings based on logical and mathematical proof. Positivism has an overreliance on empirical objectivity (and human capability to achieve it) and has little concern for the researcher's positionality, participants' voices, and research projects' social impact. Inquiry could, alternatively, be seen as a form of creativity and also activism.

Inquiry has an underlying creative character inasmuch as the truth about the world manifests itself to us only through our creative interpretation of data based on our positionality, intellectual background, and ideological agenda. In this sense, an act of capturing the truth is at best a recreation of the truth through a particular lens. In the same manner, there is no ultimate academic writing genre that can represent the truth in its totality; each writing genre allows us to communicate only a single interpretation of a phenomenon among many. Accordingly, objectivity is not observed through narrowing down research representation to one ultimate academic genre but, in contrast, by broadening genre possibilities to multiply manners of recreating the truth in various formats. Hence, viewing inquiry as a creative act will activate use of marginalized inquiry approaches in the writing class by bringing less orthodox writing genres to the centre stage, genres such as arts-based inquiry, poetic inquiry, narrative inquiry, autoethnography, duoethnography, oral history, diary writing, and so forth.

Inquiry, additionally, is potentially a form of activism inasmuch as an inquiry's findings can impact societal and political discourses. An emphasis on the social impact of research, as well as the manner in which it is conducted, can open up space for alternative writing activities in which the quality and relevance of the topic outweigh editorial checklists. It can also shift our writing evaluation practices from a stylistics oriented approach to a system of cultural capital assessment in which the main expectation from students is *writing as social action*. In this sense, language is used to construct narratives of reality that contribute to the common good. This endeavour would include mobilizing writing activities that can give voice to subjugated populations for creating alternative narratives that can challenge dominant formulations of 'the truth'.

In addition, inquiry can reflect our ignorance about the world as well as our knowledge of it. A positivist understanding of inquiry is more interested in the assertion of findings and opinions than exploration or doubt. Positivist report writing, more than anything, is concerned with formatting language that maximizes the *appearance* of objective studying and thus of controlling the world and its phenomena. If this desire is eased, textual formats will emerge that can also reflect uncertainty, anxiety, shock, emotional complexity and scepticism. Such textual engagements have, for instance, the potential of helping immigrants and refugees reflect on experiences of displacement and use writing as a tool for identity negotiation. Moving beyond positivist paradigms, thus, can multiply theme and genre possibilities to appeal to more diverse student populations.

An attempt to decolonize policies that form and impact writing education could also include considerations about the *spatial and temporal constraints of the traditional classroom*. The fact that writing courses are still offered in allotted time slots in certain official spaces (especially in our age with unprecedented digital connections) only shows the weight of the legacy of the factory model of education over policymakers' attitudes towards educational spaces. This model requires compulsory attendance at a certain place for a measurable period of time as practiced by industrial labourers. Although we often view such scheduling practices as the norm, it is a fact that most great writing was never produced in the modern classroom. The current modernist model, only a few centuries old, is only a brief experimentation compared to, at least, 3000 years of documented alternative writing practices resulting in numerous textual masterpieces (literary, academic, religious, and so on) which were created well before the Industrial Revolution. Moving beyond the traditional classroom for writing education will allow students to design their own writing processes, which are often various and defy homogeneous process models. Furthermore, practicing writing outside the classroom would create more possibilities for involving students' families and communities. It, similarly, would encourage students to forge partnerships with out-of-school writing mentors while strengthening the collaborative sides of writing as a sociopolitical engagement. Finally, regarding writing assignments as relevant beyond the borders of the classroom would let students create stronger connections between the writing instruction that they receive and other academic and professional practices that they partake in. Hence, creating fluid educational spaces can help writing assume the character of an interdisciplinary practice rather than a context-less drill.

The suggested curricular reformations would be more effective when accompanied with further research into the sociocultural and sociopolitical contexts of writing. Writing practices cannot form and evolve independently of writers' interactions with society. Unlike writers' finalized textual products, such interactions are less accessible and more difficult to study; as a result, projects of this kind do not occupy a sizable portion of writing studies literature, especially in second language writing research. Most second language writing research is interested in textual analysis of written products rather than ethnographic studies of multilingual writers' lives. More attention to power-relational and discursive dimensions of writing requires a paradigmatic shift from cognitive and syntactic views of language to theories that describe language as a form of sociocultural existence.

Besides this theoretical prerequisite, writing researchers should *borrow and develop research methods* that can help them make better sense of the para-textual communicative and hermeneutic aspects of writing. This methodological expansion would, broadly speaking, mean stepping beyond the dominant quantitative textual analyses of written products towards ethnographic qualitative projects that can provide researchers with the opportunity of spending time with writers in their contexts (Hornberger & Johnson, 2007). In tandem with this, researchers should explore using less mainstream qualitative methods such as narrative research, autoethnography and arts-based research methods that can not only help study textual products but their metatextual circumstances. In the same manner, researchers can employ methods such as visual ethnography, sonic ethnography and multimodal autoethnography in order to capture the act of writing within its organic intellectual, cultural, and political ecosystems.

Another important research implication of the study that this book was based on is the necessity of critical reflection on the Anglo-Americentric research environment (including its research paradigms and its dissemination dynamics), in which language, literacy, and writing scholars operate. Similar to practice and policy, literacy research needs to be decolonized (Zavala, 2013). Scholarship on decolonizing knowledge (Apffel-Marglin & Marglin, 1996) shows that institutional research is hardly objective and it is often used to strengthen colonial agendas. This notion matters immensely in multilingual education research, in which often researchers who are from racially and linguistically dominant groups study and teach minoritized learners.

A lingering legacy of the modernist positivist scientific method is the close association between 'research' and 'innovation', and in the same manner, 'inquiry' and 'progress'. Conducting scientific investigations for progress is a commendable endeavour, if 'progress' means improving the current situation. Nevertheless, deconstructing the connotative sphere of the word 'progress' (Apffel-Marglin & Marglin, 1996) reveals uncomfortable facts about Anglo-American research, including language and literary research. Over the past centuries, since the period in Western history popularly framed as 'the Enlightenment', progress in research has been associated with discrediting non-Western knowledges and experiences. The idea of 'progress' – as a consequence of scientific inquiry – in the colonial period meant the superiority of the modernist West over other cultures. On the other hand, in the current neoliberal structures, the Anglo-American academia heavily focuses on selling knowledge to 'developing' nations by emphasizing 'progress' in the wake of 'cutting edge' research. As a result of these trends, most Anglo-American literacy research is oblivious to non-Western, indigenous, and local scholarly conversations and pedagogical practices beyond its own orbit. Maintaining this ignorance is a grave error particularly in today's scholarly ambiance.

Ironically, as Anglo-American academia packages concepts such as intercultural competence, plurilingual education, translanguaging, out-of-school literacies, experiential learning, community involvement, multiliteracies, and so on as state-of-the-art pedagogical tools, many Native American, African, Asian and less advantaged European populations have organically taken advantage of these frameworks, although sometimes with different names, in everyday educational practices for millennia. If this irony is understood, Anglo-American research should lend itself to a decolonization process that will result in a willingness to learn from other peoples' experiences. Sometimes research innovation means rediscovering the past through *re-worlding the history of knowledge*.

What does decolonizing language and literacy research involve? Literacy research should revisit modernist 'innovation' discourses and recognize rich non-Western indigenous traditions as valuable sources of pedagogy to learn from. I, for instance, discussed how the New London Group (New London Group, 1996) framed 'multiliteracies' as a contemporary need in Western urban schools, while most forms of learning in the pre-industrial world included multiple literacies. Broadly speaking, the division of academic disciplines and school subjects has rarely been as sharp as what we have experienced in the modern and contemporary history. Learning from non-Western traditions requires the presence of non-Anglo-American scholars as equals in academic conversations. This anti-discriminatory academic relationship can take different forms; for instance, high ranked journals could specify space for international voices to speak to Anglo-American audiences. Moreover, academic journals that are entitled 'International' should accept submissions in multiple languages. Unfortunately, most often the word 'International' in the titles of Western academic journals indicates interest in a global market rather than curiosity about international experiences in their local contexts. Additionally, non-Western research methods and presentation formats should be recognized as valuable manners and mediums of academic investigation. Non-Western contexts breed language and literacy practices that can be used as convenient solutions to current education challenges in English speaking countries. These practices need to be unearthed, studied and explained by international practitioners and researchers.

On the other hand, decolonization of language and literacy research should also be performed by researchers belonging to minoritized populations mainly by proportioning their treatment of the Western academia as the main point of reference. Education has a local nature and as much as 'prestigious' institutions project themselves as capable of answering all educational questions, local questions require local solutions. In an attempt to decentralize literacy research, international scholars need to reach to one another in regional venues in the languages that could be understood by local practitioners and students' communities. Such an approach would entail a reformation of academic promotion strategies that increasingly push international scholars to publish and present in English for elevating university rankings, which are formulated, yet again, by the Western academia. In an act of decolonization of language, literacy, and writing research, Western literacy researchers should be conscious of the academic imperialism which has been eroding organic writing practices in many places in the world.

Epilogue

Modern colonial North American countries have very short histories and thus have not experienced a large variety of educational systems. Post-contact Canada and the United States, for instance, have practically had only one main single form of educational structure: the modernist industrial model, later evolved into a commercialized neoliberal format. Thus, educational policy, research and dominant practice in these territories have largely been limited to experiences of teaching and learning in standardized official classrooms. These highly centralized structures have often functioned at the price of supressing indigenous, local, and alternative pedagogies and knowledge sources (Hornberger, 2002). Although over the past decades there has been recognition of the shortcomings of these dominant educational settings, most of the suggestions and recommendations for transforming the system have not been able to fundamentally and systematically reform the system. Most of the changes have been intended to happen from within the system. North American educational apparatuses act as self-sufficient knowledge generators capable of addressing their industrial and colonial pedagogical practices by 'innovation' and 'progress' in a linear vision of history. Thus, ironically, the colonial mentality that they seek to dismantle has kept them culturally insular and indifferent to other cultural experiences. The very redemption that they are looking for, however, might be learning about the organic literacy practices that the same educational systems have eroded through colonial and industrial practices. If looked at with genuine curiosity, it could be seen that other cultures might actually be already enjoying effective practices that some progressive Western researchers and practitioners are trying to invent through discourses such as diversity, multiculturalism, multiliteracies and translanguaging.

Magda, Choman and Clarice came from cultures where educational experiences were different from those of their North American counterparts. Choman came from the Kurdistan region in the Iranian plateau, hosting populations with millennia of a large variety of literacy practices, to which the modernist educational structure is merely a recent add-on. Clarice experienced complex forms of out-of-school literacy as an underprivileged Brazilian girl in a society with unique economic challenges and complex issues with history, immigration, colonialism, and slavery. Extreme forms of educational segregation in Brazil have had minoritized populations develop creative forms of unofficial education – at times the only form of education they have access to – and also transformative approaches to pedagogy, best known among which is the Freirean critical pedagogy. Magda also, as an Eastern European, had a rich legacy of literacy practices that date back to pre-Industrial Europe. Those traditions included organic connections with literary classics, faith-based literacy engagement, community service learning, cultural reverence for the fine arts and music (beyond the written word), and also knowledge of neighbouring European languages.

In all these three contexts, multilingualism was often regarded as a fact of life. Magda, Choman and Clarice had to learn English as an internationally dominant language, but apart from that, they also spoke other languages significant in their regional contexts: Choman spoke Farsi, Magda German and Clarice Italian. This form of linguistic engagement experienced outside the English-speaking world might be unusual for most native English speakers, who typically feel satisfied with a monolingual life because of the dominance of English. In harmony with this monolingual comfort, in literacy research in the English-speaking world, there is a tendency to accept a narrative that educational trends such as multiliteracies, the multilingual turn, environmental education, and collaborative learning are the inventions of the West whereas many internationally educated learners possess complex lived experiences of such engagements and practices. Choman, Magda and Clarice are a few examples of immigrants with such rich literacy histories.

I opened this document by stating that my research project was intended to highlight the complex literate backgrounds of immigrants to Canada as a form of resistance against societal practices that devalue newcomers' experiences. This book, I hope, can illustrate educated immigrants' language and literacy practices as noteworthy examples of organic multidimensional language education possibilities. It should be noted, however, that although the participants involved in this project have successfully managed to translate some of their experiences and talents in their new home after immigration, many other skilled and educated immigrants have been less lucky, and Canadian society has a responsibility to create agreeable circumstances for them to find the place where they can fulfil their potential and maximize their contribution to their host nation.

On a different level, Clarice, Choman, Magda and I used this research to make better sense of ourselves as writers and professionals and also more consciously come together as an intellectual circle representing the larger community of practicing multilingual writers. As I previously explained, Clarice, Choman and Magda found this project a space for reflection and connection with fellow educated immigrants. Clarice said that the project helped her 'see myself as a multiliterate person and made my translingual practices more visible to me'. Clarice told us that our conversations encouraged her to write an article in Portuguese to reclaim her mother tongue and make it part of her academic life.

Magda, in one of our final conversations, reminded us 'how important it is to talk to each other'. 'We come from different parts of the world, but still we have so many similarities. That's fascinating! How can we be so different and so similar at the same time? We can only understand this through conversation'. Magda's presence in this project coincided with her career shift from textbook writing to leadership roles, and our collaboration provided her with the time and space to share her plans and visions for her new professional direction.

Choman also thought that our collective reflection was a means to overcome 'fear and how much it dominates our lives, and how much it stops us from tapping into our potentials'. Choman was happy to be a part of a community who 'fearlessly' crossed cultures and languages. She said, 'Knowing happens at different levels. There are things we know and then we learn them again, but on a deeper level. I guess this project was a new level of remembering how harmful fear is'.

I also share the same sentiments about the power of this collaborative research and feel grateful for the perspectives which Magda, Clarice and Choman shared with me. During the course of my research and writing this book, I have been teaching composition and research writing courses and have used Magda, Clarice and Choman's experiences as a source of inspiration for my everyday pedagogy with positive feedback from my students. The majority of my students in this period have been monolingual native speakers of English, yet still they state that they feel they are benefiting from the deindustrialized writing pedagogy which I have been trying to develop. It is highly possible that the belief that current genre and rhetorical *status quo* benefits dominant populations is not realistic. Perhaps a decolonized writing education should not be described as accommodation for multilingual writers and should be sought as a norm that will benefit all learners.

References

Abedi, J. (2007) The no child left behind act and English language learners: Assessment and accountability issues. In O. García and C. Baker (eds) *Bilingual Education: An Introductory Reader* (pp. 286–301). Clevedon: Multilingual Matters.

Abramitzky, R., Boustan, L.P. and Eriksson, K. (2016) *Cultural Assimilation during the Age of Mass Migration*. Cambridge, MA: National Bureau of Economic Research.

Ahern, S. (2009) 'Like cars or breakfast cereal': IELTS and the trade in education and immigration. *TESOL in Context* 19 (1), 39–51.

Alba, R. and Nee, V. (2009) *Remaking the American Mainstream: Assimilation and Contemporary Immigration*. Cambridge, MA: Harvard University Press.

Alderson, J.C. and Hamp-Lyons, L. (1996) TOEFL preparation courses: A study of washback. *Language Testing* 13 (3), 280–297.

Alexander, J. and Gibson, M. (2004) Queer composition(s): Queer theory in the writing classroom. *JAC* 24 (1), 1–21.

Allan, K. (2016) Self-appreciation and the value of employability: Integrating un(der) employed immigrants in Post-Fordist Canada. In L. Adkins and M. Dever (eds) *The Post-Fordist Sexual Contract: Working and Living in Contingency* (pp. 49–69). London: Palgrave Macmillan.

Allison, J., Haas, N. and Haladyna, T. (1998) Continuing tensions in standardized testing. *Childhood Education* 74 (5), 262–273.

Amin, N. (1997) Race and the identity of the nonnative ESL teacher. *TESOL Quarterly* 31 (3), 580–583.

Anderson, B. (1983) *Imagined Communities: Reflections on the Origin and Spread of Nationalism*. London: Verso Books.

Ansary, H. and Babaii, E. (2009) A cross-cultural analysis of English newspaper editorials. *RELC Journal* 40 (2), 211–249.

Anzaldúa, G. (2007) *Borderlands/La frontera: The New Mestiza* (3rd edn). San Francisco: Aunt Lute Books.

Apffel-Marglin, F. and Marglin, S.A. (1996) *Decolonizing Knowledge: From Development to Dialogue*. New York: Oxford University Press.

Applebee, A.N. (1992) Stability and change in the high-school canon. *The English Journal* 81 (5), 27–32.

Applebee, A.N. (1997) Rethinking curriculum in the English language arts. *The English Journal* 86 (5), 25–31.

Arasaratnam, L.A. and Doerfel, M.L. (2005) Intercultural communication competence: Identifying key components from multicultural perspectives. *International Journal of Intercultural Relations* 29 (2), 137–163.

Ashcroft, B., Griffiths, G. and Tiffin, H. (2003) *The Empire Writes Back: Theory and Practice in Post-Colonial Literatures*. London: Routledge.

Askehave, I. and Ellerup Nielsen, A. (2005) Digital genres: A challenge to traditional genre theory. *Information Technology & People* 18 (2), 120–141.

Atkinson, D. (2003a) L2 writing in the post-process era: Introduction. *Journal of Second Language Writing* 12 (1), 3–15.

Atkinson, D. (2003b) Writing and culture in the post-process era. *Journal of Second Language Writing* 12 (1), 49–63.

Ayer, A.J. (1966) *Logical Positivism*. London: Simon and Schuster.

Bacon, F. (2000) *Francis Bacon: The New Organon*. Cambridge: Cambridge University Press.

Bakhtin, M.M. (2010) *Speech Genres and Other Late Essays*. Austin, TX: University of Texas Press.

Barr, M.S. (1998) *Genre Fission: A New Discourse Practice for Culture Studies*. Iowa City, IA: University of Iowa Press.

Barton, A.C. and Tan, E. (2009) Funds of knowledge and discourses and hybrid space. *Journal of Research in Science Teaching* 46 (1), 50–73.

Barton, D. and Hamilton, M. (2000) Literacy practices. In D. Barton, M. Hamilton and R. Ivanic (eds) *Situated Literacies: Reading and Writing in Context* (pp. 7–15). London: Routledge.

Barton, D., Hamilton, M. and Ivanič, R. (eds) (2000) *Situated Literacies: Reading and Writing in Context*. London: Routledge.

Barton, M. and Cummings, R. (2009) *Wiki Writing: Collaborative Learning in the College Classroom*. Ann Arbor, MI: University of Michigan Press.

Battiste, M. (2017) *Decolonizing Education: Nourishing the Learning Spirit*. Vancouver: UBC Press.

Battiste, M. and Youngblood, J. (2000) *Protecting Indigenous Knowledge and Heritage: A Global Challenge*. Vancouver: UBC Press.

Bauder, H. (2003) 'Brain abuse', or the devaluation of immigrant labour in Canada. *Antipode* 35 (4), 699–717.

Baumann, J.F., Hoffman, J.V., Moon, J. and Duffy-Hester, A.M. (1998) Where are teachers' voices in the phonics/whole language debate? Results from a survey of US elementary classroom teachers. *The Reading Teacher* 51 (8), 636–650.

Bawarshi, A. and Pelkowski, S. (2008) Postcolonialism and the idea of a writing center. In C. Murphy and S. Sherwood (eds) *The St. Martin's Sourcebook for Writing Tutors* (pp. 79–94). New York: St. Martin's Press.

Baynham, M. and Prinsloo, M. (2009a) Introduction: The future of literacy studies. In M. Baynham and M. Prinsloo (eds) *The Future of Literacy Studies* (pp. 1–20). Cham: Springer.

Baynham, M. and Prinsloo, M. (2009b) *The Future of Literacy Studies*. Cham: Springer.

Bazerman, C., Applebee, A.N., Berninger, V., Brandt, D., Graham, S., Matsuda, P.K., … Schleppegrell, M. (2017) Taking the long view on writing development. *Research in the Teaching of English* 51 (3), 351—360.

Behrens, S.J. (1994) A conceptual analysis and historical overview of information literacy. *College & Research Libraries* 55 (4), 309–322.

Belcher, D.D. (1997) An argument for nonadversarial argumentation: On the relevance of the feminist critique of academic discourse to L2 writing pedagogy. *Journal of Second Language Writing* 6 (1), 1–21.

Belcher, D.D. (2001) Does second language writing theory have gender? In T. Silva and P.K. Matsuda (eds) *On Second Language Writing* (pp. 59–71). Mahwah, NJ: Lawrence Erlbaum.

Belcher, D.D. and Connor, U. (2001) *Reflections on Multiliterate Lives*. Clevedon: Multilingual Matters.

Benda, J. (1999) Qualitative studies in contrastive rhetoric: An analysis of composition research. See http://web.thu.edu.tw/benda/www/methcomm.htm.

Bennington, G. (2004) Saussure and Derrida. In C. Sanders (ed.) *The Cambridge Companion to Saussure* (pp. 186–201). Cambridge: Cambridge University Press.

Bermúdez, A.B. and Prater, D.L. (1994) Examining the effects of gender and second language proficiency on Hispanic writers' persuasive discourse. *Bilingual Research Journal* 18 (3-4), 47–62.

Bhabha, H. (1990) 'The third space'. In J. Rutherford (ed.) *Identity: Community, Culture, Difference*. London: Lawrence & Wishart.

Bialystok, E., Craik, F.I. and Luk, G. (2012) Bilingualism: Consequences for mind and brain. *Trends in Cognitive Sciences* 16 (4), 240–250.

Biesecker, B.A. (1989) Rethinking the rhetorical situation from within the thematic of 'différance'. *Philosophy & Rhetoric* 22 (2), 110–130.

Blanchette, J.P. (2001) Participant interaction and discourse practice in an asynchronous learning environment. Unpublished PhD thesis, University of Alberta.

Blanden, J. and Gregg, P. (2004) Family income and educational attainment: A review of approaches and evidence for Britain. *Oxford Review of Economic Policy* 20 (2), 245–263.

Blommaert, J. (2010) *The Sociolinguistics of Globalization*. Cambridge: Cambridge University Press.

Bloom, L.Z. (1990) Why don't we write what we teach? And publish it? *Journal of Advanced Composition* 10 (1), 87–100.

Blumberg, A.E. and Feigl, H. (1931) Logical positivism. *The Journal of Philosophy* 28 (11), 281–296.

Blyler, N. (1999) Research in professional communication: A post-process perspective. In T. Kent (ed.) *Post-Process Theory: Beyond the Writing Process Paradigm* (pp. 65–79). Carbondale: Southern Illinois University Press.

Blythe, H. and Sweet, C. (2008) The writing community: A new model for the creative writing classroom. *Pedagogy* 8 (2), 305–325.

Borg, E. (2003) Discourse community. *ELT Journal* 57 (4), 398–400.

Braine, G. (2010) *Nonnative Speaker English Teachers: Research*. London: Routledge.

Brannon, L., Courtney, J.P., Urbanski, C.P., Woodward, S.V., Reynolds, J.M., Iannone, A.E., ... Kendrick, M. (2008) EJ extra: The five-paragraph essay and the deficit model of education. *The English Journal* 98 (2), 16–21.

Breland, H. and Lee, Y. (2007) Investigating uniform and non-uniform gender DIF in computer-based ESL writing assessment. *Applied Measurement in Education* 20 (4), 377–403.

Britzman, D.P. (1989) Who has the floor? Curriculum, teaching, and the English student teacher's struggle for voice. *Curriculum Inquiry* 19 (2), 143–162.

Brooks, C. (1947) *The Well Wrought Urn: Studies in the Structure of Poetry*. London: Houghton Mifflin Harcourt.

Burnham, C. (2001) Expressive pedagogy: Practice/theory, theory/practice. In G. Tate, A. Rupiper and K. Schick (eds) *A Guide to Composition Pedagogies* (pp. 19–35). New York: Oxford University Press.

Campano, G. (2007) *Immigrant Students and Literacy: Reading, Writing, and Remembering*. New York, NY: Teachers College Press.

Campano, G. and Ghiso, M.P. (2011) Immigrant students as cosmopolitan intellectuals. In S. Wolf, P. Coates, P. Enciso and C. Jenkins (eds) *Handbook of Research on Children's and Young Adult Literature* (pp. 164–176). Mahwah, NJ: Lawrence Erlbaum.

Campbell, K.H. and Latimer, K. (2012) *Beyond the Five-Paragraph Essay*. Portsmouth, NH: Stenhouse Publishers.

Canagarajah, A.S. (1997) Safe houses in the contact zone: Coping strategies of African-American students in the academy. *College Composition and Communication* 48 (2), 173–196.

Canagarajah, A.S. (2002) *A Geopolitics of Academic Writing*. Pittsburgh, PA: University of Pittsburgh Press.

Canagarajah, A.S. (2006) Toward a writing pedagogy of shuttling between languages: Learning from multilingual writers. *College English* 68 (6), 589–604.

Canagarajah, A.S. (2011) Codemeshing in academic writing: Identifying teachable strategies of translanguaging. *The Modern Language Journal* 95 (3), 401–417.

Canagarajah, A.S. (2013) *Translingual Practice: Global Englishes and Cosmopolitan Relations*. New York: Routledge.

Canagarajah, A.S. and Matsumoto, Y. (2017) Negotiating voice in translingual literacies: from literacy regimes to contact zones. *Journal of Multilingual and Multicultural Development* 38 (5), 390–406. doi:10.1080/01434632.2016.1186677.

Carlsson, M. and Rooth, D. (2007) Evidence of ethnic discrimination in the Swedish labor market using experimental data. *Labour Economics* 14 (4), 716–729.

Carnap, R. (1937) *The Logical Syntax of Language* (K. Paul Trans.). London: Trench, Trubner.

Carroll, N. (2003) *Philosophy of Art: A Contemporary Introduction*. New York, NY: Routledge.

Carroll, N. and Gibson, J. (2015) *The Routledge Companion to Philosophy of Literature* Abingdon: Routledge.

Carvin, A. (2000) Mind the gap: The digital divide as the civil rights issue of the new millennium. *Multimedia Schools* 7 (1), 56–58.

Casanave, C.P. (2003) Looking ahead to more sociopolitically-oriented case study research in L2 writing scholarship. *Journal of Second Language Writing* 12 (1), 85–102.

Casanave, C.P. and Vandrick, S. (2003) *Writing for Scholarly Publication: Behind the Scenes in Language Education*. Mahwah, NJ: L. Erlbaum Associates.

Centre for Canadian Language Benchmarks (2012) *The Canadian Language Benchmarks: English as a Second Language for Adults*. Ottawa: Citizenship and Immigration Canada.

Cervatiuc, A. (2009) Identity, good language learning, and adult immigrants in Canada. *Journal of Language, Identity, and Education* 8 (4), 254–271.

Chandler, D. (1997) An introduction to genre theory. The Media and Communications Studies Site. See http://faculty.washington.edu/farkas/HCDE510-Fall2012/Chandler_genre_theoryDFAnn.pdf.

Chao, Y.J. and Lo, H. (2011) Students' perceptions of wiki-based collaborative writing for learners of English as a foreign language. *Interactive Learning Environments* 19 (4), 395–411.

Cheng, L., Watanabe, Y.J. and Curtis, A. (2004) *Washback in Language Testing: Research Contexts and Methods*. Mahwah, NJ: Lawrence Erlbaum.

Christensen, L. (1999) Critical literacy: Teaching reading, writing, and outrage. In C. Edelsky (ed.) *Making Justice Our Project: Teachers Working Toward Critical Whole Language Practice. National Council of Teachers of English* (pp. 209–225). Urbana, IL: National Council of Teachers of English.

Christensen, L. (2000) *Reading, Writing, and Rising Up: Teaching about Social Justice and the Power of the Written Word*. Milwaukee, WI: Rethinking Schools.

Christensen, L. (2009) *Teaching for Joy and Justice: Re-imagining the Language Arts Classroom*. Milwaukee, WI: Rethinking Schools.

Clifford, J. and Ervin, E. (1999) The ethics of process. In T. Kent (ed.) *Post-process Theory: Beyond the Writing Process Paradigm* (pp. 179–197). Carbondale: Southern Illinois University Press.

Cochran-Smith, M. (1995) Color blindness and basket making are not the answers: Confronting the dilemmas of race, culture, and language diversity in teacher education. *American Educational Research Journal* 32 (3), 493–522.

Cochran-Smith, M. and Lytle, S. (2006) Troubling images of teaching in No Child Left Behind. *Harvard Educational Review* 76 (4), 668–697.

Cochran-Smith, M. and Lytle, S.L. (2009) *Inquiry as Stance: Practitioner Research for the Next Generation*. London: Teachers College Press.

Coiro, J. (2008) *Handbook of Research on New Literacies*. New York: Lawrence Erlbaum Associates.

Collier, D.R. and Rowsell, J. (2014) A room with a view: Revisiting the multiliteracies manifesto, twenty years on. *Fremdsprachen Lehren Und Lernen* 43 (2), 12–28.

Connor, U. (1996) *Contrastive Rhetoric: Cross-cultural Aspects of Second-Language Writing*. New York: Cambridge University Press.

Connor, U. (2002) New directions in contrastive rhetoric. *TESOL Quarterly* 36 (4), 493–510.

Connor, U., Nagelhout, E. and Rozycki, W.V. (2008) *Contrastive Rhetoric: Reaching to Intercultural Rhetoric*. Philadelphia: John Benjamins.

Conteh, J. and Meier, G. (2014) *The Multilingual Turn in Languages Education: Opportunities and Challenges*. Bristol: Multilingual Matters.

Cope, B. and Kalantzis, M. (2000) *Multiliteracies: Literacy Learning and the Design of Social Futures*. Hove: Psychology Press.

Cope B. and Kalantzis M. (2015) The things you do to know: An introduction to the pedagogy of multiliteracies. In B. Cope and M. Kalantzis (eds) *A Pedagogy of Multiliteracies*. London: Palgrave Macmillan.

Cope, B. and Kalantzis, M. (2016) *A Pedagogy of Multiliteracies: Learning by Design*. Cham: Springer.

Couture, B. (1999) Modeling and emulating: Rethinking agency in the writing process. In T. Kent (ed.) *Post-process Theory: Beyond the Writing Process Paradigm* (pp. 30–48). Carbondale: Southern Illinois University Press.

Couture, B. (2011) Writing and accountability. In S.I. Dobrin, M. Vastola and J.A. Rice (eds) *Beyond Postprocess* (pp. 21–40). Logan, UT: Utah State University Press.

Covino, W.A. (2001) Rhetorical pedagogy. In G. Tate, A. Rupiper and K. Schick (eds) *A Guide to Composition Pedagogies* (pp. 36–53). New York: Oxford University Press.

Creswell, J.W. (2007) *Qualitative Inquiry & Research Design: Choosing Among Five Approaches* (2nd edn). Thousand Oaks: Sage.

Cubberley, E.P. (2005) *The History of Education*. Guildford: Genesis Publishing.

Cummins, J. (1994) Knowledge, power, and identity in teaching English as a second language. In F. Genesee (ed.) *Educating Second Language Children: The Whole Child, the Whole Curriculum, the Whole Community* (pp. 33–58). Cambridge: Cambridge University Press.

Cummins, J. (2001) *Negotiating Identities: Education for Empowerment in a Diverse Society* (2nd edn). Ontario, CA: California Association for Bilingual Education.

Cummins, J. (2007) Language interactions in the classroom: From coercive to collaborative relations of power. In O. García and C. Baker (eds) *Bilingual Education: An Introductory Reader* (pp. 108–136). Clevedon: Multilingual Matters.

Cummins, J. (2009a) Transformative multiliteracies pedagogy: School-based strategies for closing the achievement gap. *Multiple Voices for Ethnically Diverse Exceptional Learners* 11 (2), 38–56.

Cummins, J. (2009b) Pedagogies of choice: Challenging coercive relations of power in classrooms and communities. *International Journal of Bilingual Education and Bilingualism* 12 (3), 261–271.

Cummins, J. (2015) *Evidence-based TESOL: Teaching through a multilingual lens*. Toronto, Canada: TESOL 2015 Keynote Speech.

Cummins, J. and Danesi, M. (1990) *Heritage Languages: The Development and Denial of Canada's Linguistic Resources*. Toronto: Our Schools/Our Selves Education Foundation.

Cummins, J. and Early, M. (2011) *Identity Texts: The Collaborative Creation of Power in Multilingual Schools*. Stoke on Trent: Trentham Books.

Curtis, A. and Romney, M. (2006) *Color, Race, and English Language Teaching: Shades of Meaning*. Mahwah, NJ: Lawrence Erlbaum Associates.

Dagenais, D. (2013) Multilingualism in Canada: Policy and education in applied linguistics research. *Annual Review of Applied Linguistic* 33, 286–301. doi:10.1017/S0267190513000056.

Dahl, K.L. and Scharer, P.L. (2000) Phonics teaching and learning in whole language classrooms: New evidence from research. *The Reading Teacher* 53 (7), 584–594.

Danto, A. (1964) The artworld. *The Journal of Philosophy* 61 (19), 571–584.

De Saussure, F. (2011) *Course in General Linguistics*. New York: Columbia University Press.

Deardorff, D.K. (2009) *The SAGE Handbook of Intercultural Competence*. London: Sage.

DeCuir, J.T. and Dixson, A.D. (2004) 'So when it comes out, they aren't that surprised that it is there': Using critical race theory as a tool of analysis of race and racism in education. *Educational Researcher* 33 (5), 26–31.

De Fina, A. and Tseng, A. (2017) Narrative in the study of migrants. In S. Canagarajah (ed.) *The Routledge Handbook of Migration and Language* (pp. 381–396). New York: Routledge.

Derrida, J. (1973) *Speech and Phenomena: And Other Essays on Husserl's Theory of Signs* (B.A. David Trans.). Evanston: Northwestern University Press.

Derrida, J. (1976) In Spivak G.C. and Frye N. (eds) *Of Grammatology* (1st edn). Baltimore, MD: Johns Hopkins University Press.

Derrida, J. (1979) Scribble (writing-power). *Yale French Studies* (58), 117–147.

Derrida, J. (2001) *Writing and Difference [Ecriture et la Différence]* (A. Bass Trans.). London: Routledge.

Derwing, T.M. and Waugh, E. (2012) *Language Skills and the Social Integration of Canada's Adult Immigrants*. Montreal: Institute for Research on Public Policy.

Desforges, C. and Abouchaar, A. (2003) *The Impact of Parental Involvement, Parental Support and Family Education on Pupil Achievement and Adjustment: A Literature Review*. Nottingham: DfES Publications.

Diamond, J. (2010) Social science. The benefits of multilingualism. *Science* 330 (6002), 332–333.

DiMaggio, P., Hargittai, E., Celeste, C. and Shafer, S. (2004) Digital inequality: From unequal access to differentiated use. In K. Neckerman (ed.) *Social Inequality* (pp. 355–400). New York: Russell Sage Foundation.

Dixson, A.D. and Rousseau, C.K. (2005) And we are still not saved: Critical race theory in education ten years later. *Race Ethnicity and Education* 8 (1), 7–27.

Dobrin, S.I. (1999) Paralogic hermeneutic theories, power, and the possibility for liberating pedagogies. In T. Kent (ed.) *Post-process Theory: Beyond the Writing Process Paradigm* (pp. 132–148). Carbondale: Southern Illinois University Press.

Dobrin, S.I. (2011) *Postcomposition*. Carbondale: Southern Illinois University Press.

Dobrin, S.I., Rice, J.A. and Vastola, M. (2011) *Beyond Postprocess*. Logan, UT: Utah State University Press.

Dymetman, M. and Copperman, M. (1998) Intelligent paper. In R.D. Hersch, J. Andre and H. Brown (eds) *Electronic Publishing, Artistic Imaging, and Digital Typography* (pp. 392–406). Cham: Springer.

Edwards, S. (2017, May 16) *What Can We Learn from Canada's 'Appropriation Prize' Literary Fiasco?* JEZEBEL. https://jezebel.com/what-can-we-learn-from-canadas-appropriation-prize-lite-1795175192.

Ennser-Kananen, J. and Pettitt, N. (2017) 'I want to speak like the other people': Second language learning as a virtuous spiral for migrant women? *International Review of Education* 63 (4), 583–604. doi:10.1007/s11159-017-9653-2.

Emig, J.A. (1971) *The Composing Processes of Twelfth Graders*. Urbana, IL: National Council of Teachers of English.

Evans, B.A. and Hornberger, N.H. (2005) No child left behind: Repealing and unpeeling federal language education policy in the United States. *Language Policy* 4 (1), 87–106.

Ewald, H.R. (1999) A tangled web of discourses: On post-process pedagogy and communicative interaction. In T. Kent (ed.) *Post-process Theory: Beyond the Writing Process Paradigm* (pp. 116–131). Carbondale: Southern Illinois University Press.

Fabricant, M. and Fine, M. (2015) *Charter Schools and the Corporate Makeover of Public Education: What's at Stake?* New York: Teachers College Press.

Faez, F. (2011) Are you a native speaker of English? Moving beyond a simplistic dichotomy. *Critical Inquiry in Language Studies* 8 (4), 378–399.

Falchikov, N. (1986) Product comparisons and process benefits of collaborative peer group and self assessments. *Assessment and Evaluation in Higher Education* 11 (2), 146–166.

Faltis, C. (1997) Case study methods in researching language and education. In *Encyclopedia of Language and Education* (pp. 145–152). Cham: Springer.

Farr, M. (1993) Essayist literacy and other verbal performances. *Written Communication* 10 (1), 4–38.

Feldman, D. (2011) Beyond the classroom: Writing as therapy. *Journal of Poetry Therapy* 24 (2), 93–104.

Fields, G. and Matsuda, P.K. (2018) Advanced rhetoric and socially situated writing. In P.A. Malovrh and A.G. Benati (eds) *The Handbook of Advanced Proficiency in Second Language Acquisition* (pp. 527–546). Maden, MA: Wiley Blackwell.

Fish, S.E. (1976) Interpreting the 'variorum'. *Critical Inquiry* 2 (3), 465–485.

Fleras, A. (2014) *Immigration Canada: Evolving Realities and Emerging Challenges in a Postnational World*. Vancouver, BC: UBC Press.

Flower, L. (2003) Talking across difference: Intercultural rhetoric and the search for situated knowledge. *College Composition and Communication* 55 (1), 38–68.

Foley, M. (1989) Unteaching the five-paragraph essay. *Teaching English in the Two-Year College* 16 (4), 231–235.

Fortunati, L. and Vincent, J. (2014) Sociological insights on the comparison of writing/reading on paper with writing/reading digitally. *Telematics and Informatics* 31 (1), 39–51.

Foucault, M. (2002) *The Archaeology of Knowledge*. London: Routledge.

Frater, G. (2004) Improving Dean's writing: Or, what shall we tell the children? *Literacy* 38 (2), 78–82.

Freire, P. (1970) *Pedagogy of the Oppressed* (Myra Bergman Ramos Trans.). New York: Continuum.

Freire, P. and Macedo, D.P. (1987) *Literacy: Reading the Word & the World*. South Hadley, MA: Bergin & Garvey Publishers.

Fulkerson, R. (2005) Composition at the turn of the twenty-first century. *College Composition and Communication* 56 (4), 654–687.

Furuta, R. and Marshall, C C. (1996) Genre as reflection of technology in the world-wide web. In S. Fraïssé, F. Garzotto, T. Isakowitz, J. Nanard and M. Nanard (eds) *Hypermedia Design* (pp. 182–195). London: Springer.

Gadamer, H.G. (1975) *Truth and Method* (trans). Garrett Barden and John Cumming. New York: Crossroad.

García, O. (2011) *Bilingual Education in the 21st Century: A Global Perspective*. Chichester: John Wiley & Sons.

García, O. and Baker, C. (2007) *Bilingual Education: An Introductory Reader*. Clevedon: Multilingual Matters.

García, O. and Li Wei (2014) *Translanguaging: Language, Bilingualism and Education*. London: Palgrave Macmillan.

García, O., Skutnabb-Kangas, T. and Torres-Guzmán, M.E. (2006) *Imagining Multilingual Schools: Languages in Education and Glocalization*. Clevedon: Multilingual Matters.

Gee, J.P. (1986) Orality and literacy: From the savage mind to ways with words. *TESOL Quarterly* 20 (4), 719–746.

Gee, J.P. (1989) Literacy, discourse, and linguistics: Introduction. *The Journal of Education* 171 (1), 5–176.

Gee, J.P. (1998) What is literacy? In V. Zamel and R. Spack (eds) *Negotiating Academic Literacies: Teaching and Learning Across Languages and Cultures* (pp. 51–61). Mahwah, NJ: Erlbaum.

Gee, J.P. (1999) Critical issues: Reading and the New Literacy Studies: Reframing the National Academy of Sciences report on reading. *Journal of Literacy Research* 31 (3), 355–374.

Gee, J.P. (2008) *Social Linguistics and Literacies* (3rd edn). London; New York: Routledge.

Gee, J.P., Hull, G.A. and Lankshear, C. (1996) *The New Work Order: Behind the Language of the New Capitalism*. Boulder, CO: Westview Press.

Genette, G. (1992) *The Architext: An Introduction*. Berkeley, CA: University of California Press.

Genette, G. (1997) *Paratexts: Thresholds of Interpretation*. Cambridge: Cambridge University Press.

George, D. and Trimbur, J. (2001) Cultural studies and composition. In G. Tate, A. Rupiper and K. Schick (eds) *A Guide to Composition Pedagogies* (pp. 71–91). New York: Oxford University Press.

Giroir, S. (2014) Narratives of participation, identity, and positionality: Two cases of Saudi learners of English in the United States. *TESOL Quarterly* 48 (1), 34–56.

Giroux, H.A. (1987) Critical literacy and student experience: Donald Graves' approach to literacy. *Language Arts* 64 (2), 175–181.

Golden, A. and Lanza, E. (2013) Metaphors of culture: Identity construction in migrants' narrative discourse. *Intercultural Pragmatics* 10 (2), 295–314.

Grabill, J.T. and Hicks, T. (2005) Multiliteracies meet methods: The case for digital writing in English education. *English Education* 37 (4), 301–311.

Green, A. (2007) *IELTS Washback in Context: Preparation for Academic Writing in Higher Education*. New York: Cambridge University Press.

Grote, E., Oliver, R. and Rochecouste, J. (2014) Code-switching and Indigenous workplace learning: Cross-cultural competence training or cultural assimilation? In K. Dunworth and G. Zhang (eds) *Critical Perspectives on Language Education* (pp. 101–117). Springer.

Gunter, H.M., Hall, D. and Apple, M.W. (2017) *Corporate Elites and the Reform of Public Education*. Bristol: Policy Press.

Guo, S. (2009) Difference, deficiency, and devaluation: Tracing the roots of non-recognition of foreign credentials for immigrant professionals in Canada. *The Canadian Journal for the Study of Adult Education* 22 (1), 37.

Hancock, D.R. and Algozzine, R. (2006) *Doing Case Study Research: A Practical Guide for Beginning Researchers*. New York: Teachers College Press.

Haney, W. (1981) Validity, vaudeville, and values: A short history of social concerns over standardized testing. *American Psychologist* 36 (10), 1021–1034.

Harris, M. (1968) *The Rise of Anthropological Theory: A History of Theories of Culture*. New York: Crowell.

Haswell, R.H. (2005) NCTE/CCCC's recent war on scholarship. *Written Communication* 22 (2), 198–223.

Hatch, J.A. (2002) *Doing Qualitative Research in Education Settings*. Albany: State University of New York Press.

Hatim, B. (1997) *Communication Across Cultures: Translation Theory and Contrastive Text Linguistics*. Exeter: University of Exeter Press.

Heath, S.B. (1983) *Ways with Words: Language, Life, and Work in Communities and Classrooms*. Cambridge: Cambridge University Press.

Heath, S.B. and Street, B.V. (2008) *On Ethnography: Approaches to Language and Literacy Research*. New York: Teachers College Press: NCRLL/National Conference on Research in Language and Literacy.

Higby, E., Kim, J. and Obler, L.K. (2013) Multilingualism and the brain. *Annual Review of Applied Linguistics* 33, 68–101.

Hill, S. and Provost, F. (2003) The myth of the double-blind review? Author identification using only citations. *SIGKDD Explorations* 5 (2), 179–184.

Hobson, E.H. (2001) Writing center pedagogy. In G. Tate, A. Rupiper and K. Schick (eds) *A Guide to Composition Pedagogies* (pp. 165–182). New York: Oxford University Press.

Hochschild, J.L. (2003) Social class in public schools. *Journal of Social Issues* 59 (4), 821–840.

Holdstein, D.H. (1996) Power, genre, and technology. *College Composition and Communication* 47 (2), 279–284.

Horkheimer, M. and Adorno, T.W. (2002) *Dialectic of Enlightenment: Philosophical Fragments* (E. Jephcott, trans.). *Cultural Memory in the Present*. Palo Alto, CA: Stanford University Press. (Original Work Published 1947).

Hornberger, N.H. (2002) Multilingual language policies and the continua of biliteracy: An ecological approach. *Language Policy* 1 (1), 27–51.

Hornberger, N.H. and Johnson, D.C. (2007) Slicing the onion ethnographically: Layers and spaces in multilingual language education policy and practice. *TESOL Quarterly* 41 (3), 509–532.

Hornberger, N.H. and Link, H. (2012) Translanguaging and transnational literacies in multilingual classrooms: A biliteracy lens. *International Journal of Bilingual Education and Bilingualism* 15 (3), 261–278.

Howard, R.M. (2001) Collaborative pedagogy. In G. Tate, A. Rupiper and K. Schick (eds) *A Guide to Composition Pedagogies* (pp. 54–70). New York: Oxford University Press.

Hume, D. (2000) *An Enquiry Concerning Human Understanding: A Critical Edition.* Oxford: Oxford University Press.

Hursh, D. (2007) Assessing no child left behind and the rise of neoliberal education policies. *American Educational Research Journal* 44 (3), 493–518.

Hyland, K. (2003) Genre-based pedagogies: A social response to process. *Journal of Second Language Writing* 12 (1), 17–29.

Hyland, K. (2007) Genre pedagogy: Language, literacy and L2 writing instruction. *Journal of Second Language Writing* 16 (3), 148–164.

Innes, G. (18 Oct 2016) Degrees of debt: The failure of creative writing courses. See https://overland.org.au/2016/10/degrees-of-debt-the-failure-of-creative-writing-courses/.

Iser, W. (1980) Interaction between text and reader. In S.R. Suleiman and I.I. Crosman (eds) *The Reader in the Text: Essays on Audience and Interpretation* (pp. 106–119). Princeton, NJ: Princeton University Press.

Jakobson, R. (1960) Linguistics and poetics. *Style in Language* (pp. 350–377). MA: MIT Press.

Janks, H. (2010) *Literacy and Power.* London and New York: Routledge.

Janks, H. (2013) Critical literacy in teaching and research. *Education Inquiry* 4 (2), 225–242.

Janssen, T., Braaksma, M. and Rijlaarsdam, G. (2006) Literary reading activities of good and weak students: A think aloud study. *European Journal of Psychology of Education* 21 (1), 35–52.

Jarratt, C.J. (2001) Feminist pedagogy. In G. Tate, A. Rupiper and K. Schick (eds) *A Guide to Composition Pedagogies* (pp. 113–131). New York: Oxford University Press.

Jarratt, S.C.F. and Worsham, L. (1998) *Feminism and Composition Studies: In Other Words.* New York: Modern Language Association of America.

Jewitt, C. and Kress, G. (2003) *Multimodal Literacy.* New York: Peter Lang.

Johnson, D.M. (1992) Interpersonal involvement in discourse: Gender variation in L2 writers' complimenting strategies. *Journal of Second Language Writing* 1 (3), 195–215.

Jones, A. and Clark, N. (Monday 3 March 2014) The independent bath literature festival: Creative writing courses are a waste of time, says Hanif Kureishi (who teaches one). See http://www.independent.co.uk/arts-entertainment/books/news/the-independent-bath-literature-festival-creative-writing-courses-are-a-waste-of-time-says-hanif-9166697.html.

Journet, D. (1999) Writing within (and between) disciplinary genres: The 'adaptive landscape' as a case study in interdisciplinary rhetoric. In T. Kent (ed.) *Post-process Theory: Beyond the Writing Process Paradigm* (pp. 96–115). Carbondale: Southern Illinois University Press.

Julier, L. (2001) Community-service pedagogy. In G. Tate, A. Rupiper and K. Schick (eds) *A Guide to Composition Pedagogies* (pp. 132–148). New York: Oxford University Press.

Kaas, L. and Manger, C. (2012) Ethnic discrimination in Germany's labour market: A field experiment. *German Economic Review* 13 (1), 1–20.

Kafle, M. and Canagarajah, A.S. (2015) Multiliteracies, pedagogies, and academic literacy. In W.E. Wright and S. Boun (eds) *The Handbook of Bilingual and Multilingual Education* (pp. 241–252). Chichester: John Wiley & Sons, Ltd.

Kalan, A. (2014) A practice-oriented definition of post-process second language writing theory. *TESL Canada Journal* 32 (1), 1–18.

Kalan, A. (2016) *Who's Afraid of Multilingual Education? Conversations with Tove Skutnabb-Kangas, Jim Cummins, Ajit Mohanty and Stephen Bahry about the Iranian Context and Beyond.* Bristol: Multilingual Matters.

Kamberelis, G. (2001) Producing of heteroglossic classroom (micro) cultures through hybrid discourse practice. *Linguistics and Education* 12 (1), 85–125.

Kanno, Y. and Norton, B. (2003) Imagined communities and educational possibilities: Introduction. *Journal of Language, Identity, and Education* 2 (4), 241–249.

Kaplan, D. (1972) What is Russell's theory of descriptions? In D. Pears (ed.) *Bertrand Russell: A Collection of Critical Essays* (1st edn, pp. 277–295). Garden City, N.Y.: Anchor Books.

Kaplan, R. (1966) Cultural thought patterns in intercultural education. *Language Learning* 16 (1), 1–20.

Karwowski, M. (2010) Are creative students really welcome in the classrooms? Implicit theories of 'good' and 'creative' student personality among Polish teachers. *Procedia-Social and Behavioral Sciences* 2 (2), 1233–1237.

Keh, C.L. (1990) Feedback in the writing process: A model and methods for implementation. *ELT Journal* 44 (4), 294–304.

Kent, T. (1993) *Paralogic Rhetoric: A Theory of Communicative Interaction*. Cranbury, NJ: Associated University Presses.

Kent, T. (1999) *Post-process Theory: Beyond the Writing-Process Paradigm*. Carbondale: Southern Illinois University Press.

Kent, T. (2011) Preface: Righting writing. In S.I. Dobrin, M. Vastola and J.A. Rice (eds) *Beyond Postprocess* (pp. xi–xxii). Logan, UT: Utah State University Press.

Kerekes, J. (2005) Before, during, and after the event: Getting the job (or not) in an employment interview. In B. Bardovi-Harlig and B. Hartford (eds) *Interlanguage Pragmatics: Exploring Institutional Talk* (pp. 99–131). Mahwah, NJ: Lawrence Erlbaum.

Kerekes, J. (2007) The co-construction of a gatekeeping encounter: An inventory of verbal actions. *Journal of Pragmatics* 39 (11), 1942–1973.

Kerekes, J. (2018) Language preparation for internationally educated professionals. In B. Vine (ed.) *The Routledge Handbook of Language in the Workplace* (pp. 413–424). New York: Routledge.

Kerkman, D.D. and Siegler, R.S. (1993) Individual differences and adaptive flexibility in lower-income children's strategy choices. *Learning and Individual Differences* 5 (2), 113–136.

Kesselman, J.R. (2001) Policies to stem the brain drain: Without Americanizing Canada. *Canadian Public Policy/Analyse De Politiques* 27 (1), 77–93.

Kilomba, G. (2015) *While I write*. [YouTube Video]. See https://www.youtube.com/watch?v=UKUaOwfmA9w.

Kincheloe, J. (1993) The politics of race, history, and curriculum. In A. Castenell Louis and W. Pinar (eds) *Understanding Curriculum as Racial Text: Representations of Identity and Difference in Education* (pp. 249–262). Albany, NY: State University of New York Press.

King, E.B., Mendoza, S.A., Madera, J.M., Hebl, M.R. and Knight, J.L. (2006) What's in a name? A multiracial investigation of the role of occupational stereotypes in selection decisions. *Journal of Applied Social Psychology* 36 (5), 1145–1159.

Kitchin, R. (2014) Engaging publics: Writing as praxis. *Cultural Geographies* 21 (1), 153–157.

Kohn, A. (2000) *The Case Against Standardized Testing: Raising the Scores, Ruining the Schools*. Portsmouth, NH: Heinemann

Kong, K. (1998) Are simple business request letters really simple? A comparison of Chinese and English business request letters. *Text* 18 (1), 103–141.

Krahn, H., Derwing, T., Mulder, M. and Wilkinson, L. (2000) Educated and underemployed: Refugee integration into the Canadian labour market. *Journal of International Migration and Integration* 1 (1), 59–84.

Kramsch, C. (1997) Guest column: The privilege of the nonnative speaker. *Publications of the Modern Language Association of America* 359–369.

Krashen, S. (2002) Defending whole language: The limits of phonics instruction and the efficacy of whole language instruction. *Reading Improvement* 39 (1), 32–42.

Kubota, R. and Lehner, A. (2004) Toward critical contrastive rhetoric. *Journal of Second Language Writing* 13 (1), 7–27.

Kuhn, T.S. (1970) *The Structure of Scientific Revolutions* (2nd Enl. edn). Chicago: University of Chicago Press.

Ladson-Billings, G. and Tate, W.F. (1995) Toward a critical race theory of education. *Teachers College Record* 97 (1), 47–68.

Lam, W.S.E. (2000) L2 literacy and the design of the self: A case study of a teenager writing on the internet. *TESOL Quarterly* 34 (3), 457–482.

Lamarque, P. (2008) *The Philosophy of Literature*. Wiley-Blackwell.

Lambert, R. (1999) Language and intercultural competence. In J. Lo Bianco, A.J. Liddicoat and C. Crozet (eds) *Striving for the Third Place: Intercultural Competence Through Language Education* (pp. 65–72). Melbourne: Language Australia.

Lankshear, C. and Knobel, M. (2003) From 'reading' to the 'New literacy studies'. In C. Lankshear and M. Knobel (eds) *New Literacies: Changing Knowledge in the Classroom* (pp. 3–22). Philadelphia, PA: Open University Press.

Lareau, A. (1987) Social class differences in family-school relationships: The importance of cultural capital. *Sociology of Education* 60 (2), 73–85.

Lawson, A. (2004) Postcolonial theory and the 'settler' subject. *Essays on Canadian Writing* 56 (Fall 1995), 20–36.

Lea, M.R. and Street, B.V. (1998) Student writing in higher education: An academic literacies approach. *Studies in Higher Education* 23 (2), 157–172.

Leki, I. (2003) Coda: Pushing L2 writing research. *Journal of Second Language Writing* 12 (1), 103–105. 10.1016/S1060-3743(02)00128-5.

Levis, J.M. and Levis, G.M. (2003) A project-based approach to teaching research writing to nonnative writers. *Professional Communication, IEEE Transactions On* 46 (3), 210–220.

Lillis, T. and Curry, M.J. (2006) Professional academic writing by multilingual scholars: Interactions with literacy brokers in the production of English-medium texts. *Written Communication* 23 (1), 3–35.

Littlewood, W. (1981) *Communicative Language Teaching: An Introduction*. Cambridge: Cambridge University Press.

Lo Bianco, J., Liddicoat, A.J. and Crozet, C. (1999) *Striving for the Third Place: Intercultural Competence Through Language Education*. Melbourne: Language Australia.

López, G.R. (2003) The (racially neutral) politics of education: A critical race theory perspective. *Educational Administration Quarterly* 39 (1), 68–94.

Lorente, B.P. (2017) *Scripts of Servitude: Language, Labor Migration and Transnational Domestic Work*. Bristol: Multilingual Matters.

Loux, M. (2002) *Metaphysics: A Contemporary Introduction* (2nd edn). London: Routledge.

Lycan, W.G. (2000) *Philosophy of Language: A Contemporary Introduction*. London: Routledge.

Lysaker, J. (2014) Writing as praxis. *The Journal of Speculative Philosophy* 28 (4), 521–536.

Macdonald, D. (2004) Curriculum change in health and physical education: The devil's perspective. *Journal of Physical Education New Zealand* 37, 70–83.

Mathieu, P., Parks, S.J. and Rousculp, T. (eds) (2011) *Circulating Communities: The Tactics and Strategies of Community Publishing*. Lanham: Lexington Books.

Matsuda, P.K., Canagarajah, A.S., Harklau, L., Hyland, K. and Warschauer, M. (2003) Changing currents in second language writing research: A colloquium. *Journal of Second Language Writing* 12 (2), 151–179.

McKinley, J. (2013) Displaying critical thinking in EFL academic writing: A discussion of Japanese to English contrastive rhetoric. *RELC Journal* 44 (2), 195–208.

McNeil, L. (2002) *Contradictions of School Reform: Educational Costs of Standardized Testing*. London: Routledge.

Meddings, L. (2009) In S. Thornbury (ed.) *Teaching Unplugged: Dogme in English Language Teaching*. Peaslake, Surrey: Delta.

Merchant, G. (2007) Writing the future in the digital age. *Literacy* 41 (3), 118–128.

Merriam, S.B. (1998) In Merriam S.B. (ed.) *Qualitative Research and Case Study Applications in Education* (2nd edn). San Francisco, CA: Jossey-Bass Publishers.

Messias, E. (2003) Income inequality, illiteracy rate, and life expectancy in Brazil. *American Journal of Public Health* 93 (8), 1294–1296.

Miller, E.R. (2014) *The Language of Adult Immigrants: Agency in the Making*. Bristol: Multilingual Matters.

Moll, L.C., Amanti, C., Neff, D. and Gonzalez, N. (1992) Funds of knowledge for teaching: Using a qualitative approach to connect homes and classrooms. *Theory into Practice* 31 (2), 132–141.

Montero, M.K. and Rossi, M.A. (2012) Exploring oral history methodology as a culturally responsive way to support the writing development of secondary English language learners. *Oral History Forum D'histoire Orale 32* (Special Issue 'Making Educational Oral Histories in the 21st Century'), 1–26.

New London Group (1996) A pedagogy of multiliteracies: Designing social futures. *Harvard Educational Review* 66 (1), 60–92.

Nir, B. and Berman, R.A. (2010) Complex syntax as a window on contrastive rhetoric. *Journal of Pragmatics* 42 (3), 744–765.

Noguera, P. (2003) *City Schools and the American Dream: Reclaiming the Promise of Public Education*. New York: Teachers College Press.

Norton, B. and Pavlenko, A. (2019) Imagined communities, identity, and English language learning in a multilingual world. In X. Gao (ed.) *Second Handbook of English Language Teaching* (pp. 703–718). Cham: Springer.

Nunnally, T.E. (1991) Breaking the five-paragraph-theme barrier. *The English Journal* 80 (1), 67–71.

Odell, S.J. (2006) *On the Philosophy of Language*. Belmont, CA: Thomson, Wadsworth.

Ogden, C.K. and Richards, I.A. (1946) *The Meaning of Meaning*. Fort Washington, PA: Harvest Book.

Olson, G.A. (1999) Toward a post-process composition: Abandoning the rhetoric of assertion. In T. Kent (ed.) *Post-process Theory: Beyond the Writing Process Paradigm* (pp. 7–15). Carbondale: Southern Illinois University Press.

Ong, W.J. (2013) *Orality and Literacy*. Abingdon: Routledge.

Ortega, L. (2013) SLA for the 21st century: Disciplinary progress, transdisciplinary relevance, and the bi/multilingual turn. *Language Learning* 63, 1–24.

Paasi, A. (2005) Globalisation, academic capitalism, and the uneven geographies of international journal publishing spaces. *Environment and Planning A: Economy and Space* 37 (5), 769–789.

Pager, D. and Shepherd, H. (2008) The sociology of discrimination: Racial discrimination in employment, housing, credit, and consumer markets. *Annu Rev Sociol* 34, 181–209.

Prior, M.T. (2019) 'I am an adult now': Re-storying an 'abuse' narrative through categorization. *Pragmatics and Society* 10 (3), 423–451.

Parkinson, H.J. (5 Mar 2014) I agree with Hanif Kureishi – creative writing courses are a waste of time. See https://www.theguardian.com/books/booksblog/2014/mar/05/hanif-kureishi-creative-writing-courses-waste-of-time.

Passig, D. and Schwartz, G. (2007) Collaborative writing: Online versus frontal. *International Journal on E-Learning* 6 (3), 395–412.

Pavlenko, A. (2001) Language learning memoirs as a gendered genre. *Applied Linguistics* 22 (2), 213–240. 10.1093/applin/22.2.213. See http://resolver.scholarsportal.info/resolve/01426001/v22i0002/213_llmaagg.

Perry, K.H., Shaw, D.M., Ivanyuk, L. and Tham, Y.S.S. (2017) Adult functional literacy: Prominent themes, glaring omissions, and future directions. *Journal of Language and Literacy Education* 13 (2), 1–37.

Petraglia, J. (1999) Is there life after process? The role of social scienticism in a changing discipline. In T. Kent (ed.) *Post-process Theory: Beyond the Writing Process Paradigm* (pp. 49–64). Carbondale: Southern Illinois University Press.

Phelps, L.W. and Emig, J.A. (1995) *Feminine Principles and Women's Experience in American Composition and Rhetoric*. Pittsburgh: University of Pittsburgh Press.

Phillipson, R. (1992) *Linguistic Imperialism*. New York: Oxford University Press.

Phillipson, R. (2008) The linguistic imperialism of neoliberal empire. *Critical Inquiry in Language Studies* 5 (1), 1–43.

Phillipson, R. (2009) *Linguistic Imperialism Continued*. New York: Routledge.

Piccardo, E. (2013) Plurilingualism and curriculum design: Toward a synergic vision. *TESOL Quarterly* 47 (3), 600–614.

Piccardo, E. (2014) The impact of the CEFR on Canada's linguistic plurality: A space for heritage languages. In P. P. Trifonas and T. Aravossitas (eds) *Rethinking Heritage Language Education* (pp. 183–212). Cambridge: Cambridge University Press.

PISA (2012) *Untapped Skills: Realising the Potential of Immigrant Students*. Paris: Organization for Economic Cooperation & Development.

Polinsky, M. (2011) *Heritage Languages*. New York: Oxford University Press.

Popper, K.R. (1972) Objective knowledge: An evolutionary approach.

Posey-Maddox, L. (2014) *When Middle-Class Parents Choose Urban Schools: Class, Race, and the Challenge of Equity in Public Education*. Chicago: University of Chicago Press.

Prior, P.A. (1998) *Writing/Disciplinarity: A Sociohistoric Account of Literate Activity in the Academy*. Mahwah, NJ: L. Erlbaum Associates.

Prior, P.A. (2010) Remaking IO: Semiotic remediation in the design process. In P.A. Prior and J.A. Hengst (eds) *Exploring Semiotic Remediation as Discourse practice* (pp. 206–234). Cham: Springer.

Prior, P.A. and Hengst, J.A. (2010) *Exploring Semiotic Remediation as Discourse Practice*. Basingstoke: Palgrave Macmillan.

Pullman, G. (1999) Stepping yet again into the same current. In T. Kent (ed.) *Post-process Theory: Beyond the Writing Process Paradigm* (pp. 16–29). Carbondale: Southern Illinois University Press.

Quine, W.V. (2013) *Word and Object*. Cambridge, MA: MIT Press. (Originally published in 1960).

Ramjattan, V.A. (2017) Racist nativist microaggressions and the professional resistance of racialized English language teachers in Toronto. *Race Ethnicity and Education* 1–17.

Ransome, J.C. (1941) *The New Criticism*. Norfolk, CT: New Directions.

Reynolds, J. (2018) Jacques Derrida. See http://www.iep.utm.edu/derrida/.

Riazi, M., Shi, L. and Haggerty, J. (2018) Analysis of the empirical research in the *Journal of Second Language Writing* at its 25th year (1992–2016). *Journal of Second Language Writing* 41, 41–54. doi:10.1016/j.jslw.2018.07.002.

Richards, I.A. (2014) *Practical Criticism*. Abingdon: Routledge.

Ritchie, J. and Boardman, K. (1999) Feminism in composition: Inclusion, metonymy, and disruption. *College Composition and Communication* 50 (4), 585–606.

Rivard, L.O.P. (1994) A review of writing to learn in science: Implications for practice and research. *Journal of Research in Science Teaching* 31 (9), 969–983.

Robillard, A.E. (2006) 'Young scholars' affecting composition: A challenge to disciplinary citation practices. *College English* 68 (3), 253–270.

Romano, T. (2000) *Blending Genre, Altering Style*. Portsmouth, NH: Boynton/Cook.

Root, R.L. (2003) Naming nonfiction (a polyptych). *College English* 65 (3), 242–256.

Rosenblatt, L.M. (1994) *The Reader, the Text, the Poem: The Transactional Theory of the Literary Work*. Carbondale, IL: SIU Press.

Russell, D. (1999) Activity theory and process approaches: Writing (power) in school and society. In T. Kent (ed.) *Post-process Theory: Beyond the Writing Process Paradigm* (pp. 80–95). Carbondale: Southern Illinois University Press.

Russell, B. (1905) On denoting. *Mind* 14 (56), 479–493.

Rydell, M. (2018) Being 'a competent language user' in a world of Others – Adult migrants' perceptions and constructions of communicative competence. *Linguistics and Education* 45, 101–109. doi:10.1016/j.linged.2018.04.004.

Rymes, B. (2014) Communicative repertoire. In B. Street and C. Leung (eds) *Routledge Companion to English Language Studies*. New York: Routledge.

Sacks, P. (1999) *Standardized Minds: The High Price of America's Testing Culture and What We Can Do to Change It*. Cambridge, MA: Perseus Books.

Sandhu, P. (2016) *Professional Identity Constructions of Indian Women*. Amsterdam: John Benjamins.

Samovar, L.A. and Porter, R.E. (2001) *Communication Between Cultures* (4th edn). Belmont, CA: Wadsworth/Thomson Learning.

Sampson, F. (2007) Writing as 'therapy'. In S. Earnshaw (ed.) (pp. 312–319). Edinburgh: Edinburgh University Press.

Sayegh, L. and Lasry, J. (1993) Immigrants' adaptation in Canada: Assimilation, acculturation, and orthogonal cultural identification. *Canadian Psychology/Psychologie Canadienne* 34 (1), 98–109.

Sayer, A. (2000) *Realism and Social Science*. London: Sage.

Schecter, S.R. and Cummins, J. (2003) *Multilingual Education in Practice: Using Diversity as a Resource*. Portsmouth, NH: Heinemann.

Schellenberg, G. and Maheux, H. (2007) *Immigrants' Perspectives on their First Four Years in Canada*. Ottawa: Statistics Canada.

Schilb, J. (1999) Reprocessing the essay. In T. Kent (ed.) *Post-process Theory: Beyond the Writing Process Paradigm* (pp. 198–214). Carbondale: Southern Illinois University Press.

Schmidt, S. (2017, 15 June) Yoko Ono set to receive credit with John Lennon as songwriter of 'Imagine'. *The Washington Post*. See https://www.washingtonpost.com/news/morning-mix/wp/2017/06/15/yoko-ono-will-receive-credit-with-john-lennon-as-songwriter-of-imagine/?utm_term=.e3827cf43434.

Scollon, R. and Scollon, S. (1981) *Narrative, Literacy, and Face in Interethnic Communication*. Norwood, NJ: Ablex.

Scollon, R. and Scollon, S. (1997) Point of view and citation: Fourteen Chinese and English versions of the 'same' news story. *Text* 17 (1), 83–125.

Shafer, G. (2012) Living in the post-process writing center. *Teaching English in the Two Year College* 39 (3), 293–305.

Shin, N.L. and Otheguy, R. (2013) Social class and gender impacting change in bilingual settings: Spanish subject pronoun use in New York. *Language in Society* 42 (4), 429–452.

Siegler, R.S. (1988) Individual differences in strategy choices: Good students, not-so-good students, and perfectionists. *Child Development* 833–851.

Simon, R. (2011) On the human dimensions of multiliteracies pedagogy. *Contemporary Issues in Early Childhood* 12 (4), 362–366.

Simon, R. (2014) Making critical sense and critical use of the common core state standards. *Language Arts* 91 (4), 271.

Simon, R. and Campano, G. (2013) Activist literacies: Teacher research as resistance to the' normal curve'. *Journal of Language and Literacy Education* 9 (1), 21–39.

Simon, R. and Campano, G. (2015) Hermeneutics of literacy pedagogy. In J. Rowsell and K. Pahl (eds) *The Routledge Handbook of Literacy Studies* (pp. 472–486). Abingdon: Routledge.

Simon, R., Bailey, A., Brennan, J., Calarco, A., Clarke, K., Edwards, W., ... McInnes-Greenberg, E. (2014) 'In the swell of wandering words': The arts as a vehicle for youth and educators' inquiries into the holocaust memoir 'night'. *Penn GSE Perspectives on Urban Education* 11 (2), 90–106.

Simon, R., Evis, S., Walkland, T., Kalan, A. and Baer, P. (2016) Navigating the 'delicate relationship between empathy and critical distance' youth literacies, social justice and arts-based inquiry. *English Teaching: Practice & Critique* 15 (3), 430–449.

Simpson, J. and Whiteside, A. (eds) (2015) *Adult Language Education and Migration: Challenging Agendas in Policy and Practice*. New York: Routledge.

Sinor, J. and Huston, M. (2004) The role of ethnography in the post-process writing classroom. *Teaching English in the Two Year College* 31 (4), 369–382.

Skilton-Sylvester, E. (2002) Literate at home but not at school: A Cambodian girl's journey from playwright to struggling writer. In G.A. Hull and K. Schultz (eds) *School's Out: Bridging Out-of-School Literacies with Classroom Practice* (pp. 61–90). New York: Teachers College Press.

Skutnabb-Kangas, T. (2000) *Linguistic Genocide in Education – or Worldwide Diversity and Human Rights?* Mahwah, NJ: Lawrence Erlbaum Associates, Publishers.

Skutnabb-Kangas, T. (2006) Linguistic human rights in education? In O. García and C. Baker (eds) *Bilingual Education: An Introductory Reader* (pp. 137–144). Clevedon: Multilingual Matters.

Skutnabb-Kangas, T. and Cummins, J. (1988) *Minority Education: From Shame to Struggle* (1st edn). Clevedon: Multilingual Matters.

Skutnabb-Kangas, T. and Heugh, K. (2012) *Multilingual Education and Sustainable Diversity Work: From Periphery to Center*. New York: Routledge.

Smith, K. (2006) In defense of the five-paragraph essay. *English Journal* 95 (4), 16–17.

Soltero, S.W. (2004) *Dual Language: Teaching and Learning in Two Languages*. Boston: Pearson.

Stake, R.E. (1995) *The Art of Case Study Research*. Thousand Oaks: Sage Publications.

Statistics Canada. (2011) Immigration and ethnocultural diversity in Canada. *Statistics Canada*. See http://www12.statcan.gc.ca/nhs-enm/2011/as-sa/99-010-x/99-010-x2011001-eng.pdf.

Steinman, L. (2003) Cultural collisions in L2 academic writing. *TESL Canada Journal* 20 (2), 80–91.

Storch, N. (2005) Collaborative writing: Product, process, and students' reflections. *Journal of Second Language Writing* 14 (3), 153–173.

Street, B.V. (1984) *Literacy in Theory and Practice*. New York: Cambridge University Press.

Street, B.V. (1993a) *Cross-Cultural Approaches to Literacy*. New York: Cambridge University Press.

Street, B.V. (1993b) Introduction: The new literacy studies. In B.V. Street (ed.) *Cross-Cultural Approaches to Literacy* (pp. 1–22). New York: Cambridge University Press.

Street, B.V. (2003) What's 'new' in new literacy studies? Critical approaches to literacy in theory and practice. *Current Issues in Comparative Education* 5 (2), 77–91.

Sugiharto, S. (2015) The multilingual turn in applied linguistics? A perspective from the periphery. *International Journal of Applied Linguistics* 25 (3), 414–421.

Swain, M. (2006) Languaging, agency and collaboration in advanced second language proficiency. In H. Byrnes (ed.) *Advanced Language Learning: The Contribution of Halliday and Vygotsky* (pp. 95–108). New York: Continuum.

Swales, J. (1990) *Genre Analysis: English in Academic and Research Settings*. Cambridge: Cambridge University Press.

Taft, M., Kacanas, D., Huen, W. and Chan, R. (2011) An empirical demonstration of contrastive rhetoric: Preference for rhetorical structure depends on one's first language. *Intercultural Pragmatics* 8 (4), 503–516.

Tate, G., Rupiper, A. and Schick, K. (2001) *A Guide to Composition Pedagogies*. New York: Oxford University Press.

Taylor, Y. (2008) Good students, bad pupils: Constructions of 'aspiration', 'disadvantage' and social class in undergraduate-led widening participation work. *Educational Review* 60 (2), 155–168.

Templer, B. (2004) High-stakes testing at high fees: Notes and queries on the international English proficiency assessment market. *Journal for Critical Education Policy Studies* 2 (1), 1–8.

Tharp, T.L. (2010) 'Wiki, wiki, wiki – what?' assessing online collaborative writing. *English Journal* 99 (5), 40–46.

Thatcher, B., Amant, K.S. and Sides, C.H. (2017) *Teaching Intercultural Rhetoric and Technical Communication: Theories, Curriculum, Pedagogies and Practice*. Abingdon: Routledge.

Trimbur, J. (1990) Essayist literacy and the rhetoric of deproduction. *Rhetoric Review* 9 (1), 72–86.

Trimbur, J. (1994) Taking the social turn: Teaching writing post-process. *College Composition and Communication* 45, 108–118.

Uysal, H.H. (2010) A critical review of the IELTS writing test. *ELT Journal* 64 (3), 314–320.

Vasudevan, L. and Campano, G. (2009) The social production of adolescent risk and the promise of adolescent literacies. *Review of Research in Education* 33 (1), 310–353.

Ventola, E. and Mauranen, A. (1991) Non-native writing and native revising of scientific articles. In E. Ventola (ed.) *Functional and Systematic Linguistics* (pp. 457–492). Berlin: Mouton de Gruyter.

Vessey, R. (2018) Domestic work = language work? Language and gender ideologies in the marketing of multilingual domestic workers in London. *Gender and Language* 13 (3), 314–338. doi:10.1558/genl.35581.

Weaver, C. (1988) *Reading Process and Practice: From Socio-psycholinguistics to Whole Language*. Portsmouth, NH: Heinemann Educational Books.

Weidmann, N.B., Benitez-Baleato, S., Hunziker, P., Glatz, E. and Dimitropoulos, X. (2016) Digital discrimination: Political bias in internet service provision across ethnic groups. *Science (New York, N.Y.)* 353 (6304), 1151–1155. 10.1126/science.aaf5062 [doi].

Weissberg, R. (2011) *Bad Students, Not Bad Schools*. Piscataway, NJ: Transaction Publishers.

Wenger, E. (1998) *Communities of Practice: Learning, Meaning, and Identity*. Cambridge: Cambridge University Press.

Wenneras, C. and Wold, A. (1997) Nepotism and sexism in peer review. *Nature* 387, 341–343.

Wennerberg, H. (1967) The concept of family resemblance in Wittgenstein's later philosophy. *Theoria* 33 (2), 107–132.

Wesley, K. (2000) The ill effects of the five paragraph theme. *The English Journal* 90 (1), 57–60.

Wiley, T.G. (2007) Accessing language rights in education: A brief history of the US context. In O. García and C. Baker (eds) *Bilingual Education: An Introductory Reader* (pp. 89–107). Clevedon: Multilingual Matters.

Withrow, F.B. (2004) *Literacy in the Digital Age: Reading, Writing, Viewing, and Computing*. Lanham: Rowman & Littlefield Education.

Wittgenstein, L. (1953) *Philosophical Investigations* [*Philosophische Untersuchungen*] (G.E.M. Anscombe Trans.) (3rd edn). New York: Prentice Hall.

Wittgenstein, L. (2004) Tractatus logico philosophicus. In D.F. Pears and B.F. McGuinness (eds) *Tractatus Logico Philosophicus*. New York: Routledge.

Wixson, K.K., Dutro, E. and Athan, R.G. (2003) The challenge of developing content standards. *Review of Research in Education* 27 (1), 69–107.

Woodin, T. (2008) 'A beginner reader is not a beginner thinker': Student publishing in Britain since the 1970s. *Paedagogica Historica* 44 (1–2), 219–232.

Yagelski, R.P. (2012) Writing as praxis. *English Education* 44 (2), 188–204.

Yelland, N., Cope, B. and Kalantzis, M. (2008) Learning by design: Creating pedagogical frameworks for knowledge building in the twenty-first century. *Asia-Pacific Journal of Teacher Education* 36 (3), 197–213.

Yin, R.K. (2009) *Case Study Research: Design and Methods* (4th edn). Los Angeles, CA: Sage Publications.

York, L.M. (2002) *Rethinking Women's Collaborative Writing: Power, Difference, Property*. Toronto: University of Toronto Press.

Zafar Khan, S. (2009) Imperialism of international tests: An EIL perspective. In F. Sharifian (ed.) *English as an International Language: Perspectives and Pedagogical Issues* (pp. 190–205). Bristol: Multilingual Matters.

Zavala, M. (2013) What do we mean by decolonizing research strategies? Lessons from decolonizing, Indigenous research projects in New Zealand and Latin America. *Decolonization: Indigeneity, Education & Society* 2 (1), 55–71.

Zavarzadeh, M. and Morton, D. (1986) Theory pedagogy politics: The crisis of 'the subject' in the humanities. *Boundary 2* 15 (1/2), 1–22.

Zhu, Y. (1997) An analysis of structural moves in Chinese sales letters. *Text* 17 (4), 543–566.

Zuengler, J. and Miller, E.R. (2006) Cognitive and sociocultural perspectives: Two parallel SLA worlds? *TESOL Quarterly* 40 (1), 35–58.

Index

aboriginal people 20, 61
academic writing *see also* essayist literacy
    Anglo-American bias 17, 43, 83, 125, 128, 180, 184
    collaborative writing 93, 96
    dominance of 17
    as gatekeepers of 'quality' of writing 89
    intercultural rhetoric 126
    multilingual writing 112, 114–15
    multiliterate practices 119
    ontologies of writing 69–70, 76, 77, 78
    participant histories 38–9
    perceptions of 'good' 43
    power 96
    publishing 89–92
    report writing 180, 188
    rhetorical traditions 86–7
accent/accented writers 37, 102–3, 146, 147, 155, 157, 182
activist literacies 83, 86
adult education 140
aesthetics 69, 114
agency 17, 84–8, 101, 185–6
agility
    discursive agility 63, 79
    genre agility 67, 79, 80, 108, 129, 167, 173, 179, 180
    rhetorical agility 113, 156
    semiotic agility 61–2, 79, 118, 130, 167, 179, 180
Alexander, J. 83
Algozzine, R. 27, 28, 29
ambiguity of language, innate 12
Anglo-American bias
    academic writing/rhetorical traditions 17, 43, 83, 125, 128, 180, 184
    cultural values 151
    deindustrialization of writing pedagogy 173–4
    devaluation of non-Anglo experience/tradition (brain abuse) 2, 43, 58–9
    genres 156
    against multilingualism 130
    race and gender-based othering 155
    research dissemination environment 88–93, 191–2
animation 73, 119
Ansary, H. 21
anti-colonial resistance 60
Anzaldúa, G. 19
Arasaratnam, L.A. 122
argumentative writing 84, 107, 169, 173
artistic skills 119
arts-based inquiry 177
assertiveness, rhetoric of 83–4
assessment 88, 101, 107, 116, 129, 168–71, 178, 186–8 *see also* standardized tests
assimilation 87, 126, 151–6
Atkinson, D. 16
audiences for writing 88–93, 184
authentic pedagogy 117
authentic writing contexts 97, 115, 162, 163, 164, 166, 179, 187
autoethnography 23, 24, 177, 191
autonomous model of literacy 14
Ayer, A.J. 11, 12

Babaii, E. 21
'bad' students 132–6
Bakhtin, M. 68
Barr, M.S. 53
Barton, A.C. 23
Barton, D. 6, 14–15, 51, 52
'basic skills' 163, 173
Bauder, H. 1, 2, 43, 59, 140
Bazerman, C. 158
Behrens, S.J. 163
Belcher, D.D. 6, 7, 23–4
belief systems, engagement with 51, 52

Benda, J. 21
Berman, R.A. 21
Bermúdez, A.B. 19
Bhabha, H. 48, 121
Bialystok, E. 110
Blanchette, J.P. 53
Blommaert, J. 83
Blumberg, A.E. 12
Blyler, N. 17, 74
Blythe, H. 98
Borg, E. 53
bounded systems 27
brain abuse 2, 43, 59
brain drain 1
Breland, H. 19
Britzman, D.P. 177
business writing 77, 127, 154

Campano, G. 22–3, 83, 157–8
Canada
    aboriginal people 20, 61
    assimilationism 151, 152–3
    education system 169, 193–4
    immigration policies 61, 140
    migration 157
    ontologies of writing 70
    participant histories 31–50
    publishing 91, 92
    as setting for case studies 1–2, 3, 4,
        8, 27–9
*Canadian Language Benchmarks: English
    as a Second Language for Adults* 8–9
Canagarajah, A.S. 7, 16, 83, 107, 115, 118
canonical curriculum 64, 80, 142–6, 160
capitalism 83, 126, 127, 188 *see also*
    neoliberalism
Carnap, R. 11, 12, 174
Casanave, C.P. 24
case study approach 27–9
case study database 31–2
categorical aggregation 31
Centre for Canadian Language
    Benchmarks 8
children's literature 65–6
Christensen, L. 83, 87, 163
class 21–3, 25, 133, 186
Clifford, J. 17, 85
close reading 68
Cochran-Smith, M. 23
co-construction 74, 142, 183, 187
code-switching 115–16, 181
coding of data 31–2
cognitive skills 9, 94, 97, 110–11, 133, 172
co-learning with children 46

collaboration in writing 9, 93–104, 175,
    182–4
collaborative writing pedagogy 16, 93, 94
colonialism 53, 59, 60, 118, 126, 151–2,
    157, 169, 188, 192
communication, writing for 69, 75–6, 80,
    110, 164
Communicative Language Teaching (CLT)
    163
communicative performance 149
communicative repertoires 70
communities, writing 80, 93, 96–104, 123,
    126, 175, 182–4
community publishing 104, 185
community-service pedagogy 16, 87, 187–8
composition studies 16–17, 18
Connor, U. 6, 20, 21, 23–4, 86, 121, 124,
    125
Conrad, Josef 2
conscientization 67
consciousness, forms of 52–3
context, reading/writing in 6
contrastive rhetoric 6, 20–1, 86–7, 124–30,
    155
conversational skills 149–50
Cope, B. 62, 117, 118
co-researchers, participants as 31
cosmopolitanism 158
co-writing 93, 104, 175
creative discourse narrative formation 61
creative inquiry, writing as 76, 189–90
Creative Writing programmes 36
Creswell, J.W. 27, 28, 29
critical collaborations 94–7
critical consciousness 67
critical curriculum 64
critical distance 55–6
critical literacy 64, 163
critical pedagogy 67, 85, 194
critical theory 83, 112
critical writing 43
cultural capital 190
cultural collage, literacy as 55–61
cultural pluralism 189
cultural studies pedagogy 16, 83
culturally responsive pedagogy 145
culture
    adjusting to a new 45, 48
    crossing/borrowing from 55–6, 80,
        103, 105, 122–4, 128–31
    cultural conformity 151–6
    cultural repertoires 105–31, 134
    and definitions of 'good' writing 68
    empirical research 20–1

hegemony of American 123
intercultural competence 121–30
literacy as culture 55–6
literate culture, definition 28–9
monoculturalism 49, 145
multiculturalism 118, 151
culture-sharing groups 29
Cummins, J. 6, 15, 19, 23, 52, 67, 83, 139, 140, 156, 160, 186
curriculum development
choice of canon 64, 80, 142–6, 160
critical curriculum 64
decentralization 116, 187
decolonization of writing curricula 188–93
and discourse narratives 60
diversifying 80, 142–6, 160–1
dominant curricula 142–6
implications for the future 176, 186–93
intercultural competence 124, 129
mono-literacy 118
open-ended and suggestive 187

Danto, A. 89, 91, 104, 182
data coding 31–2
data collection 29–31
De Fina, A. 31–2
Deardorff, D.K. 124
decolonization of writing curricula 188–93
deficit mentalities 72, 140, 157
deindustrialization of education 159, 172, 186–93
Derrida, J. 3, 12, 54, 68, 82, 88, 104, 110, 122
descriptive case studies 28
différance 12, 54, 110, 122
digital technologies
digital literacy practices 166–8
for family conversations 41
genre flexibility 77
internet writing 24
interviews via 29
multiliteracies 23
multimodality 53, 61–3, 79, 80, 105–6, 167–8, 177, 181
new semiotic possibilities 61–3
online collaborative writing 93
online writing communities 98
publishing writing 185
semiotic migration 62
virtual learning environments 53, 63
discourse additives 60–1
discourse analysis 24

discourse communities 53
discourse exchanges 13
discourse maps 59
discourse narratives 59–61
discourse negotiation 66
discourse practices 54–66
discourses of literacy 51–3
discursive agility 63, 79
discursive consciousness 59, 60
dissemination of writing 88–93, 126, 184–5 see also publishing
diversity 15, 105–6, 118, 146
Dobrin, S.I. 3, 23
documentary evidence 30–1
Doerfel, M.L. 122
Dogme movement 163
'doing' language 12
drama 119
drills 97, 101, 106–7, 163, 164
duoethnographies 177

Early, M. 6, 15, 19, 52, 67, 83
editing 141–2, 147–8
educational institutions see also academic writing; teachers
activation of agency 101
assessment 88, 101, 107, 116, 129, 168–71, 178, 186–8
choice of canon 64, 80, 142–6, 160
collaborative writing pedagogy 94, 96–7
decolonization of writing curricula 188–93
discursive legacies 52, 53
dissemination of writing 93
dominant curricula 142–6
favouring certain types of writing 73
fluid pedagogy 66
as gatekeepers of 'quality' of writing 69, 89, 184
'good' and 'bad' students 132–6
industrialized education 2, 25, 97, 99, 116, 120, 129–30, 143, 169–70, 173–86, 190–1
intercultural competence 124
mainstream writing pedagogy 67
mechanics of learning writing 163–6
multiliteracies 117, 119
multisemioticity 120
plurilingualism 113–14, 116
power relations 83, 87–8, 104, 139–42
providing for multilingualism 116–17
public funding for 47, 136, 138–9, 160
recognition of minority languages 85

rubrics 25–6, 73, 105, 107, 129, 150–1, 173, 178, 187, 188
school literacy traditions 58, 59, 66
standardized tests 107, 116, 129, 168–71, 186–7, 188
streaming models in education 25
and students' native literacy discourses 54–5, 136
technology 63
writing communities 80
English
as favoured academic language 89
hegemony of American 123
as a lingua franca 147
testing 169–70
English as an additional language
assessment 169–70
discourse practices 54
native/non-native dichotomy 146–51
participant histories 38–9, 41, 42, 45, 100, 134, 139
and students' native literacy discourses 55
texts in 64
writing and power 83
Ennser-Kananen, J. 19
epistemological tool, writing as 75–7, 119, 179–80
epistemology 11
errors 141–2
Ervin, E. 17, 85
essayist literacy
in academic writing 107, 109, 173
assessment 169–70
dominance of 17, 162, 180, 188
in educational institutions 77, 80, 83–4, 106–7
power differentials 83
essentialist pedagogies 106–7, 125, 173
ethnicity see race and ethnicity
ethnography
autoethnography 23, 24, 177, 191
as basis of this study 3, 29–31
case study methods 28–9
future research 87, 191
second language research generally 4, 6, 10, 22, 24, 25
in writing classrooms 120
ethnolinguistic communities 99, 101

Faltis, C. 27
family literacy traditions 56–8, 66, 95–6, 136–7, 145, 167
family resemblance 108–9, 110, 113

Farr, M. 83, 106, 107
Farrokhzad, Forough 144
Farsi 33, 35, 36, 64, 111, 112, 114, 123
feedback 141, 179, 184 see also assessment
Feigl, H. 12
feminist scholarship 18, 83, 111–12
fiction writing
multilingual writing 111, 114
multiliterate practices 119–20
ontologies of writing 75, 78
participant histories 35–6, 37
publishing 91
writing as praxis 85
Fields, G. 70
fluid discourses, literacy practices as 65–6
'forbidden' books 144
Foucault, M. 12, 13
Freire, P. 6, 52, 67, 84–5, 163, 194
French 36, 157
Fulkerson, R. 82
functional knowledge 9
functional literacy theory 163, 164
funds of knowledge 6, 15, 23

Gadamer, H.G. 71, 179
García, O. 16, 110, 115
gatekeepers 69, 89, 91, 170, 184
Gee, J.P. 4, 6, 13, 15, 52, 53, 60, 62, 136
gender 6, 18–20, 25, 37, 83, 86, 153–6
Genette, G. 68
genre
challenging dominant genres 17
families of 108–9
flexibility and fluidity 67, 77–9
genre agility 67, 79, 80, 108, 129, 167, 173, 179, 180
genre pedagogy 68
genre plurality 107–8, 186, 189
genre theory 6
transgenre writing 78–9
George, D. 16, 83
Ghiso, M.P. 157–8
Gibson, M. 83
globalization 106, 118, 121, 122, 130
'good' and 'bad' students 132–6
grammatical knowledge 9, 115, 141, 148–9, 163–6, 174
'great writing' 68, 69, 80, 177
Guo, S. 58

Hamilton, M. 14–15, 51, 52
Hancock, D.R. 27, 28, 29
Harris, M. 29
Hatch, J.A. 27, 29

Hatim, B. 21
healing, writing for 76
Heath, S.B. 14, 22, 27, 53, 83
hegemony 41, 47, 98, 121, 123, 125, 142–3, 152
Hengst, J.A. 53
hermeneutic guessing 69, 80
hermeneutic horizon 71
hermeneutic tool, writing as 12–13, 67, 68–72, 79, 80, 89, 179, 180
hidden discourses 177
hierarchies 62, 77–8, 83, 91–2, 107
Hobson, E.H. 16
holistic teaching 25, 156, 163, 164
horizons of understanding/interpretation 71–2
Hornberger, N.H. 110, 169, 191, 194
Howard, R.M. 16
human rights 16, 38, 169
Hungarian 44–5, 165
hybrid discourse practices 53, 177
hybrid styles of writing 43
Hyland, K. 6, 68

identity
    challenging dominant genres 17
    in the classroom 142
    ethnolinguistic communities 101
    and gender 19
    hyphenated identities 37, 101
    identity texts 19, 83, 177
    identity-based literacy learning 52
    ideological coercion 141
    imagined communities 102–3
    intercultural competence 121–30
    internet writing 24
    intertextual identities 75
    multilingual writing 111, 112
    negotiation of 45, 48, 58, 88, 155, 176, 190
    and power 87
    rhetorical migration 156
    and the turn to sociocultural contexts 6, 15
    writing as a tool for identity creation 76–7, 86, 87–8
    writing as resistance 153
    writing identities 178
ideological coercion 141
ideological hegemonies 47
ideological model of literacy 14
ideological stance 69
IELTS (International English Language Testing System) 107, 169, 171

'illiteracy' 53
imagined communities 99, 102–3
imperfect written products 72
imperialism 42, 59, 169, 188
indigenous knowledge 89, 118, 175, 192, 194
industrialized education 2, 25, 97, 99, 116, 120, 129–30, 143, 169–70, 173–86, 190–1
inquiry, writing as a tool of 75–7, 80, 189–90
institutional theory of writing 89
intellectual associations (loose) 98–104, 175, 183
intercultural (contrastive) rhetoric 6, 20–1, 86–7, 124–30, 155
intercultural competence 121–30, 157, 159, 178, 192
intercultural dialogue 48
intercultural practices 16
interlingual processes 116
inter-literary experiences 114
international awareness 158–9
international networks 95
international professionals 39
internet writing 24 see also digital technologies
intersectional discrimination 153–4
intertextuality 64, 75, 113
interview data 29
invisible communities 101–3, 175

Jakobson, R. 70, 179
Janks, H. 52, 67, 163
Jarratt, C.J. 18, 67, 83
Jewitt, C. 52
job application writing 77, 84, 89
Johnson, D.M. 18–19
Journal of Second Language 5
journalistic writing 21, 33–4, 38, 62, 78, 85, 98
journals, academic 89–90, 92, 193
Julier, L. 16, 87

Kalan, A. 17, 33
Kalantzis, M. 62, 117, 118
Kamberelis, G. 53
Kanno, Y. 102
Kaplan, D. 12, 20, 86, 125
Kent, T. 3, 16, 17, 69, 179
Kesselman, J.R. 1
Kilomba, Grada 82–3
Kincheloe, J. 160
Kong, K. 21
Kramsch, C. 148

Kress, G. 52
Kubota, R. 86, 125, 129
Kurdish 33, 35, 36, 38, 64, 70, 120

Ladson-Billings, G. 152
Lam, W.S.E. 24
Lambert, R. 122
Language Instruction for Newcomers to
      Canada (LINC) 8–9
language learning 51
language-games 12
languaging 51–2
learning, writing for 76
Lee, Y. 19
Lehner, A. 86, 125, 129
Leki, I. 5, 6
less visible intellectual associations
      98–104, 175, 183
libraries 139
life events 67, 72–5, 89
lingua francas 147
linguistic imperialism 42
linguistic performance 121, 149, 150, 164
linguistic repertoires 105, 111, 113, 115,
      134, 181
linguistic rights 157, 169
linguistic turn 11
literacy, definition 27
literacy events 14
literacy narratives 59, 176, 177–8
literacy practices 51–81
literacy regimes 83
literacy studies 13–16, 18–26
literacy tools and artefacts, as data source
      31
literary circles 97–8
literary theory 68
literate culture, definition 28–9
literate legacies 15, 23, 27–50, 80, 176
literate lives, definition 27
literate-illiterate dichotomy 53
Littlewood, W. 163
lived experiences 28, 86, 123, 132–61
Lo Bianco, J. 122
logical positivism 12
Lorente, B.P. 20
Loux, M. 106
Lycan, W.G. 11
Lytle, S. 23

Macdonald, D. 143
Maheux, H. 58
mainstream curricula 142–6
Matheiu, P. 104

Matsuda, P.K. 6, 7, 70
Mauranen, A. 21
McKinley, J. 21
meaning making 12–13, 71, 80, 109–10
mechanics of learning writing 163–6
Meddings, L. 163
member checking 31
mentors 99–100, 104, 175
Merriam, S.B. 28
metalingual features 71, 179
metatextuality 16, 18, 191
micro-interactions 140–1, 142, 160–1, 178,
      182, 186
micropolitics 91, 135
migration
      assimilation 151–6
      and class 21–3
      cosmopolitanism 158
      English language testing 169–70
      and functioning in Canada 8
      importance of narratives 31–5
      as intellectual catalyst 156–9
      intercultural competence 123–4, 178
      lived experiences 132–61
      native/non-native dichotomy
            146–51
      power relations 140
      race and gender 19–20
      semiotic migration 62
      systematic devaluation of education/
            knowledge 48
Miller, E.R. 94
mimicry 151–2
Moll, L.C. 6, 15, 23
monoculturalism 49, 145
monolingual ideologies 2, 49, 111, 145,
      188, 195
monoliteracy 118
Montero, M.K. 87
MOOCs (Massive Open Online Courses)
      75
Morton, D. 143
mother tongue instruction 157
motherhood 46
multi-authored works 94, 96, 183
multiculturalism 118, 151
multilingual education 15–16
multilingual turn 15–16
multilingualism 23–6, 110–11
multiliteracies 6, 15, 23–6, 52, 62, 105–6,
      110, 117–21, 181, 192
multimodality 53, 61–3, 79, 80, 105–6,
      167–8, 177, 181
multiple/collective case studies 28, 31

multisemioticity 117–21, 177, 181
multitextuality 106–10

narrative research 6, 24, 191–2
narratives
    discourse narratives 59–60
    discursive consciousness 59
    literacy narratives 59
    and migration 31–2
    subjectivity 56
native literacy discourses 55, 60, 66, 105–6,
    108, 128
native/non-native dichotomy 142, 146–51
nativist microaggressions 146
negative feedback 141
neocolonialism 169, 188
neoimperialism 188
neoliberalism 20, 126, 138, 172, 185, 188–9
neopragmatism 11
New Criticism 68
New Literacy Studies 11, 13–16, 22, 27, 53,
    60, 117
New London Group 6, 15, 23, 52, 62,
    105–6, 110, 117–18, 192–3
newcomers 1–3, 4, 8–9, 45, 48, 52, 84, 140,
    177
1984 (Orwell) 42, 64, 144
Nir, B. 21
No Child Left Behind 169
non-written semiotic elements 116, 117–21
Norton, B. 102

objectivity 56, 60, 189
observation 30, 54, 120
Odell, S.J. 12, 54
Ogden, C.K. 68
Ong, W.J. 53
online writing communities 98
ontologies of literacy 53, 54–66, 79,
    165–6
ontologies of writing 66–81
ontology 11
oracy traditions 40, 57, 60, 70, 80, 87, 107,
    119–20, 127, 149
organic writing practices 7, 98, 186–7
Orwell, George 42, 64, 144
Otheguy, R. 22
othering 152, 153, 155
out-of-school writing experiences 23, 25,
    74–5, 97–8, 120, 175, 187, 190–1

paradigmatic communication 70
participant histories 4, 31–50, 136–9
participatory research 93

patriarchy 155
Pavlenko, A. 6, 18, 102
Perry, K.H. 163
Persian literary canon 144
persuasive writing 19, 84, 107, 188
Pettitt, N. 19
phenomenon of study 27–9
philosophy 11, 12, 13, 68, 73, 82, 104,
    106–10, 118
phonics 163
Piccardo, E. 16, 113
PISA (Programme for International Student
    Assessment) 22
Plato 68
plurilingualism 16, 24, 25, 85, 110–17, 192
plurisemiotic literacy learning 52
poetry 57, 64, 78, 80, 83, 114
Poets, Essayists and Novelists (PEN)
    Canada 33
policies 8, 52, 139, 160, 186–93
pop music 41, 42, 123
Portuguese 39, 42, 44, 58, 112, 114
positionality 69, 85, 93, 177
postcolonialism 60–1, 83, 118, 151–2
post-composition era 23
postmodernism 5
postpositivism 5, 11, 189
postprocess writing theory 16–17, 69,
    74, 85
poststructuralism 3, 5, 11, 12, 107, 110
poverty 34, 39–40, 57, 60, 100, 136–9, 142
power
    in the classroom 60, 139–42
    Foucault on 13
    hegemony 41, 47, 98, 121, 123, 125,
        142–3, 152
    intercultural rhetoric 125
    and the mechanics of learning writing
        163–4, 165
    native/non-native dichotomy 150–1
    ontologies of writing 67
    power differentials 81, 82–104,
        181–2
    ranking/judging literacy practices 60
    teacher agency 186
    writing as hermeneutic design 67
    writing-as-power 82, 88–9
'practicing writers' 7, 28–9, 50
practitioner research 22–3
pragmatics 149
Prater, D.L. 19
praxis 82, 84–8, 104
primary discourse 60
Prior, P.A. 24, 53, 61

process theory 74
professional writers 7
project-based approaches to teaching
    writing 87
projection 71
Prussian model of education 143
psychology 94, 97, 133
public funding 47, 136, 138–9, 160
publishing 37, 43–4, 73, 88–94, 104, 111,
    126, 128, 184–5
purposive sampling 31

quality of writing 68–9, 76–7, 80, 89, 177
queer composition 67, 83
Quine, Willard Van Orman 11

race and ethnicity
    assimilation 153–6
    in the classroom 160
    empirical research 19–23, 25
    'good' and 'bad' students 133
    impact on literacy practices 56–7
    intercultural competence 123
    native/non-native dichotomy 146–7,
        148, 149, 150
    participant histories 31, 48
    power relations 84, 182, 186
    race-neutral education 152
    United States 61
radical semiotic interactions 118, 180–1
Ransome, J.C. 68
reader-response theory 88
readership, engagement with 69–71
report writing 77, 83, 126, 180, 188, 190
resistance, writing as 35, 73, 85–6, 153,
    195
rhetoric of assertion 17
rhetorical agility 113, 156
rhetorical patterns 6
rhetorical traditions 20, 86–7, 107, 113,
    125–30, 156, 189
Riazi, M. 5
Richards, I.A. 68
Rossi, M.A. 87
rubrics 25–6, 73, 105, 107, 129, 150–1, 173,
    178, 187, 188
Russell, B. 12
Russell, D. 17, 74
Russian 47, 165
Rydell, M. 150
Rymes, B. 70, 180

sampling 31
Sandhu, P. 20

Saussure, Ferdinand de 109–10
Sayer, A. 107
Schellenberg, G. 58
school literacy traditions 58, 66
scientific inquiry 107, 192
Scollon, R. 21, 27, 52, 53, 121
Scollon, S. 21, 27, 52, 53, 121
secondary discourse 60
self-confidence 86
self-marketing 49, 84
self-publication 91, 185
semantic relationships 71, 105
semiotics
    multiliteracies 110
    multisemioticity 117–21, 177, 181
    non-written semiotic elements 105,
        116, 117–21
    plurisemiotic literacy learning 52
    radical semiotic interactions 118,
        180–1
    semiotic agility 61–2, 79, 118, 130,
        167, 179, 180
    semiotic migration 61–3
    semiotic webs 111, 117
    writing as semiotic activity 16, 17, 54
Shamlou, Ahmad 144
Shin, N.L. 22
Siegler, R.S. 133
signification 13, 17, 54, 109–10, 117, 122
Simon, R. 83, 93
single process, writing is not 17
single-author preferences 94, 96
situated linguistic engagement 27
situated literacy 6, 83, 117
Skilton-Sylvester, E. 23
Skutnabb-Kangas, T. 110, 111
Smith, K. 107
social class 21–3, 25, 133, 186
social impact 87–8
social media 30, 62, 167
social practice, writing as 73–4, 190
social practices, shared 15, 17
social skills 58
social turn 11, 12, 13–18, 51, 94
sociocultural, shift to the 5–6
socioeconomic status 34, 39–40, 57, 60,
    100, 136–9, 142
sociolinguistic knowledge 9
soft skills 84
song writing 37, 57, 78, 96
Stake, R.E. 29, 31
standardized tests 107, 116, 129, 168–71,
    186–7, 188
strategic competence 9

streaming models in education 25
Street, B.V. 13–14, 22, 27, 53, 83
stylistics 69, 162–6, 172, 178, 179–80, 184
subjectivity 56, 60
Swain, M. 51–2
Swales, J. 77
Sweet, C. 98

Tan, E. 23
Tate, W.F. 152
teachers
    collaborative writing pedagogy
        96–7
    consciousness of power relations 84,
        87
    going beyond dominant curricula
        145–6
    'good' and 'bad' students 135
    intercultural competence 159
    intercultural rhetoric 129
    in Iran 137–8
    literate legacies 176–7
    micro-relations 140–2
    mobilizing teacher agency 185–6
    multiliteracies 181
    multisemioticity 120
    native/non-native dichotomy 150–1
    in neoliberal industrialized education
        172–3
    pedagogical implications 175–86
    power relations 140, 160
    role in construction of literacy
        narratives 60
    and students' identity creation
        176
techne of writing 17, 80–1, 184
technical writing
    collaborative writing 94–5
    genre flexibility 78
    hermeneutic tools 70
    intercultural rhetoric 127, 128
    multilingual writing 112–13
    participant histories 45, 49
    report writing 188
technology see digital technologies
TESL (Teaching English as a Second
    Language) 43
textbook writing 44–5, 47, 49, 75, 94–5,
    112, 129
texts
    identity texts 19, 83, 177
    ideological load 63–4
    intercultural competence 122–3
    intertextuality 64, 75, 113

as life events 67
and linguistic/cultural repertoires
    105–31
metatextuality 16, 18, 191
multilingual texts 111, 114, 116, 179,
    181, 189
multitextuality 106–10
and power 84, 103
as product of social relationships
    94
as sources of literacy discourses
    63–4
and their readers 88–93
textual analysis 4, 6, 19
textual knowledge 9
Thatcher, B. 129
therapy, writing as 76
'thesis-support-conclusion' template
    43
third spaces 48, 121
TOEFL (Test of English as a Foreign
    Language) 19, 107, 169, 170, 171
Toronto 8, 36, 39, 44, 101
transdisciplinary writing education
    187–8
transformational potential of writing
    85
transformative pedagogy 82, 194
transgenre writing 78–9
translanguaging 16, 115, 181, 192
translation 181
translingual lives 80, 110–17
translingual practices 181
triangulation 29
tribalism 91, 92, 104
Trimbur, J. 16, 83, 106, 107
'truth' 13, 189–90
Tseng, A. 31–2

underground writing circles 35, 97, 99
unfinished writing projects 73
United States 38, 61, 123, 151, 157, 169,
    193

Vandrick, S. 24
Ventola, E. 21
Vessey, R. 20
virtual learning environments 53, 63
vivo codes 31

Washington Post 96
Wei, L. 16
Weissberg, R. 133, 135
Wiley, T.G. 157

Wittgenstein, L. 3, 11, 12, 54, 108, 110, 113
women of color 19–20, 154–5 *see also* gender; race and ethnicity
writing, definition of 67
writing centre pedagogy 16
writing communities 80, 93, 96–104, 123, 126, 175, 182–4
writing identities 178
writing theory 16–18
writing trajectories 178

writing-as-power 82, 88–9
writingworld 89, 90, 91, 182–4

Yagelski, R.P. 85
Yin, R.K. 28, 29
York, L.M. 94, 96
YouTube 63, 73, 119

Zavarzadeh, M. 143
Zhu, Y. 21
Zuengler, J. 94